INNOVATIONS A~~~ ~~~~~~~~~~
INTERNAL FAMILY SYSTEMS THERAPY

Martha Sweezy and Ellen L. Ziskind's *Internal Family Systems Therapy: New Dimensions* quickly established itself as essential reading for clinicians who are interested in IFS by illustrating how the model can be applied to a variety of therapy modalities and patient populations. Sweezy and Ziskind's newest volume, *Innovations and Elaborations in Internal Family Systems Therapy*, is the natural follow-up to that text. Here Richard Schwartz and other master IFS clinicians illustrate how they work with a wide variety of problems: racism, perpetrator parts, trauma, addiction, eating disorders, parenting and grief. The authors also show creative ways of putting into practice basic IFS techniques that help parts to unblend and to unburden both personal and legacy burdens.

Martha Sweezy, PhD, is an assistant professor at Harvard Medical School and has a therapy and consultation practice in Northampton, Massachusetts. She is co-editor *of Internal Family Systems Therapy: New Dimensions*, and co-author *of Intimacy From the Inside Out: Courage and Compassion in Couple Therapy*.

Ellen L. Ziskind, LICSW, CGP, has been affiliated with Harvard Medical School at Cambridge Hospital, Beth Israel Deaconess Medical Center and was on the faculty at Boston Institute for Psychotherapy, Two Brattle Center and Northeastern Society for Group Psychotherapy. She is co-editor of *Internal Family Systems Therapy: New Dimensions* and has a psychotherapy/ consultation practice in Brookline, Massachusetts.

INNOVATIONS AND ELABORATIONS IN INTERNAL FAMILY SYSTEMS THERAPY

Edited by Martha Sweezy and Ellen L. Ziskind

Routledge
Taylor & Francis Group

NEW YORK AND LONDON

First published 2017
by Routledge
711 Third Avenue, New York, NY 10017

and by Routledge
2 Park Square, Milton Park, Abingdon, Oxon, OX14 4RN

Routledge is an imprint of the Taylor & Francis Group, an informa business

Library of Congress Cataloging-in-Publication Data
Names: Sweezy, Martha, editor. | Ziskind, Ellen L., editor.
Title: Innovations and elaborations in internal family systems therapy /
    edited by Martha Sweezy and Ellen L. Ziskind.
Description: New York, NY : Routledge, 2016. Includes bibliographical
    references and index.
Identifiers: LCCN 2016014598 | ISBN 9781138024380 (hbk : alk. paper) |
    ISBN 9781138024373 (pbk : alk. paper) | ISBN 9781315775784 (ebk)
Subjects: LCSH: Psychotherapy patients—Family relationships. |
    Family psychotherapy.
Classification: LCC RC489.F33 I56 2016 DDC 616.89/14—dc23
LC record available at https://lccn.loc.gov/2016014598

ISBN: 978-1-138-02438-0 (hbk)
ISBN: 978-1-138-02437-3 (pbk)
ISBN: 978-1-315-77578-4 (ebk)

Typeset in New Baskerville
by Apex CoVantage, LLC

We dedicate this book to the outstanding teachers, therapists, and learners of our vibrant IFS community. We also dedicate it—only partly tongue-in-cheek—to polarities, which are illustrated in every chapter. Without the mighty persistence of our polarized protectors we would never find the whole truth of our experience.

Contents

Contributors

Frank G. Anderson, MD, completed his residency and served as a clinical instructor in psychiatry at Harvard Medical School before becoming the executive director and vice chairman of the Foundation for Self Leadership. He co-leads a 5-day intensive training for the Center for Self Leadership called Internal Family Systems (IFS), Trauma and Neuroscience. He is the author of "Who's Taking What," about neuroscience, psychopharmacology and IFS therapy, for the volume *Internal Family Systems Therapy: New Dimensions*. He has long been affiliated as a lecturer and senior supervisor at the trauma center at Justice Resource Institute in Boston. He maintains a private practice in Concord, Massachusetts.

Jeanne Catanzaro, PhD, is a clinical psychologist in private practice in Brookline, Massachusetts. A former director of the partial hospitalization program at the Renfrew Center of New York City, she has worked extensively with clients with eating disorders and trauma. Her current interests include how to use IFS to facilitate long-term positive health choices.

Pamela Geib, EdD, has been affiliated with Harvard Medical School at Cambridge Hospital and the Family Institute of Cambridge. She currently co-leads training in the Toni Herbine-Blank's Intimacy From the Inside Out couple therapy program. She co-founded and co-teaches the yearlong seminar "Challenges in Applying IFS: Mastering the Basics." She sees couples and individuals in her private practice and consults to therapists and groups.

Pamela K. Krause, LCSW, is a senior trainer for the Center for Self Leadership, teaching Levels 1 and 2. She also teaches workshops on how to use direct access. She coauthored a chapter in *EMDR Therapy and Adjunct Approaches With Children* and authored a chapter in *Internal Family Systems Therapy: New Dimensions*. She has a private practice near Harrisburg, Pennsylvania, working with adults, adolescents and children.

Paul Neustadt, MSS, LICSW, is an IFS co-lead trainer, an AAMFT approved supervisor, and has a private practice in Arlington, Massachusetts, where he specializes in couples therapy, parent coaching, and IFS consultation. For 17 years he was the director of a community counseling and prevention program for children, adolescents, and their families, and he taught couples and family therapy at a family therapy institute and in two graduate programs.

Lawrence G. Rosenberg, PhD, supervises at Cambridge Health Alliance/ Harvard Medical School and has a psychotherapy and consultation practice for individuals and couples in Cambridge, Massachusetts. Drawing on an integrative perspective, he has written and presented on IFS, sexuality, gay/lesbian/bisexual/transgender development, trauma, and supervision.

Richard C. Schwartz, PhD, began his career as a systemic family therapist and an academic at the University of Illinois and at Northwestern University. Grounded in systems thinking, Dr. Schwartz developed the internal family systems model in response to clients' descriptions of various parts within themselves. In 2000, he founded the Center for Self Leadership (www.selfleadership.org), which offers three levels of trainings and workshops in IFS for professionals and the general public, both in this country and abroad. A featured speaker for national professional organizations, Dr. Schwartz has published five books and over 50 articles about IFS.

Derek Scott, RSW, has a therapy and consultation practice based in London, Canada, and works primarily online. He lectures in the Department of Thanatology at the University of Western Ontario and has authored several chapters on IFS and grief in the books *Counting Our Losses: Reflecting on Change, Loss, and Transition in Everyday Life; Principles and Practice of Grief Counseling;* and *Techniques of Grief Therapy Assessment and Intervention*. He has created a video demonstration of working with grief from an IFS perspective that may be seen on his website: www.derekscott.co

Ann L. Sinko, LMFT, is an IFS senior trainer for the Center for Self Leadership. She has been an adjunct professor at Central Connecticut State University in the Marriage and Family Therapy Program for 20 years. Ann conducts continuing education workshops on legacy burdens and creative externalization of parts, and is in private practice in Portland, Connecticut.

Janna Malamud Smith, LICSW, is a lecturer at Harvard Medical School and has a therapy and consultation practice in the Boston area. She is the author of four books and many articles. Website: www.jannamalamudsmith.com

Martha Sweezy, PhD, is an assistant professor at Harvard Medical School and has a therapy and consultation practice in Northampton, Massachusetts. She is co-editor/co-author of the book *Internal Family Systems Therapy: New Dimensions*, co-author of the book *Intimacy From the Inside Out: Courage and Compassion in Couple Therapy*, and author of two articles on IFS in peer reviewed journals, www.marthasweezy.com

Cece Sykes, LCSW, has been a senior trainer with the Center for Self Leadership for over 10 years and has operated a psychotherapy and consultation practice for 30+ years in Chicago. She specializes in recovery from trauma and addiction, and co-authored two articles on systemic treatment of sexual abuse. She also developed the Heart Lessons of the Journey retreat for an ongoing study of therapist personal narratives. Cece lectures internationally on these and other related topics, www.cecesykeslcsw.com

Acknowledgments

The editors thank Elizabeth Graber, Meira Bienstock and Autumn Spalding of Routledge for their unfailing courtesy and support. And we thank Susan Callaghan for her patient, skillful work in designing the beautiful cover of this book.

Introduction

Janna Malamud Smith

February 2014

Isn't it odd? Here we are. Briefly, accidently, inconclusively. Yet filled with haste and purpose. From the instant we arrive, we labor to survive; and, to do so, we race to grasp the life-and-death rules of our environment. We pay close attention.

Everything rests on learning lessons. Say that one time when we are out walking, the bent blades of grass signal a lion lying in wait. We get away, but carry the scar of the paw swipe. The next 100 times we walk, the bent blades signal nothing, yet we recall and react to the lion. (At least, a "part" of us does.)

Or, say we see fear in our parents' faces because they see the lion when we do not. This time there is no paw swipe, just a contagious terror. The memory of the adults' fearful expression wakens our trepidation when we again notice the bent blades of grass. Learning from others' intense emotions may save us from the actual, physical paw wound. (A "part" holds that knowledge.)

Or, say we neither encounter the lion nor directly see the fear-ridden face, but we are admonished: When you are walking, always listen for sounds, watch for bent grass.

We learn from our own experiences; from witnessing others, particularly when they are close kin; or from attending to instruction. (We have "parts" who absorb and recite back such instruction to us.)

In his book *The World Until Yesterday,* Jared Diamond describes how, living among different New Guinean peoples for many years, he was repeatedly struck by their continual talking and the detail it contained.

> I have been impressed by how much more time New Guineans spend talking with each other than do we Americans and Europeans. They keep up a

running commentary on what is happening now, what happened this morning and yesterday, who ate what and when, who urinated when and where,
and minute details of who said what about whom or did what to whom. They
don't merely fill the day with talk: from time to time through the night they
wake up and resume talking.

(2012, p. 273)

Diamond speculates that the talkativeness is partly a response to the huge
risks of the New Guinea environment. No detail is too small to consider with
care, to scrutinize and discuss; everyone seeks to increase safety by pooling
knowledge. You might say that each of our minds contains something like
a group of talkative New Guineans. Internal family systems (IFS) calls them
"parts." The parts carry our experiences and remind us at every juncture
what they think we need to know in order to best cope. At least, according
to them.

Our crucial lessons are not simply about fear, but encompass an almost
infinite array of signs to be memorized concerning physical and emotional
survival. A sweet scent signals that the fruit on the fig tree is ripe. An aunt
whom we trust offers us our first fig. We comprehend from her gesture
that it is a safe food to eat. Whenever we smell that particular sweetness,
we know to look around until we can find and pick that ripe fruit. And we
fondly recall our aunt. If we're lucky, we might even feel a sense of safety
remembering her solicitousness. Conversely, should we stick something
rotten or poisonous into our mouths, we can see from her expression of
disgust or urgency, or hear in her rushed words, or feel from her fingers in
our mouth, that we are not to eat that thing again.

We may not enjoy our aunt's sharp actions, but we learn very early that to
survive we must not alienate our older siblings and adult kin. So we attend
closely to learning how to get along. When we are very young, our feelings
are as impressionable as soft clay to a thumbprint. Before long, aspects of
our characters become as ornery and fixed as clumps of stinging nettles.
(Perhaps character is in part the adhesions of many stuck-together impressions.) And as we become more aware, and we begin to possess language,
our awareness takes the form of stories we tell ourselves about all that has
been impressed upon us and all that we've observed and felt.

We are guided through a maze of daily encounters, pleasures and dangers by our complex, lesson-absorbing minds, with which we try to make
sense of the chaos, to perceive the patterns, to draw survival rules from all
the bits of experience with which we continually collide.

If you are reading this page, chances are good you already know the
basics of the internal family systems model. To reiterate briefly: IFS is a form
of psychotherapy that is about how our minds draw lessons from the bent
grass blades, the parental expressions, the aunt's offering of figs, the family
rules—and all the attendant feelings about the layered, talkative, distorted

way that these memories and impressions reside dynamically within us—to help us survive.

Richard Schwartz divides our parts into two sorts: protectors and exiles. Protectors are either proactive (referred to as managers) or reactive (referred to as firefighters). Exiles carry our deepest pain—often from having experienced extreme lessons when emotion was intense. Managers are our most common, active guides through daily life. Firefighters are hair-trigger emergency managers who race in when they perceive an urgent situation.

Our parts all carry stories. They function as the vehicles through which our minds attempt to generalize from particular lessons in the hope of guiding us safely along subsequent paths. Each part has taken certain experiences to heart and repeatedly applies what it has learned. We must be very perceptive to learn quickly enough; yet that same acute awareness makes us vulnerable to intense psychic pain. Indeed, sometimes it seems we have evolved paradoxically such that the very sensitivity that allows us to survive renders the world quasi-unbearable to us. Our parts attempt to broker the balance between our need for such awareness and its often painful impact.

Each of our parts may hold but a small portion of our larger story. And, when an initial impression is strong, or the same impression is repeated many times, parts may overgeneralize the value of a lesson they believe they learned. Sometimes bent grass is just bent grass. A manager may divert us too quickly from the path; an exile's cueing may goad us to sweat, arousing a firefighter to help us run away—when, really, this time there's no cause.

Fortunately, Schwartz tells us, along with our parts, we have a "Self." This Self helps parts work together such that the useful knowledge possessed by each can better apply itself to the moment. The Self, according to Schwartz, is primarily a positive, spacious state of being—one with compassion, calm and curiosity. When we can readily access it, the Self allows us to gain a larger perspective on all the mini-lessons reiterated by our busy managers, and to choose among them; to offer them smaller or larger realms of jurisdiction and, at moments, to override them.

The presence of parts in people's minds is vividly illustrated in George Saunders's short story "Victory Lap" (2013) in which he uses the ongoing commentary in his characters' heads as a way both to reveal them to us and to recount an attempted kidnapping/rape. Saunders is a wonderful writer, but the additional gift he offers us here is illustrating both how fundamental parts and their opinions are within our minds, and how someone who is not a therapist describes them. The ugly assault is foiled because the adolescent protagonist, Kyle, at home alone after school, violates all his parents' rules and acts to save his teenage neighbor, Alison. Saunders's use of parts is so precisely as Schwartz describes them, and as clinicians encounter them, that the parallel is a bit uncanny. Yet, as far as I know, Saunders knows nothing about the IFS model. Schwartz often comments on particular rules governing parts, and Saunders's spontaneous representation of these rules offers a one-off bit of evidence.

Here is a moment in Kyle's mind. You can see how each time he moves about his family home, his father's voice offers heavy-handed instructive (hilarious) commentary. In IFS language, Kyle has an overbearing, omnipresent "Dad part"—a manager—working very hard, continually nagging at him: "Scout, Dad said in his head, has anyone ever told you that even the most neatly maintained garage is going to have some oil on its floor, which is now on your socks, being tracked all over the tan Berber?" (Saunders, 2013, p. 12).[1]

Here's 15-year-old Alison. She's also home alone. Feeling consciously happy—and, it seems, unconsciously anxious. She kisses a photo of her parents and herself as a little girl. Saunders's text reveals how she works with her parts to try to comfort herself, and to manage the anxiety of an apparently young part, in this moment represented as a baby deer.

> Sometimes, feeling happy like this, she imagined a baby deer trembling in the woods.
>   Where's your mama, little guy?
>   I don't know, the deer said in the voice of Heather's little sister Becca.
>   Are you afraid? she asked it. Are you hungry? Do you want me to hold you?
>   Okay, the baby deer said.
>   (Saunders, 2013, pp. 5–6)

A hunter breaks into Alison's reverie and kills the baby's mother. Alison befriends the hunter and attempts to render him nonthreatening. While her self-soothing is not completely successful (the baby deer keeps asking what happened to its mother), it is a spontaneous illustration of working with one's own parts to create more calm. (The dialogue also nicely illustrates Schwartz's insistence that parts—as opposed to the dangerous folk in the real world—will not hurt us if we are not afraid of them.)

The actual assailant has no name. After he makes an error while trying to force Alison into his van, he finds himself hearing the voice of his dead, abusive stepfather, Melvin. (The passage also suggests the existence of a traumatized young exile within the adult kidnaper—one who carries the memories of having been beaten and, apparently, sexually abused): "Melvin appeared in his mind. On Melvin's face was the look of hot disappointment that had always preceded an ass whooping, which had preceded the other thing. Put up your hands, Melvin said, defend yourself" (Saunders, 2013, p. 19).

At the critical moment, Kyle's "giddy part"—which seems to be a firefighter—takes over, and lets him break loose of all his mental rules (other managers) and act. Kyle grabs the new highly prized geode from his father's collection, runs after the kidnapper and throws the geode through the van's windshield to smash the kidnapper's head and to save Alison:

> Then he was running. Across the lawn. Oh God! What was he doing? Jesus, shit, the directives he was violating! Running in the yard (bad for the sod); . . . hopping the fence, which stressed the fence, which had cost a pretty penny; leaving the yard, leaving the yard barefoot; . . . and, not only that, oh God, suddenly he saw what this giddy part of himself intended, which was to violate a directive so Major and absolute that it wasn't even a directive.
>
> (Saunders, 2013, p. 22)

Kyle's adrenalized assault saves Alison. "Victory Lap" demonstrates how intuitively familiar we all are with parts, even if no psychotherapy before IFS has worked with them so explicitly, particularly in relationship to the Self. Saunders's narration further reminds us that our waking minds are all-stories-all-the-time. We are never internally quiet, never without a constant commentary—sometimes subliminal, or delivered in images or inchoate feelings; other times more distinctly "voiced."

Saunders's remarkable tale also leads us to an important recognition lately described by Michael Gazzaniga, an esteemed neuroscientist. At the center of our critical brain function, he tells us, is a storyteller. Thanks to machine imaging and careful experiments, Gazzaniga has discovered how, in our left hemisphere, we possess an "interpreter," who rapidly creates coherent retrospective accounts that we overlay upon our otherwise incoherent experience. Here is *The New York Times* description:

> The interpreter creates the illusion of a meaningful script, as well as a coherent self. Working on the fly, it furiously reconstructs not only what happened but why, inserting motives here, intentions there—based on limited, sometimes flawed information.

One implication of this is a familiar staple of psychotherapy and literature: we often know little about who we are, all we really know is the story as we've retrospectively told it, usually subconsciously, usually bending information and nudging it here and there to fit our narration. "The storyteller never stops, except perhaps during deep sleep" (Carey, 2011).

Those of us who use the IFS model, or write fiction like Saunders, would hypothesize that many internal storytellers—or parts—contribute to, or perhaps compete to be the voice of, this master narrative. Each part, and the experiences it carries, is both a building block of these essential internal stories and a reporter on particular interior perspectives—or lessons learned.

Furthermore, the fact that we can recognize ourselves—or at least variations on our own minds—as mirrored back to us in fiction suggests that there might be a deep grammar involved in parts representations, and that neither writers, nor the rest of us, create parts from thin air, but perhaps by unconsciously overlaying our particulars onto innate structures.

Schwartz believes that our parts are multidimensional and real. And, at the least, we must work with them as if each one were a real person. We should treat them as fellow members of a village, or the characters in Saunders's story—as whole beings each with his or her own subjectivity, assumptions, and knowledge. Certainly, parts are as real as any of our self-perceptions. And the admonition from Schwartz to deal with parts respectfully offers a glimpse of the value system of his model.

My larger point is that one feels with IFS therapy that Schwartz has found a straightforward, simplified language to conceptualize some fundamental processes of mind. In IFS therapy, people are encouraged to identify their parts, to get to know them, to help them unblend, to speak with them, to listen carefully to their stories and when possible, to liberate them from at least some of the pain they carry. By unburdening the particularly vulnerable, pained exile parts, the therapy seeks to relax and harmonize the whole inner system, and free energy for other purposes.

Is IFS a better psychotherapy than the many others out there? We cannot be certain because, like most psychotherapies, it has not yet been fully researched. Yet, even un-researched, IFS can demonstrate that it flexes therapeutic muscle both as a method of healing and in the ethics of its approach. In his classic work *Persuasion and Healing* (1961), Jerome D. Frank reviewed many types of psychotherapeutic, communal and religious healing, and attempted to identify the common effective elements of approaches used across societies and centuries. IFS manifests these elements.

According to Frank, psychotherapy is a type of "influence" characterized by a trained, socially sanctioned healer; a sufferer who seeks relief; and "a circumscribed . . . structured series of contacts between healer and sufferer" that "tries to produce . . . changes in the sufferer's emotional state, attitudes, and behavior." Psychotherapies heal the patient, Frank tells us, by offering new learning, awakening hope, arousing emotion, enhancing the patient's sense of mastery and helping him "overcome his demoralizing sense of alienation from his fellows" (1961, pp. 2–3, 329).

If you are familiar with IFS, you will immediately hear how well Frank's schema fits with it. But here I want to highlight those aspects of IFS that are congruent with Frank's description and yet distinctive. While Frank does not discuss the relative ethics of different forms of psychotherapy, his book stimulated my thinking about the subject as relevant to IFS. So, when I refer to the ethics of IFS, I am noting underlying values within its method that determine how it seeks to facilitate change.

At the core of the IFS position is the assumption that both the therapist and the sufferer are fully human, and that the sufferer is to be approached as an equal. IFS training repeatedly sends this message to therapists. It says,

"We are all in this together." Sufferer and therapist are merely in different chairs. IFS is not interested in cataloging or sorting pathology (for example, "dysthymia versus major depressive episode") nor in describing schemas of causality of the "A cold mother creates a schizophrenic child" sort. While this choice may occasionally be problematic because it risks creating a naïveté about the gravity of some people's conditions (for example, acute psychotic episodes), one of its strong virtues is in diminishing the extent to which sufferers are "othered" or objectified.

IFS therapists are trained in intensive training groups in which they repeatedly take turns in the roles of therapist, sufferer and witness. This unusually "democratic" process intensifies the group bond and reinforces practitioners' belief in the healing powers of the method. The therapist's personal experience of having suffering (exiles) relieved by IFS also enhances his or her ability to offer hope. (When he teaches, Schwartz repeatedly reminds therapists that they must be "hope merchants.")

Also distinctive, and ethically significant, is the way IFS shifts the balance of power and agency toward patients by encouraging them to heal their own parts. Schwartz (2013) states that IFS is a relational therapy and that the therapist's steady, warm presence is essential. He describes healing as a parallel process occurring between therapist and patient, and between the patient's Self and parts. Yet, while the therapist offers structure and guidance, assists the patient at tough moments and provides a witnessing/comforting presence, his or her role is not often a focus in the treatment. Instead, the therapist's Self-energy gradually enhances the patient's Self enough to empower it to heal suffering parts.

Anyone who has watched Schwartz work knows that personal authority and confidence in the method enhance patient response. But the position of therapist is worn differently than in transference-focused therapies. Rather than emphasizing the therapist's power to heal, IFS focuses on relationships among the sufferer's parts and the relationship of parts to Self. While the therapist's Self-energy and compassion create the context for the therapeutic work, IFS emphasizes that the patient does the most to heal him- or herself.

Indeed, one reason many patients easily embrace IFS is that the naming of parts quickly rebalances the ways in which they view themselves. To have an "irritable" part is radically different from being an irritable person. The latter is totalizing and defining; the former, descriptive and inviting of curiosity. This difference allows emotions and states of mind to be held more lightly and encourages self-reflection, or curiosity.

In general, IFS offers a straightforward method that concretizes internal processes left more abstract in other psychotherapy approaches. In IFS, the sufferer is repeatedly told—in different ways—that he or she is suffering because his or her parts are burdened by the painful memories they carry, and because, to protect exiles from feeling overwhelmed by that pain, their managers and firefighters are overworking and exhausting themselves. Although all parts wish to assist the patient, they are often unaware of each other, not working in harmony and not functioning under the more spacious guidance of the Self.

The first phase of treatment focuses on going inside: learning about parts, inviting them to unblend, working with them individually and building trust among them. The second phase involves the Self witnessing the exile's injuries along with its consequent emotional pain and burdensome beliefs, and ends with a ritual unburdening.

In this process, IFS therapists consistently model the importance of holding empathy and positive regard for all parts. This attitude is necessarily qualified because there are distinctions to be made between intentions and behavior. For example, a firefighter who suggests we repeatedly cut ourselves to relieve numbness or intense pain is likely to be promoting a behavior that attempts to protect us from what it fears is unbearable psychic pain. As a desperate adolescent, trapped and unaware of other possibilities or resources, cutting may have seemed like the best alternative to promote survival. But in the present adult moment, that firefighter is pointing toward a behavior that is harmful and forecloses new possibilities. Thus it inhibits learning better ways of bearing feelings. Still, the idea that all parts seek to protect us by conveying their lessons (however mislearned) raises patients' self-compassion and thus morale. It quickly begins lowering the internal battling among polarized parts.

A fascinating larger question about IFS is the degree to which its emphasis on "parts" may turn out to improve psychotherapeutic healing. Schwartz and many IFS practitioners believe that approaching parts directly allows for particularly effective change, and the chapters that comprise this book will demonstrate many instances of the method and its achievements. Whatever we eventually learn from research, the very fact that our minds (as independently shown by fiction writers, poets and dramatists) recognize the existence of parts, and are so readily able to create full characters, suggests that IFS has pulled an essential process of mind into our psychotherapeutic work.

NOTE

1. All quotes from "Victory Lap" are reprinted with permission from the author.

REFERENCES

Carey, B. (2011). *Decoding the brain's cacophony*. Retrieved from www.nytimes.com/ 2011/11/01/science/telling-the-story-of-the-brains-cacophony-of-competing-voices. html?pagewanted=3&_r=0

Diamond, J. (2012). *The world until yesterday.* London, England: Penguin Books.
Frank, J. D. (1961). *Persuasion and healing: A comparative study of psychotherapy.* Baltimore, MD: Johns Hopkins Press.
Saunders, G. (2013). *Tenth of December.* New York: Random House.
Schwartz, R. C. (2013). The therapist-client relationship and the transformative power of self. In M. Sweezy & E. L. Ziskind (Eds.), *Internal family systems therapy: New dimensions* (pp. 1–23). New York: Routledge.

Chapter 1

Getting Unstuck

*Pamela K. Krause, Lawrence G. Rosenberg
and Martha Sweezy*

INTRODUCTION

From neophyte to seasoned clinician, all therapists experience the occasional impasse or rupture in their work. These events are often embodied in behavior: something like forgetting an appointment, arriving late, avoiding uncomfortable content and not being willing to try something the therapist suggests; or something dramatic and urgent, like frequent phone calls and voice mail messages, intractable despair, crises in the therapy relationship, suicidal emergencies. Since these behaviors are generally about something that remains unspeakable for the client, most of the time we don't easily understand their meaning. The moments in which we know something is amiss but feel uncertain about how to proceed can evoke our anxious, shaming and agenda-driven parts. In a parts-to-parts struggle, either internally or in the therapeutic relationship, we lose Self-leadership and fail to contain the moment with curiosity, clarity and calm. We are stuck. For this reason, therapeutic dilemmas have been of great interest to generations of clinicians from every school.

We (the authors) postulate that every therapy impasse occurs because the client, the therapist or both are so *blended* with their parts that they cannot access the qualities of the Self, ranging from curiosity to compassion, that are needed to proceed constructively. This is the internal family systems (IFS) equivalent of transference and countertransference. When blended parts assert their judgments, emotions and body sensations, they motivate all of us, client and therapist alike, to act as we wish, and we don't have the perspective to recognize their influence. Instead we believe *this is who I am* and *my view is correct*.

When we (again, all of us) are in a balanced state, our protectors are bolstered by Self-energy and we rely on them to navigate and function in the world. However, when situations activate our exiles (usually out of awareness) and evoke feelings like loneliness, worthlessness and yearnings for redemption, our protectors take over or *blend* to prevent us from feeling overwhelmed. An activated protector may blend spontaneously, or it may remain chronically blended, doing its job so automatically, repetitively and compulsively over many years that its behavior is our dominant character style. When desperate exiles drive protectors to be powerfully assertive, leaving virtually no access to the clarity and calm of Self-energy, anyone can feel very ill and meet criteria for diagnoses like major depression, psychosis or PTSD. Metaphorically speaking, this is a coup d'état: *The Self has been thrown into the trunk and a part is driving the car!*

CHAPTER OVERVIEW

To get a clear perspective and see the best course of action during a difficult clinical interaction, we must have a critical mass of Self-energy. Therefore, the solution for resolving stuck moments in therapy for both therapist and client is unblending, a state in which parts are differentiated from the Self. We wrote this chapter because helping parts to unblend can be easier said than done. An exile may fear the invitation to unblend as a prelude to being banished again. A protective part may fear unblending for any number of reasons: the part needs to feel more connected to the therapist, it feels threatened by a polarized part, it is guarding a secret that has yet to be disclosed or the therapist does not have enough Self-energy to calm its fears. Whatever the reason, we can always be curious about the cause of stuckness. And the first target of our curiosity should be us: Am I (the therapist) leading from my Self or from a part?

We divide the chapter into four sections. The first offers some basic guidelines for preventing and working with stuckness. The second presents case vignettes that illustrate some options for helping a wary internal system take the leap of unblending. The third presents case vignettes that illustrate common obstacles to unblending: a Self-like part in the lead (in either therapist or client), polarities and a system that's been through extreme trauma. And the fourth section presents a case that illustrates being innovative in response to feeling stuck.

GUIDELINES FOR PREVENTING AND WORKING WITH STUCKNESS

Cultivate Self-Energy

The capacity to be calm, curious and compassionate is essential for preventing and working through therapeutic impasses. It is our responsibility, therefore, to know what triggers our system by use of introspection, supervision and personal therapy. When we are able to come to sessions without an agenda and trust the process, we are implicitly reassuring the client's protectors (Schwartz, 1995).

Be a Good Parts Detector

In order for our parts to trust the Self in considering their differing perspectives and making wise decisions, we need to be excellent *parts detectors*. A perpetual stance of wonder can be very helpful in this regard: *Who (in the other person) am I talking to? Who (inside me) is talking and reacting?*

Be Aware of the Vulnerable Part Behind the Fierce Protector

Having identified a part, we must then wonder about its role: *Is this a protector, an exiled protector* (a part, often young, who seems to be an exile but when asked will endorse protecting another part), *or an exile?* Almost all internal systems lead with protectors. Again, curiosity is key: *Who is being protected?* As we illustrate later, one good way to find out is to ask the question: *What are you afraid would happen if you stopped what you're doing?*

Be Aware of Polarizations

Extreme parts contribute a great deal to stuckness. Remember that they always come in pairs, and the anxiety their disagreements generate reinforces their polarization and drives their extremity. If one forceful protector is present, another is in the wings whether we hear its voice or not.

Proceed Slowly With Patience, Persistence, and Perspective

As we illustrate throughout the chapter, we should move only as quickly as the client's system allows.

UNBLENDING

Ways of Beginning a Session

We might start the session by asking *What are you curious about today?* Or *Is there a part who needs your attention?* The target part will be embedded in a cluster of concerned parts, and IFS has developed procedural options, called *parts-detecting*, for exploring this micro-system, especially by repeatedly asking the client *How do you feel toward this* (the target) *part?*

If the client names a feeling toward a target part that is not something along the lines of curiosity, caring or compassion, then a reactive part is speaking and we have a couple of options: (1) ask the reactive part for permission to continue with the target part; (2) externalize both the target part and the reactive part through the client's imagination, on a whiteboard or paper, in a sand tray or with objects in the room like pillows or scarves, and then ask who needs attention first; or (3) use direct access with the reactive part, the technique (illustrated in Table 1.1) in which the therapist's Self talks directly to the client's part.

Proceeding With Either Direct Access or In-Sight

The IFS model presents two ways of working with a client's internal system: in-sight and direct access. Unless we have reason to think otherwise, we begin by assuming that we will use in-sight, the technique in which the client's Self communicates with the client's parts. When this fails, we opt for direct access because a blended part will almost always talk to the therapist's Self.

While many clinicians prefer the ease of collaboration between the client's Self and parts, both in-sight and direct access have benefits. The

Table 1.1 Selecting a Target Part

1. **Ask the client directly:** *What shall we work on? What are you curious about today?*
2. **Reflect back the client's words in parts language:** *I hear that a part of you is* (angry, sad, doesn't know what to do, etc.). *Would you like to get to know your* (anger, sadness, confusion . . .) *better?* If the client objects to the word *part*, you can switch to words like *feeling, sensation* or *thought* while you keep thinking in terms of parts.
3. **Guided awareness:** *Take a breath, go inside, open up space, and notice any feelings or concerns that would like your attention. Who wants to go first?*
4. **Follow up on a part from a previous session:** *Last session, you were getting to know part X. Let's start by checking with that part to find out how it's doing.*

former is particularly efficient and helps clients engage with their parts between sessions; the latter is helpful in traumatized systems when hyper-vigilant protectors need to experience a connection with the Self of the therapist before they can trust the Self of the client (Schwartz, 1995). To complicate matters slightly, direct access has two modalities: *explicit* direct access in which the therapist openly asks permission to speak to the blended part, and *implicit* direct access in which the Self of the therapist appears to be talking directly to the client, but is, in fact, speaking directly to a blended part of the client, just as the client's Self does with in-sight. This dialogue looks like regular talk therapy, but the therapist is mindful that she's speaking to a part. We illustrate both kinds of direct access as well as in-sight next.

Explicit Direct Access

Explicit direct access is easy to identify because the therapist asks the client for permission to speak directly to a part. For example, Laura was a 20-year-old woman who had recently returned home from college following hospitalization for a suicide attempt. Laura started seeing me (Pam) weekly, and after several sessions she was able to use in-sight with some of her protectors. During the third month of therapy, Laura said, "I've been thinking of killing myself again."

I replied, "Would you like to know more about the part who thinks about killing you?" Laura was interested. As she focused, the part appeared as a revolver. "How do you feel toward the revolver part?" I asked.

"I hate it!" Laura exclaimed. Despite much reassurance, neither the one who hated the revolver part nor a variety of other reactive parts were willing to allow direct contact between the revolver and Laura. They were all too afraid of what the revolver might do if Laura gave it attention. So I said to Laura, "Can I talk directly to the revolver? I don't want to turn it loose in your system, but if I can find out more about it I'm confident we can address its concerns." This statement served to raise at least some hope in her system and the other parts gave permission for direct access. "I'd like to talk with the revolver. Are you there?" I said.

Laura replied, "Yes."

"You think about killing Laura?" I asked.

"Yes and don't try to talk me out of it," the revolver replied. "If you put me in the hospital again, I swear I'll kill her. You know I almost succeeded the last time because those people in the hospital are so stupid."

"I'm not talking about the hospital right now," I said. "I just want to get to know you better. I know you're trying to protect Laura, and I wonder why you do it this way. Would you be willing to tell me about yourself?"

No one had ever asked the revolver to talk before. Intrigued, it replied, "I'm the end game. I'm here to stop all the pain when it gets to be too much." "What kind of pain?" I asked.

"That empty, hollow feeling. Nothingness," the revolver replied.

"You think about killing her to keep her from feeling hollow and empty. Do you want to kill her?" I asked.

"Not really but nothing else has worked," the revolver replied. "Therapy has been a huge flop. I hate feeling drugged out by all the crappy meds they have her on, her parents are a nightmare, and Tom just dumped her. I really don't have a choice."

"What if I told you that there is another way?" I said, being the *hope merchant*—the one who is certain that feelings can change and exiles can heal (Schwartz, 1995). "We can find the part who feels empty and hollow and heal it so it doesn't have to feel that nothingness any more."

"Yeah, right!" the revolver replied. "There is no way you can do that."

"Yes there is," I said. "I know how to help her do that. Have you been watching what we've been doing over the last couple of months?"

"Yes."

"So I bet you've already begun to see what we can do. We only need two things from you. First, we'll ask you to step back when Laura and I are together so Laura can help the one who feels empty. Second, obviously, we can only do this if Laura is alive, so I'm going to ask you to give us some time to work on it."

"How much time?" the revolver asked.

"How much are you willing to give us?" I asked.

"Three months," the revolver said.

"Okay," I replied, "but here's the deal. It's unlikely that we'll be able to finish everything by then but we can make good headway, so you'll know if what I say is actually possible. And if you see it is then the deal continues."

"All right," the revolver said.

"Now, you may get triggered during the next three months. If that happens would you talk to me before you do anything?"

"Fair enough," the revolver said.

"Great!" I said. "If it's okay I'd like to talk with Laura again. Laura, how do you feel toward the revolver after hearing all that?"

"I don't hate it any more," Laura said. "I see that in a strange kind of way it's trying to help me."

"How does the revolver respond to you saying that?"

At this point, I was transitioning back to in-sight in the service of forming a relationship between Laura's Self and the revolver. After this, with the cooperation of the revolver, we were able to make contact with Laura's empty feeling exile. As I predicted, the revolver got alarmed several times over the next three months. But it always talked with me and/or Laura and we were able to reassure it. At the end of the three months, also as I predicted, the work was not complete but there had been enough change in the level of Laura's emotional pain that the revolver felt great hope and no urgency to kill her. Laura's case illustrates explicit direct access and also how to move between direct access and in-sight during a session, which is a perfectly good option.

When an Extreme Protector Won't Back Off

The case of Laura and her suicidal part raises the question of when an impasse might lead to hospitalization. Sometimes a client's protectors are dangerous and uncooperative and the clinician must make a Self-led choice regarding safety. At any time, this decision can be confusing and stressful for the therapist. Dangerous client parts (suicidal, self-harming, substance abusing, food restricting, bingeing/purging, etc.) can evoke parts with intense feelings and powerful agendas in the therapist, including parts who are afraid, intellectual, caretaking or frozen, to name just a few. So the first step for the IFS therapist is to embody as much Self-energy as possible and calm her parts so they can unblend. Asking yourself *How do I feel toward this part of my client?* is crucial. Remember, the therapist wants to establish a Self-led relationship with dangerous parts of the client because healing in the IFS model occurs in the Self-to-part relationship.

If the therapist's parts do not step back, she will be engaged in a part-to-part interaction (her parts interacting with the client's parts), which is likely to increase the client's risk. For example, if the client has a suicidal part, one of the therapist's managers might try to contract with the client to not kill herself; or if it is a bingeing part, the therapist might have a manager who offers advice or food plans to moderate the part's behavior; or the therapist might be taken over by a frightened exile and seek to hospitalize the client immediately. Conflicts between the therapist's managers and the client's firefighters can easily escalate into a dangerous impasse. In contrast, the curiosity and compassion of the Self helps dangerous parts feel understood, increasing the chance that they will negotiate. If the therapist can be Self-led and develop a relationship with the dangerous part, then hospitalization may not be necessary.

However, if a dangerous part refuses to negotiate, no matter how it is welcomed, then the therapist must act as a lifeguard and may make a Self-led decision to hospitalize. For example, Tara, an 18-year-old girl who had just started IFS therapy, quickly found an exile who felt empty and untethered. Tara was able to communicate with this exile using in-sight during therapy sessions but was not yet able to take care of it between sessions, in part because just as she began therapy a classmate had introduced her to heroin. Tara was open with me (Pam), saying that heroin was the only thing that had ever made the emptiness go away. Her delighted firefighter not only refused to give up the heroin but used more and more often over the next few weeks.

I tried negotiating with it by saying things like, "I understand that this feels better to you, but you've also said that you have the same feeling when Tara can meet with that exile here in therapy. Is that true?"

"Yes," it replied, "but I only see you two hours a week. There's lots of crap happening every day, and I can't take it anymore."

"I know it's really tough and we're working as quickly as we can," I said. "Tara is going to be able to help the little one who feels empty more and more every week. I know you want that. Would you consider backing off a bit, maybe getting high less frequently? How about switching to pot or something less dangerous?"

"Nope. Nothing, I mean nothing, works like the heroin," the part replied.

"I get why you want to do heroin then. But at the same time I'm concerned about you and Tara. Your help is putting her in danger—she could die and you'd die with her. I know you're not trying to kill her, but it's getting more and more likely that heroin will. Once we release that empty feeling everyone inside will feel better, but we can't get there if Tara's dead. I know you won't like this but I can't let her be in danger any longer. Let's talk about inpatient rehab."

"I don't want to kill her, but I can't stop because I don't want to feel like this anymore."

"I know. That's why I want to get Tara to a safe place. Then we can continue our work."

With her parents' support, Tara entered a rehab program and discontinued the heroin use. When she got out we continued, and she was eventually able to unburden the exile who felt empty. To date, she has not used heroin again. This example illustrates how welcoming a dangerous part can require more than listening, understanding and offering compassion— it can also require the therapist to face danger with courage. When the heroin-using part insisted on continuing, I spoke for my concerns and set a limit. Even though the part didn't like what I said and didn't want Tara in rehab, it did feel connected to me. Believing my promise that help was coming, it let her return to therapy.

Implicit Direct Access

Here is an example of using implicit direct access with a client who just described feeling angry with her mother. We might say, "You've just described having a disagreement with your mother where you felt rejected and got angry. Would you like to know more about the parts who responded that way?" If Josie says *yes* we can help her explore the anger using in-sight. If Josie ignores the question or says *no*, we begin using implicit direct access. "No, I just want you to know how awful my mother was," Josie says.

"I can see it's important for you to tell me about this," the therapist responds. "Would you be willing to let me know why it's so important to you?" **(Therapist speaks directly to the part: implicit direct access.)**

"Everyone always tells me: *Let it go, she doesn't mean it.* No one ever supports me!"

"What's it like for you when no one supports you?" **(Implicit direct access.)**

"I feel alone, like I don't matter."

"And what happens when you feel like you don't matter?" **(Implicit direct access.)**

"I don't know . . . I get mad I guess. I just can't stand it."

"It makes sense to me that feeling so alone is hard to stand. What happens when you get mad about it?" **(Implicit direct access.)**

"It helps for a little while but in the end I just feel more alone. Nothing fixes this."

"Getting mad distracts you from feeling alone, but afterward you feel worse." **(Implicit direct access.)**

"Yeah. This sucks."

"What is it like to be telling me about feeling alone?" **(Implicit direct access.)**

"It's different. At least you listen."

"There is a very important story here—the story of a part who feels alone and unimportant. How about we find this part and help it?" **(An invitation to switch to in-sight.)** If the client is willing, she can accept this invitation to shift to a Self-to-part, in-sight based relationship with her parts. But if she is still not interested in switching and says, "I just really need you to hear this," the therapist continues to be curious and listens to the part's story.

"Okay," the therapist replies, "tell me what happened." **(Implicit direct access.)**

In-Sight

When a client's Self is available to work with his parts, we call the approach in-sight. In this mode, IFS therapy tends to go along smoothly because, by definition, the client has enough Self-energy to be in relationship with whichever parts need attention. The more Self-energy the client has, the smoother the process will be. The following client is experienced with IFS and able to use in-sight.

"My girlfriend told me I was bullying her this week," Hugh reported to me (Martha).

"Do you recognize what she's talking about?" I said.

"It was on Sunday. I guess I was just in a bad mood."

"Shall we check with that part?"

"Sure," he said, closing his eyes.

"Where do you find it?"

"The muscles in my jaw. It's like this grim, clenched jaw thing."

"How do you feel toward it?"

"I actually wasn't aware of this part but now I'm really noticing it. I wonder what's going on." **(The Self.)**

"How does it respond?"

"It's swearing and calling her a bitch—sorry—now I feel really bad for Sarah." **(A part with some Self-energy.)**

"What do you say to the one who feels bad?"

"I'm asking it to wait. I know Sarah deserves an apology but I want to find out more about this clenched jaw part." **(The Self.)** He was silent for a few moments. "Oh, wow, this is my little dad part. My father could go from charming leprechaun to rude, entitled asshole in no time flat. I'm asking who he protects. It's the lost boy of course. I'm reminding him that I take care of the boy **(the Self)**. He wonders if everyone is mad at him for doing this job—I have a lot of parts with strong feelings about my father."

"Would he let you take over with the boy so the other parts don't get mad at him anymore?"

"Yes. He's lonely."

"Does he get that you can do this?"

"He didn't know but he's getting it now."

As we hear, Hugh was able to get into a Self-led relationship with his little dad part quickly despite the disapproval of the other parts toward the little dad. This illustrates how a session moves along smoothly with in-sight once the client's parts have developed enough trust in the client's Self. Since a therapy is less likely to get stuck when the client's system has the Self-energy to engage in in-sight, the lion's share of what we discuss in this chapter is devoted to variations on direct access.

OBSTACLES TO UNBLENDING IN EITHER THE THERAPIST OR THE CLIENT

Polarizations

Painful early experiences evoke powerful emotional and behavioral responses, which can override the child's access to Self-energy. When the internal system gets knocked off balance, protectors' belief that safety lies in opposite directions seems to be the balancing act of a burdened system (Schwartz, 1995). Every system has polarizations (Rosenberg, 2013), yet they differ in intensity and we may wonder what causes one person's polarity to be more extreme than another's. The answer seems to be: Why use a cannon to kill a fly when a flyswatter is sufficient? Protectors are only as aggressive as they need to be in the job of protecting an exile or protecting the system from the exile's feelings. Generally speaking, the more wounded the system's exiles, the more intense the behavior of protectors.

When circumstances cause polarized parts to escalate in intensity and each side grows more entrenched, unblending becomes unpopular on both sides of the fence. Nevertheless, when a polarization is so intense that neither side is interested in a relationship with the client's Self, we have the option of asking them to unblend simultaneously. My experience (Pam) with Harry is a good example. Harry had had some success as a screenwriter but still felt unseen, unheard and worthless. He wrote numerous scripts, which he urgently tried to sell, a part of him believing that if he could write an Academy Award–winning one, he would no longer feel worthless. He came to therapy because he was having trouble staying motivated and found himself lying around the house smoking pot, which made his hardworking part frantic.

As I listened to Harry describe his parts, I began to notice my parts either aligning or polarizing with his. One of mine agreed with his hardworking part and another wanted to suggest programs to help Harry stop smoking pot. I also noticed a part saying *What's the matter with smoking pot? It's a great way to take the edge off, and in the big picture it's not the worst firefighter in the world.* As I noticed these parts, I asked them to give me space to listen to Harry. When I asked Harry where he would like to begin, he said, "I'd like to spend some time with the hardworking part so I can make it stronger." I asked Harry to remember a recent time when he felt motivated and to notice this in his body. He replied, "I can't feel my body." One of my parts reacted strongly to this, saying, *Oh no, this is going to be a tough client!* And another admonished, *You didn't do a very good job explaining this.* As I asked these parts to step back, I suggested to Harry that his hardworking part might be in his head. Would he check?

Harry said, "My head is filled with thoughts about what I could be doing."

After he listened to the hardworking part in his head I asked him the classic unblending question, "How do you feel toward it?"

Replying from a polarized part, Harry said, "Oh I hate it!"

I asked him to find the one who hated the hardworking part and ask it to step back. Then I checked again to find out how Harry felt toward the hardworking part. His response was the same so I said, "Ask this part: What will happen if you relax enough to let me get to know the hardworking part?"

It replied, "All I will ever do is work!"

I said, "Let it know that we don't want you to work all the time and that we can help with that." After a moment I checked once more to see how he felt toward the hardworking part.

He replied, "I still hate it."

We had now asked the part (probably the pot smoker) who hated the hardworking part to step back three times, and it was unwilling. So we needed to make it the target. I asked Harry to find it in his body. He said it was a vague tension throughout. When I asked how he felt toward it, he replied, "I hate it."

At this point, it's safe to say that many of my parts were reacting. Some were irritated with Harry, others were irritated with me and one was trying desperately to figure out what to do. I started by reassuring them that Harry and I would be okay if they stepped back. Returning to Harry, I walked us through the same basic steps of asking this last part (the hardworking part) to step back. When it would not, I asked what it was afraid would happen if it did.

It said, "If I do, Harry will just lie around and smoke pot all day."

In this way, I knew that the hardworking part had returned and that neither it nor the pot smoker was willing to step back for fear of the other gaining control. If polarized parts are willing to unblend simultaneously, the therapist can help the client get to know both at the same time. When I asked if they would do this, they agreed.

Then, displaying the first touch of Self-energy, Harry said, "I'd like to know them better."

"Tell them you want to know them both and they have to take turns."

The hardworking part wanted to go first, and the pot smoker agreed. The hardworking part said, "I work hard to write screenplays that are interesting, and I know if you show them to enough people someone will make one of them into an Academy Award–winning movie. I'm smart and creative and people will see my value when my movie wins an award."

I made sure Harry asked the hardworking part what it was afraid would happen to Harry if it didn't work so hard. It replied, "He'll lie around all day smoking pot and he'll feel worthless," indicating that the hardworking part was also afraid of an exile who felt worthless.

When Harry invited the pot smoker to speak, it said, "Why do you want to go out there and put yourself on the line by showing people your screenplays? You keep getting rejected and then you feel like crap (*aka worthless*). It's much safer to stay at home and numb out."

It was now clear to Harry that both the hardworking part and the pot smoker were trying to keep him from feeling worthless. He also knew that neither had ever succeeded. At the same time, having discovered their shared goal, these polarized protectors were feeling less irritated with each other. So I helped Harry become the hope merchant.

"If the worthless feeling part felt better, would these two have to work so hard?"

Table 1.2 De-escalating Polarities

To de-escalate a polarity, follow this series of steps with both parts:
1. Ask which part would like to talk first. (Part A wanted to.)
2. Make sure there is a Self-to-part relationship between the client and Part A, and check periodically to make sure Part B has not blended. (*How do you feel toward Part A?* usually suffices to detect blended parts.)
3. Find out about Part A's job and what it is worried will happen if it stops doing it. This question reveals either a polarized protector or an exile.
4. Do the same with Part B.

"They would not," Harry replied.

"Ask if they're willing to watch and see what you can do to help the part who feels worthless," I said.

"They accept," he reported.

As Harry's experience illustrates, protective parts can be so radically at odds and distrustful of each other's influence that neither is willing to budge. When this occurs we can arrange a moment of mutual unblending, which makes space for the transformative presence of the client's Self (see Table 1.2).

When the Therapist Is Blindsided by a Hidden Polarity

Polarized parts can also take turns blending, sometimes at dizzying speeds, proffering contrary requests or responses of which the client shows no awareness, causing us to feel confused about who's talking. For example, Ian, a 34-year-old man with a history of trauma, opened his first session with me (Larry) with this statement: "I'm looking for a warm, nurturing therapist who really gets what I've been through." I nodded sympathetically. He went on to tell the story of an often terrifying, always sad and lonely childhood. I liked Ian and felt we had launched a warm connection. But the next week he came in stiff and glowering. "When I spoke about my childhood last week you looked sad," he said. There was a long pause, after which he concluded with breathtaking coldness, "I find it disgusting when other people get emotional about my life."

Internally I could feel my startled, shamed and frustrated protectors springing to the barricades. I asked them to trust me. After taking a moment to breathe, I nodded and replied, "I'm just beginning to get to know you, Ian. Last week you had a part who spoke of wanting warmth and connection. Now I hear you also have part who doesn't want that. Both of them are welcome here."

Ian continued to eye me coldly. "I don't know what you're talking about," he said. "I've had a lot of therapists and I guess you're going to be another one of them." Before I could reply, however, he went on, "I need you to understand." Since naming his polarity had done nothing to unblend the parts, I decided to try implicit direct access. But which part should I address first? I wasn't sure, so I just nodded and waited. "If you think I want your sympathy I guess I should leave now," he said, answering my question.

"It doesn't feel good when people have feelings about you," I said.

He sat back, noticed he still had his coat on and took it off, tossing it on the other side of the couch. "What good does pity do? No one ever helped me when I needed it. Talking just makes things more dangerous."

"Then your feelings make perfect sense," I said.

As this illustrates, when a client vacillates between opposite attitudes like idealizing and devaluing we're hearing from only one (blended) part at a time while another part watches from the wings. We can ally in this hidden polarity with entire innocence and be blindsided later on by the other part. Because the client has no access to the Self in this situation, holding the perspective that he needs both sides of the polarity for self-protection is our job alone, as is preparing our protectors for accusations of misattunement so we can remain calm, curious and courageous.

When a Self-Like Part Steps in for the Self

In both client and therapist, Self-like parts can be hard to distinguish from the Self (see Table 1.3). This is another common sticking point. The part is a manager who displays qualities similar to the Self but does not have the ability to heal. It will be empathic rather than compassionate, which is an important distinction. When we empathize, our exiles identify with the client's exiles, which is a threat to our protectors who fear being overwhelmed. When we feel compassion, even if our exiles identify with the client's exiles, our protectors don't mobilize because the Self is unafraid of being overwhelmed (Schwartz, personal communication, March 17, 2014).

From an IFS perspective, then, Self-like parts are well-meaning poseurs whose job is to prevent emotional overwhelm. In general, the Self-like part seeks to silence the exile by trying to help it feel better without letting it tell its story. Their strategies include calming or comforting an exile before it is ready to be comforted (clients often describe this as a smothering kind of mothering); being a gentle intellect that explains why bad things happened to the exile; or by removing sensations and feelings from the exile's visual witnessing process (clients say this is *like a Plexiglas screen* in front of the exile, or they say they feel *neutral* toward the exile, or *detached* while witnessing the exile). Here is an example.

Charlotte was a 51-year-old woman who had been in therapy off and on her whole life for depression and credited her spiritual practice with saving her life. Several months into working with me (Martha), the polarized protectors who dominated her life (a good girl part and an angry part) were just beginning to unblend enough for her to glimpse a 3-year-old exile. "She says she's always alone," Charlotte reported. "She's sad and mad. Everyone in the family makes fun of her. And they don't explain anything. They never answer her. Why?" Without missing a beat, she went on, "Well, nothing can be done about all that! It's in the past."

"How does the little girl respond to that?" I asked.

"She turned her back. But she'll be okay," Charlotte went on blithely. "She needs to understand that what's done is done."

"Who said that?" I asked.

"I did," Charlotte replied. "What can we do about reality beyond accepting it? I practice acceptance every day."

"May I talk directly to the part who's responsible for accepting?" I asked. Charlotte blinked. "It's a part of you," I asserted. "A part whose job must be very important for it to need to work every day." After a moment, Charlotte nodded. "So are you there?" I asked.

"Yes," Charlotte replied, speaking for the part.

"What do you do for Charlotte?" I asked.

"I save her," the part replied.

"What if we could save her without you having to work so hard?" I asked, introducing the idea of new options.

As this vignette illustrates, if we miss the underlying agenda and mistake a Self-like part for the Self, the exile's response (turning away, clamming up or disappearing) will give it away. In training, IFS therapists are encouraged to develop a good relationship between their Self and their Self-like parts (often therapist parts), who inevitably act as an agent of the status quo. In contrast, the Self is the agent of change and healing.

Table 1.3 *Qualities of the Self and Self-Like Parts*

Self	Self-Like Parts
Curiosity from the heart	Curiosity may be from the head
Calm	Calm
Compassion	Empathy
Connected to parts	Unable to heal other parts despite any connection
Does not try to change a part	Often wants other parts to change
No agenda	Has an agenda
Open, receptive energy	Energy often seems *moving toward*
Heart open	Heart covered

THE ROLE OF INNOVATION IN UNBLENDING:
GETTING CREATIVE WITH A SADISTIC PROTECTOR

In order to survive her first 18 years of extreme trauma at the hands of her parents and a high school teacher, Rhonda's dissociative identity disorder (DID) system was layered with parts whom she could see and name, and whose roles ranged from frontline worker to hidden exile. Some of these parts helped her function at a high level professionally and provided the appearance of being present even though she was mostly dissociated. And then there were parts, like the one who sliced her skin with a razor blade, who provided some immediate relief from intense inner conflict and self-blame. When I (Larry) guided Rhonda to learn more about her cutting part, it said it wanted to cut out *the badness.* Remaining curious, I said, "Tell me more about the badness."

"We're stupid, ugly, bad, unlovable," she replied.

"How do you know?"

"The bad man says so."

"Who is the bad man?"

"He has John's voice."

John was a high school teacher, a sadist who had spotted Rhonda's vulnerability (a childhood of extreme abuse) and had turned her high school years into a nightmare of brutal sexual assaults followed by savage humiliations. "How are you feeling toward the bad man?" I asked.

Rhonda squirmed, "Very scared. He says we should die."

"Yes, it makes a lot of sense that many parts are afraid of him," I said.

"He wants control so he can do things his way."

"Please ask the bad man to give you some space. Maybe he could sit in this chair over here?"

She went inside; then shuddered. "He won't listen to me. He doesn't care."

Shifting tactics, I asked, "May I speak directly to the bad man?"

"No," she said. "He won't talk to you."

"Why not?"

"He won't say."

I tried talking to the bad man anyway. "I understand that you speak inside Rhonda with John's voice. Is that right?"

"He won't talk to you," Rhonda repeated.

I asked the bad man, "Are you afraid something bad will happen if you talk to me?" No response. This was the first time that Rhonda and I had encountered a part who would not communicate with either of us. My figuring-it-out part hypothesized that the bad man was not truly a part of Rhonda but represented John's parasitic energy buried in Rhonda's system. Over the next two sessions, I guided Rhonda in a couple of attempts to exorcise the bad man by having her imagine giving him back to John. These attempts not only failed, but they also (along with some other events in her life) precipitated a new round of deeper and more urgent cutting. In response, her other parts retreated far inside and I was getting very worried.

I reviewed this stuck dilemma with my supervision group, who suggested that I view the bad man as a protective part with whom I should ally. I realized with some embarrassment that my insistent, anxious manager had gotten into a war of control with him over Rhonda, whose body had literally become a bloody battleground. In the next session, I said to the bad man, "I believe I've misunderstood you. I see that you're trying in your own way to help Rhonda. I apologize for not recognizing this sooner." I held out my hand. "I'm extending my hand to you in friendship."

Rhonda, agitated, said, "He won't talk to you."

Then, out of the blue, an idea from the 1960s science fiction movie *Fantastic Voyage* came to me. In the movie, scientists shrink down to enter the body of their colleague to save him from a deadly blood clot. I asked Rhonda, "If you can imagine me becoming very small, would you and your parts give me permission to enter your system and look for the bad man?"

Rhonda went inside and consulted with her parts. Then she opened her eyes, "Yes, that's okay. But they're afraid the bad man will hurt you."

I said, "I thank your parts for their concern and for giving me permission. I'm strong and I'm bringing a special flashlight to find where the bad man is so I can talk with him." I continued with a hypnotic-like suggestion, "I'm becoming very, very small and I'm coming inside slowly." Because I had some parts who felt cautious about doing this "shrinking the shrink" intervention, I kept checking with her, "Is this okay for you and your parts?"

Rhonda slowly replied, "They can see you. It's okay."

As I greeted her different parts, I explained, "I'm looking for the bad man," and Rhonda reported that her parts were stepping back, fearful of coming into contact with him. Fairly quickly, I announced, as though I had just discovered a child playing hide-and-seek, "Ahhh . . . I see where the bad man is hiding! Hello." Rhonda reported that the bad man backed away from me, so it was clear that he was seeing me. I added, "I'm glad to meet you."

The bad man said to me, "What are you doing here?"

"I come as a friend. I understand that you have a powerful role in Rhonda's system."

"She is very bad and dirty. Her badness needs to be cut out," he responded.

"I know that you really want the badness out of Rhonda," I said. "I also want to help her get the badness out. To accomplish that, I'd like to get to know you better. Maybe we can find a way to work together." I held out my hand to him literally and also figuratively within Rhonda's system. "Will you take my hand?"

Rhonda shuddered again and trembled with approach–avoidance agitation. I kept extending my hand to him. Tentatively, the bad man, using Rhonda's hand, reached out and took mine. We held our grasp. Remembering that every extreme protector is paired with a suffering exile, I offered, "I'm sending you strong compassion for all the suffering you've endured over the years."

Still holding my hand, the bad man retorted, "I'm not suffering."

"I know you're strong," I said. "And I believe that you have suffered immensely in your own way, which is why you so desperately want to cut out Rhonda's badness."

Rhonda, as the bad man, turned away with a pained expression and a low moan, "Ohhh . . ." Our hands released.

I persisted, "I see that you're hurting, aren't you? Could Rhonda and I get to know you better so we can get the hurt out?"

Softening, he whispered, "Okay."

Before continuing, I wanted to make sure Rhonda was sufficiently co-conscious to hear our conversation. So I asked, "Before we talk more, could I speak to Rhonda for a moment?"

He replied, "Yes. I can get her, but she can't get to me."

As was typical when Rhonda shifted from one part to another—or to herself—her eyes closed, she briefly entered a dissociated state and then her body posture and facial expression changed as she transitioned. She scratched her head and opened her eyes to look at me. "Hi," she said.

"How are you doing?"

"I'm okay."

"Did you hear my conversation with the bad man?"

"Not much. He takes up a lot of space."

"I'd like to return to talking with him. Let's ask him to give you more room."

Rhonda shifted again and the bad man returned. I said, "Thank you for coming back. Would you be able to get a little smaller so Rhonda could have some space to hear our conversation?" After some negotiation he agreed. I began, "We've been calling you *the bad man*. Do you have a name?" (Almost every part in Rhonda's DID system was named.)

"Robert," he replied.

"Good to meet you, Robert." We shook hands again. "How old are you?"

"Different ages. First I was four. But I'm also grown up and big."

"Were you big when you were four?"

"No. But I was mad. And the others," he said, meaning Rhonda's protectors and exiles, "got afraid and tried to push me back. So I got bigger. And with John—very big."

In response to my questions over the next few sessions, Robert told his story. He was a youngster with a giant's rage, which had so frightened Rhonda's interacting-with-the-world protectors that they had exiled him—permanently, they hoped. But now that Rhonda was hearing and feeling the excruciating psychic and physical pain of parts who had endured severe neglect and torture, her protectors were no longer able to say that her experiences were *not so bad* and Robert had come up from the deep recesses determined to cut the badness out of her. I proclaimed my fury at all the people who had assaulted Rhonda, asserting that if John were alive he would be incarcerated for his crimes. Over much more time, as we slowly helped each traumatized part to unburden and heal (including those who were enraged), Robert grew increasingly quiet. Admitting that his job was stressful and exhausting, he said he was glad that his work was coming to an end and he was pleased to have some rest.

As this interchange illustrates, Rhonda's bad man was a young part, not a parasitic manifestation of her perpetrator's savagery. I had made assumptions about him because I didn't know him, and I didn't know him because I had not yet convinced him that it was safe to communicate with me—so we had gotten stuck. Getting unstuck from my assumptions about him enabled me to take a creative leap and reach out with curiosity rather than judgment, which finally enabled him to find his voice.

CONCLUSION

When a client repeatedly insists that we are misattuned or unempathic (stirring our confused or anxious parts), or gets under our skin by being aggressive (stirring our scared or shamed parts), or tunes out and negates us (stirring our helpless or angry parts) we are stuck in a way that can be difficult to tolerate. The IFS answer to this kind of impasse is, of course, *Therapist, help your parts unblend and get into Self! Find and heal your exile.* But, as we know, it ain't always easy. There are many ways of getting unstuck and we've illustrated some in this chapter, but there is no single answer for handling the problems that arise in therapy. Growing in the role of therapist requires us to be curious about ourselves and guided by our intuition. When we are Self-led we can mix knowledge, skill, and the conventions of IFS with courageous innovation. Creativity may mean accommodating parts of the client who don't respond as we expect, being curious about a part who won't cooperate or being confident that we can do something even when a part declares it's not possible. The difference between an experienced and an inexperienced clinician is not who gets stuck—we all get stuck. Rather, the experienced clinician has had more time and opportunity to experience Self-energy, which buys her the freedom to experiment. Being Self-led is the most essential ingredient when we practice IFS.

REFERENCE

Rosenberg, L.W. (2013). Welcoming All Erotic Parts: Our Reactions to the Sexual and Using Polarities to Enhance Erotic Excitement. In M. Sweezy & E. L. Ziskind (Eds.), *Internal family systems therapy: New dimensions* (pp. 1–23). New York: Routledge.
Schwartz, R. C. (1995). *Internal family systems therapy.* New York: The Guilford Press.

Chapter 2

An IFS Lens on Addiction
Compassion for Extreme Parts

Cece Sykes

INTRODUCTION

Viewed through the lens of internal family systems (IFS), addiction as I see it is an unremitting cyclical process characterized by a power struggle between two well-intentioned teams of protective parts, each attempting to bring balance to the client's internal system. In IFS we categorize these teams as *managers* whose role is providing stability and improved function-ing and *firefighters* whose traditional role is putting out the fire of shame and worthlessness that lies buried in *exiles*, our most vulnerable parts (Schwartz, 1995). In this chapter, however, I use the term *distractor* instead of fire-fighter in order to emphasize that these protectors serve a vital function beyond dousing emotional flare-ups; they complement our driven, hard-working managers by introducing pleasure, novelty, comfort and relief into everyday life (Sykes, 2001). If we only had the desire to be safe and stable, what a humdrum existence we would face!

When protectors respond to acute emotional pain by going into sur-vival mode, their drive intensifies. The manager's aim for stability esca-lates into harsh self-criticism, creating a rigid mantle of responsibility and the demand for perfection, traits that clients often overidentify with and find difficult to recognize as harmful. Meanwhile the intentions of distrac-tors to shift gears away from responsibility and toward rest intensifies into compulsive cravings for mood-altering substances, food, sexual activity or other dissociative practices. This escalating, polarized struggle between two teams of protective parts who are trying to control or medicate under-lying emotional pain is foundational to what I call the addictive process (see Figure 2.1).

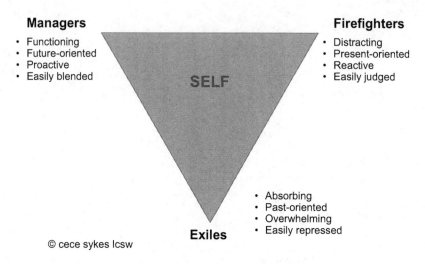

Managers

- Functioning
- Future-oriented
- Proactive
- Easily blended

Firefighters

- Distracting
- Present-oriented
- Reactive
- Easily judged

SELF

- Absorbing
- Past-oriented
- Overwhelming
- Easily repressed

Exiles

© cece sykes lcsw

Figure 2.1 *Polarization: Extreme Balancing Act*
© Cece Sykes LCSW

CHAPTER OVERVIEW

This chapter illustrates how to interact compassionately with the client's entire system, safely intervening with the polarizations at the center of the addictive process. Although it is beyond the scope of the chapter to cover all types of addictive behavior, I use the same treatment paradigm to address substance addictions, disordered eating, self-harm, suicidal urges, and gambling. Since distractor behaviors occur on a continuum of intensity, and even positive or neutral behaviors can become compulsive, understanding the intention behind any repetitive behavior is important. Therefore, I often help clients explore their more ordinary activities (working, exercising, sleeping, fantasizing, social media use) so that we can draw a picture of all their methods for relaxing or distracting from stress.

The chapter also examines the role of the therapist. The compelling nature of the addictive process can act as a gilded invitation for the caretaking and controlling parts of the therapist to rush to the rescue—or the helm. Rescuing may work, but only temporarily. In contrast, when clients develop Self-leadership and self-compassion there are long-lasting benefits. In the case descriptions that follow I include moment-to-moment commentary on my decisions about what to pursue, what to avoid and how I help my activated parts.

One topic I do not attempt to address here is the cause of addiction, other than to say that it differs for each client. Addictive processes often help clients who are recovering from complex or relational childhood trauma to cope with overwhelming pain and feel armored against further injury, but not everyone with an addiction problem has a history of trauma. On the other hand, we can assume at the outset of treatment that anyone experiencing addiction has also experienced deep feelings of shame, worthlessness and isolation. In IFS we guide our clients to listen to their inner dialogue, whatever the origin of their struggle.

MILO: NEVER AN EXCUSE, ALWAYS A REASON

Milo's early relational trauma, including living with two addicted parents, had fostered extreme needs for self-soothing and self-reliance during adolescence. Though he'd had some recovery from drinking, he was still using marijuana daily when he came to see me. He was 52 years old, married, working successfully as an accountant and he identified pot smoking as his only concern. He had started using drugs and alcohol when he was 10 years old and had gone into his first round of recovery in his early 30s. He had then married and remained clean from substances until he resumed smoking pot 5 years before we met. He reported enjoying his work and said his marriage was okay, though he did acknowledge that his connection with his wife felt perfunctory and stagnant.

Milo was very troubled by his daily need for pot, which occurred primarily in the evenings after work and on the weekends. He didn't know why getting high was so important and he didn't like the consequences. He hid the habit from his wife and felt tired, groggy and depressed the next morning. These symptoms were increasing with age yet he found himself unable to quit for more than a few days at a time.

History: How Milo's Firefighters Got Started

During the first few sessions I wanted to get a big-picture sense of what was happening to his exiles when he began using drugs and alcohol so I asked Milo to tell me about his early family life. I also knew that listening with an openhearted, accepting attitude would invite his more extreme parts to speak up. Milo reported that his early years were chaotic and stressful. His parents drank heavily, and during their frequent fights, he and his brother hid in the closet or out in the yard. Before Milo was 9, his father left and started a new family. By the time Milo was 13, his mother's drinking and uncontrolled rages had escalated, motivating him to spend less and less time at home. Hanging out with other neglected young teenagers, he began to get high regularly and started dealing street drugs. Eventually, he dropped out of high school and supported himself by taking short-term jobs and selling drugs, while continuing his own heavy using.

First Steps: Start With Managers

At the outset of therapy, urgent distractor activity is compelling enough to draw the attention of both client and therapist. Although it's tempting to dive into the obvious dysfunction of the team on the using (distractor) side of the addictive polarity, distrustful managers are generally far too blended with the client to allow this. Therefore, treatment generally begins by initi-ating a strong connection with managers, who need to be appreciated and acknowledged for their legitimate anxiety about compulsive behavior. Man-agers may be harsh, belittling and shaming but they're not crazy! They need to know that both therapist and client understand how extreme distractor behaviors have played out as poor judgment, bad decisions and endless suf-fering. They need to feel valued for being forced to take over after the risk-taking distractors create more chaos. The therapist's job is to sell the client's managers on the hope that distractors will perk up and take an interest in alternatives if the client can get enough Self-energy to extend curiosity.

The Benefits of Parts Language

As Milo shared stories about the disintegration of his family and his attempts to adapt to the losses, loneliness and neglect, I began to use parts language to reframe his narrative. I paid particular attention to naming distractors, like Milo's drug user and drug seller parts, as protectors who held a positive intention for him. I also made a point of noticing his disapproving manag-ers and his (mostly) suppressed exiles. Parts language gives the client the opportunity to view even overwhelming emotions as a temporary state, not an unchangeable truth. As we met Milo's parts, I especially wanted him to notice the distinct behaviors on each side of his addiction polarity and to see how they were reacting to each other.

"So, I'm hearing that you had these smart young parts who figured out how to take care of things. The 13-year-old guy was really good at making sure you had a little money—and some friends, too."

"Yeah, I guess he was a savvy little drug dealer, that's true," Milo said, expressing grudging admiration. "We were on our own out there. We were crazy. We didn't give a damn about school or anything else. But we had some fun, I can tell you that!"

"There were real risks to being out there on your own—no parents, no one at home, no one to help if you got in trouble. How did that affect you?"

"I managed. I made it okay."

I noted that Milo's minimizing parts were protecting him from noticing his early abandonment. I paused, realizing that my caretaking managers might have subtly triggered his minimizers when I disregarded the fun he mentioned in favor of focusing on the risks he faced. I knew it was important to validate the ways in which risk-taking, self-reliance and absence of authority can be exciting to distractor parts. So I slowed down and made time for his distractors to reminisce and tell a few stories. When I judged that they felt more accepted I tried again, offering a gentle probe and hoping that we could now name some of his exiled vulnerability. "Right, you guys were having a good time out there. And you figured out how to do it," I said. "And yet, I wonder what it was really like that nobody noticed what you were doing, that you were taking care of yourself all alone."

"Well, yeah, I guess it was kind of rough. When I did head back home, either my mom was gone or she was drunk and acting crazy. Pretty soon I'd just go right back out the door."

"Yeah, so when you were home with your mom, in the house, with all that drinking and craziness, you had a part who felt alone or kind of abandoned? Which makes sense. It sounds like your mom was not available."

I was working on detecting his parts now, helping him differentiate between his distractors and the exile they protected. I didn't expect Milo to pay close attention to his isolated, abandoned part at this early stage (it was too early for extended witnessing), but I wanted to give him time to notice, from Self, how tough his childhood had been.

"And then some strong parts got you back out the door to be with your friends so your more tender parts could go underground again. Is that right?" I added.

Milo nodded, "I guess so. I know I hated being home. Nobody actually gave a shit."

At this point we had a clear picture of the serious neglect and stress in Milo's environment when he started using. Now I hoped we could begin to befriend this lonely 13-year-old boy. "Yeah, it sounds like being home was really hard. So that street kid part would help you go back out to find your friends. Then you wouldn't notice so much what it was like to be home." I paced my responses slowly so we could puzzle it out together. Although I didn't want my seasoned, know-it-all parts to jump ahead of Milo's parts, my role was to help him notice that his distractor and his exile were linked.

Milo nodded, reflecting back on those days. "Yeah, we were a bunch of misfits but I felt real good with those kids. Plus, I was good at selling dope. I could make money."

Connecting With Self-Destructive Distractors

Clients and therapists alike often view distractors as one-dimensional and bad, wild or crazy. But when we direct the client to inquire about its mission, the part will often express its intent to provide comfort or relief from pain and share fears of the dire consequences if it were to stop. Although distractors can be maddeningly single-minded and uninterested in change, once we appreciate that they're standing up to a barrage of hostility from the managerial team, even while warding off the emotional pain of exiles, we can honor their courage and stamina. "As you describe this time in your life, I wonder if you can see him right now, the 13-year-old hanging with his buddies on the street?"

"Yeah," Milo shrugged, "I can."

"Great. Keep that image in your mind's eye and see if you can connect with him, on the inside, to let him know that you're near him."

Milo closed his eyes and nodded.

"As you watch him, what feelings come up?"

"He's a real bad kid. He's messed up," Milo said. "Nothing we can do about that."

Now we were hearing from Milo's judgmental critic, a manager who was reacting negatively to the teenage drug user and seller. Though my caretaking manager was tempted to challenge this manager by suggesting that Milo not be so hard on himself, I decided it was more important to name and accept the critic, who was an integral part of Milo's addictive process. "So another part of you is critical of the boy and believes he's just a bad, messed-up kid?" I said.

Illustrating why treatment generally starts with inner critics, Milo said, "Well, yeah! He was a scammer. He was a little delinquent."

This manager had no patience for the boy's very real dilemmas and didn't understand his risk-taking. "Right, true," I said. "This young guy was acting pretty wild. I get that he was messing up—your critic is right. So, Milo," I said, hoping to open the door for some compassion by reframing his term *messed up*, "I wonder if you could acknowledge to the critic that you get its point of view: this 13-year-old was in trouble." We both took a moment to reflect before I went on. "Let's ask the critic what would happen if it didn't criticize the 13-year-old."

"Well, what I was doing was kind of fucked up."

"Right. It was a bad situation. Let's reassure the critic that you hear its concern about the drugs. But see if right now it would let you take over so we can get curious about what the 13-year-old needs."

Milo shrugged but closed his eyes, "Well, I do kinda feel sorry for the kid. Where else is he gonna go?"

"You feel sorry for him. But let's see, does it seem like you feel compassionate toward him and sad for what he went through or like you have to fix him up and make him feel better?"

"Well what's wrong with helping him feel better?" Milo asked, opening his eyes. Although I started to explain, Milo interrupted with urgency. "He needs help, doesn't he? I want to help him!"

I realized that a protector who wanted to rescue the boy had blended with Milo, which is common when a client first feels connected to a part who is trapped in traumatic circumstances. I wanted Milo to recognize this rescuer part (also seen as *codependent* in addiction treatment). At the same time, a voice inside me warned *If you push the rescuer to unblend, Milo's parts will resist.* Taking this warning to heart, I decided to try appreciating the rescuer before asking it to relax so Milo could share Self-energy with the 13-year-old. Taking a breath, I plunged in, "Well, yes, this boy definitely needs help, and I appreciate the part who wants to save him. But at the same time the most compassionate thing we can do is *listen* to him. Once we know what he wants us to know, I promise we'll be able to help him."

"Okay, okay, I get it," Milo said. "I'll let the rescuer know that I'm here to handle this. I can see the kid is feeling bad. . . . Okay, he says he'll trust me to do it."

"Great. Thank him. Now can you let the 13-year-old know that he's not alone? He's with you. And ask what he's trying to do for you when he's out there selling pot."

Milo shook his head, tears suddenly welling up, "Poor kid!" He was silent for a few seconds. "He says he's not afraid. He can take care of himself."

"Yes, he can," I echoed quietly. "Let him see that you understand. He does such a good job taking care of himself. Show him how you feel toward him. He has a tough job."

While we waited I noticed that my own overly self-reliant parts were resonating and moved by this boy who had so much on his shoulders. I acknowledged them and went back to tracking Milo's inner inquiry. "Ask him what he's afraid would happen to you if he weren't making money for you and getting high?" I wanted Milo to hear the positive intentions of this hardworking distractor.

"I wouldn't make it," Milo said. "He says I'd fall apart."

I knew the part was referring to Milo's exile, the part who was at risk of breaking down.

I said, "Is he maybe noticing another part, one who got overwhelmed or was afraid he truly wouldn't survive?"

Milo nodded through tears, "Oh yeah, yeah."

"Okay, well, let him know that you're with him now and you can feel how bad it got."

Milo nodded, "He's only five. He's hiding behind the garage."

"Can you stay with him?"

At this point I felt some indecision about which way to go. One option was to stay with the 5-year-old, an exile who clearly deserved plenty of tenderness and attention. But we had just started hearing from the 13-year-old, who was also deeply in need of understanding and compassion. I could feel my parts getting overwhelmed about how much need there was in Milo's inner world. I took a deep breath and sent the breath to the anxiety in my chest where my own rescuers and fixers live, telling them, *Yes you're right there is a lot to do here! But we can't do it all right now.* "So your 5-year-old is here and we know a little something about how much was going on for him. And your 13-year-old part is here, too. We know both of them are hurting and need your support. In this moment, I'm leaning towards continuing with the street kid, but we can do whatever feels right to you."

Milo nodded, "Let's stick with the street kid."

"Okay, just let the 5-year-old know that you see him and ask if it would be okay to come back to him later, when things settle down." Milo nodded. "So Milo, you're with the 13-year-old right now, right? Let him know that you can see how close he is to the little one who was afraid of dying."

"I'm telling him that I get that he was being strong so I wouldn't lose it."

"How do you feel toward the 13-year-old now that you see what he was up against?"

"Oh, I feel bad. I do! He didn't really have a choice out there."

"Ask him to show you more about how it was for him to be a dealer and keep money coming in for you."

Milo listened. "He says he liked it. He liked getting his own money."

"He enjoyed being self-sufficient, making it happen for himself, is that it?"

"Well, it's not like I coulda got any money from my mother. She was using, too," Milo said.

I made a mental note to find out how Milo's parts felt about his mom being a fellow user and so, de facto, a peer. Tempting though it was to explore that trailhead now, I felt it was more important to stay with the 13-year-old. "Let's appreciate how truly alone he was and how he did what he had to do," I said.

"Yeah," Milo said, "he sure did."

"And ask him," I went on, fleshing out the part's positive intentions, "when he helped you get high, what did he want for you?"

"He wanted me to feel good," Milo said right away. "Have a little fun."

"Right, feeling good and having some fun, we all need that. And ask him what he feared would happen if he didn't help you feel good and get some fun in?"

"I'd feel bad!" Milo said, as if stating the obvious.

"Right, you would. There's a part who's been feeling really bad. Ask if he'd like you to help take care of the little guy who felt bad?"

Milo was quiet before saying, "Yeah. I felt pretty damn bad at home."

"So let the 13-year-old know that you understand how he was protecting this little guy who felt so bad at home. How do you feel toward him now that you see what he was doing?"

"He was something else, wasn't he?" Milo said admiringly.

"Yes, he was. He did what he had to do. Let him know you really get it. He was involved with some pretty wild stuff, and he took a lot of risks. But he had a lot to protect you from, didn't he?"

Milo agreed and lingered with the 13-year-old, admiring his courage as well as noticing how protective he had been and all that he had had to contend with. Distractors don't benefit from being *excused* for their risk-taking and its harmful consequences, but through a relationship of sustained, compassionate inner inquiry, we do discover that we can appreciate their motives and sacrifices.

The Spectrum of Self-Awareness and Self-Energy

In IFS when we speak of being *in Self* we are referring to a centered state of embodied self-awareness and self-acceptance, combined with a deep sense of how we connect to others. Milo's compassion for his young parts illustrates the progression from parts being blended with us to a Self-to-part connection. Many clients with addictive process are a long way from any prevailing sense of Self-energy. Instead, they struggle with a chronic sense of parts overload and a fear that they are not really capable of changing. Though I initially developed the Self Spectrum graph in Figure 2.2 for training purposes, the continuum also serves as a gauge for clients to

Figure 2.2 Self Spectrum: Degrees of Consciousness

notice each bit of headway they are making with their inner connections to parts and in the small shifts that occur in relationships with others. This can be particularly useful for people with a slow recovery pace because it highlights the incremental process of building Self-energy through identifying and unblending from parts.

The Importance of Intention

Milo's childhood neglect molded his inner system into one that was run by extreme protectors, including derisive, harsh managers and a self-destructive 13-year-old drug user who lived on the street corner. These parts had the tough task of keeping Milo functioning and distracted from the raw emotions of the panicked, isolated 5-year-old who threatened to overwhelm him. By building relationships with them, Milo learned that their goal was to keep him alive, self-reliant and upbeat. The more he understood them, the more they looked to him for perspective, letting go of their wary distrust of each other. Building a strong connection with protective parts cultivates the inner trust and self-regulation that is so important for clients to feel before tackling the needs and vulnerability of exiles.

Getting in Relationship, Not in Control

Clients like Milo whose addictive processes started when they were young often find their adult propensities for self-destruction incomprehensible. Until they begin their inner inquiry, their vulnerability has been so exiled that they don't know why their distractors can't stop using, especially when the stakes are so high. Making daily choices without a clue about one's own motivation naturally opens the door for more intense self-criticism, which further intensifies the desire to control distractor behavior. Rather than urging the client to get in control of this problem behavior, a battle won and lost many times, we guide him to get in relationship with his problem parts. If the client can engage in the compassionate inquiry at the core of the IFS model with both exiles and protectors, he is likely to achieve desperately needed self-awareness and understanding.

Milo's Work

To summarize the work of our sessions, when Milo began therapy he was disturbed that he couldn't stop smoking marijuana and, with his polarized protector teams vying for the driver's seat, he was making little headway.

I helped him hear the voices inside and notice their action urges: the critics who disapproved of and judged his substance use and the distractors who wanted him to deny the risks they took and who minimized the intensity of his isolation. As he became curious about the motivations of these protectors, he recognized both the ones who feared acting out with drugs and the ones who gave him the thrill of surviving on the street with his peers. This process of helping his protective parts to differentiate ultimately led Milo to connect with his exiled 5-year-old, at which point he came to appreciate the full impact of neglect and danger during his childhood. Milo continued his therapy for some time, creating strong inner connections and compassionate relationships with various young exiles who needed attention. He did eventually stop using marijuana, go to couples therapy with his wife, rediscover his love of music and pick up the banjo again.

DAN: EXTERNAL POLARITIES

While Milo came to therapy wanting to change at least one behavior (pot smoking), Dan, the next client described, initially admitted to no conscious dissatisfaction with his addiction. He found it pleasing and comforting and claimed he only came to therapy at the insistence of his wife and couple therapist. This posed a challenge: how to avoid joining with his externalized managerial team, his wife and couple therapist, while guiding him to recognize that he was in the middle of an inner manager/distractor polarity.

Dan was a bright, charming 48-year-old advertising executive who had a history of ongoing infidelities, other risk-taking sexual behavior and regular drinking (the distractor team) along with chronic overwork (the manager team). After finding evidence of an affair for the third time, his wife had one foot out the door and his couple therapist had advised him to begin individual treatment. His entitled distractors were continually challenging and presented my managers with many opportunities for a power struggle.

At the outset, Dan's distractors minimized the impact of his extramarital activities. He said he wasn't sure he could be faithful and wasn't sure he wanted to be. He had a handful of ongoing sexual relationships and couldn't imagine life without them. Yet he did admit to feeling mystified that, even in high school and long before the ties of marriage, he had always cheated on girlfriends and lied about it.

Since distractor parts involved with the addictive process are very talented at blaming others, my first goal was to avoid having Dan label the concerns of his wife and couple therapist as his real problem. I clarified that he needed to choose his own goals for therapy, which might differ from theirs. Dan was able to acknowledge some mild curiosity, "Well, actually I wouldn't mind figuring out this thing I have going with women."

I began by asking him about his childhood, his early experiences with his parents and his dating history. His father was financially successful, angry and critical. He had had a long, fairly public extramarital affair and had recruited Dan and his brothers to be involved in it while warning them to keep it secret from their mother. His mother, in contrast, had spent a lot of time ill in bed, and Dan had never felt close to her.

I often create a multigenerational genogram with clients, outlining the family history of trauma and addictive behaviors and exploring legacy patterns. My goal is to locate burdening beliefs that have been passed down the generations and to generate compassion and self-respect for the client's efforts to tackle behaviors that his family never addressed. Dan observed that various extended family members and both his brothers had serious alcohol issues. Other clients may be lucky enough to observe a legacy of recovery in their families.

Dan stated that he started dating in high school, met his future wife in college and quickly got married while continuing an affair. After identifying his numerous risk-taking behaviors as parts whom we should get to know better, I asked Dan what he wanted to call the part who picked up girlfriends.

"Well, let's call him my sexy guy."

"Sounds good. So with a picture of him in your mind's eye, how do you feel toward your sexy guy?"

"I like him a lot!" Dan immediately closed his eyes, beamed and launched into a description of a recent sexual encounter.

Since letting this part take over now would have encouraged it to do so again, I interrupted. "Right now I would say you're seeing the world through his eyes, as though he's you—all of you. He sounds proud and pleased, like he really helps you have good times, is that right?" Though my question was reasonable, I could sense a part who was judging Dan, especially his gleeful tone. Internally, I accepted my part and asked it to relax. Despite my judging tone, Dan's broad smile didn't flag.

"Yeah, he lets me have fun. I mean a lot of fun!"

With my humorous part helping my judgmental part step back, I smiled, nodded and said, "I think I've got the picture."

Dan's smile relaxed in turn, and his puffed up part seemed to let go a little. Already I was appreciating how easy it would be to develop a therapist/manager versus client/distractor polarity with Dan's sexy guy part. Having gathered more Self-energy, I went on. "My hope is for to you to get to know your sexy guy. I mean really know him, rather than have him tell us about what he does for you. He is definitely a lot of fun, but sometimes when he gets going things can become pretty challenging for you. So getting to know him might be helpful. Can he appreciate how that might work, maybe a little?"

"Maybe sometimes," Dan said, hesitant but not defensive.

"You've said you don't really understand the way you interact with women, right? What is it like for you when you have parts who do something, many times over, that you don't understand?" I was fishing, hoping to flush out other parts in his system related to this womanizing part—maybe judging managers or fearful exiles under the surface—but it didn't work.

"I'm pretty good at not thinking about that," Dan said quickly.

"Right, yes, I bet you are," I smiled, no judgment up. "But that is what you said you wanted, right? To understand what happens with you and women a little better." Dan nodded gamely. "Okay, so let's see if we can connect with the sexy guy again and maybe listen to what he has to say. Can you see him, Dan? Maybe get an image of him in action in your mind's eye?"

"Like I said, he's helping me have a good time. You know I work my ass off. I deserve this. I need to relax and enjoy myself every once in a while!" This was his distractor expressing a very common defense, complaining that managers work too hard. And when the client has managerial parts who chronically overwork and feel resentful, as Dan did, the accusation is essentially true.

"Right, you've told me how hard some parts of you push to take on extra days and so forth, to be sure you get things done. And you've said that you have parts who then feel exhausted and resentful. So what you're saying is this part has girlfriends on the side to help you feel good, despite overworking, is that right?"

"Yes," Dan said.

"Can we take a minute to acknowledge the part who works extra hard?" I asked. "I have no doubt that part needs your attention, too. Let him know we'll get there." Dan acknowledged his hard worker. "So if it's okay right now, let's go back to the sexy guy. Is he there? From what you've been telling me, he helped you a lot. And yet he's also gotten you into some dicey situations. Like right now your wife has kicked you out of the house, which hasn't been easy to handle."

Although I knew Dan would not readily have a conversation about consequences at this point, I was trying to bring his attention to the benefits of building a relationship with his addict part: doing so would eventually mean less trouble for him. Dan nodded with a sigh, as if busted but not very concerned. "Okay, Cece! Yeah. True! Sexy guy can go a little overboard." (A small unblend.) "But he's still having a blast, I gotta tell ya!" (Blended again.)

I could feel a tiny pain in my chest, the feelings of my exile who had been betrayed in a past relationship. I sent a deep breath with the message, *Not now. We will connect later.* And though I did not ask my vigilant feminist part to leave, I did ask her to take a back seat. I started again, "Okay, Dan, we can agree to the fact that hooking up with these women is a good time for you. No question about that!"

Dan smiled, his sexy guy ready to elaborate with another juicy story. But I cut him off again, albeit with a light tone, "I got it. I really do! It's a good time. I believe you." I knew the sexy guy desperately needed help, and if he would unblend, Dan would be there to help him. To make this happen I had to burst his bubble of sexual reverie. "And I know I just cut you off," I acknowledged, knowing I was speaking directly to his sexy guy. "But here's the deal. I don't want to moralize, like you've been a bad person. I'm also not here to stop you from enjoying your memories. It's not my job to take anything away from you. But right now I wonder if we could try something new, something that might lead you to understand your sexy guy better. Like maybe there is a back story behind this story he likes to lead with?" I sat back and waited. I could almost see Dan's inner debate: indulge in that distractor pleasure or admit his world was crumbling and maybe, just maybe, try something different that could be of benefit.

"Okay, Cece," he said, reluctantly. "Fine, fine, we can do this your way."

Dan's tone was accommodating and I could feel that he had more Self-energy, but I also sensed an irritated part who was pretending to be powerless. It didn't want Dan to be responsible for this decision so it was acting as if he had been forced to give in to my request. Since I wasn't going to take charge I put the problem squarely back in Dan's court. "Well, okay, you're right," I said. "I do have an agenda and I would like to see you connect with the sexy guy in a different way, which, yes, would be my way. You're totally right about that. But it's up to you. I'm not going to pressure you. I do think you would get somewhere. But we can also stop here, no problem. It's your call."

There was an edge of discomfort in his smile and laughter. He didn't answer right away. "All right," he said, finally. "So I just gotta be with my sexy guy, right?"

"Yep, that's it," I said. "It's just about you hearing from him."

"Well, maybe that would be good. He's been around for a long time."

Internally, I heard a part say, *We're on the road now!* "So ask him what he's afraid would happen if he weren't helping you get more women?"

"He says I'd be bored," Dan answered.

The fear of boredom, of no distractions, no adrenalin rush, is common with parts who are accustomed to the intensity of addictive process. "Ask him what would happen if you got bored?"

"Well, I'd have nothing to do. I'd just be sitting around, going nowhere," he said.

I continued, "Ask him what would happen if there was nowhere to go, like what would be bad about that?"

"Well I'd feel like shit, that's what! I'd have nothing to do and I'd feel like a loser!" Dan exclaimed. "When I was in high school I spent a lot of time alone in my bedroom. I actually knew I was fucking depressed. But what was I supposed to do? My father was an asshole and my mother was fucking useless. I was a real hot shot, a big basketball star!" He shook his head. "It didn't matter. I just felt like a total fucking loser. And there was nothing I could fucking do about it."

I was not sure Dan would be able to stay with this level of vulnerability, but since the memory had popped up strongly, I wanted to see if he could get some connection with the part. So I nodded and said, "This was such a crucial time for you. These are strong feelings. Can you let this kid know that you're aware of him now?"

Dan sat head down, shoulders slumped, the weight of the part bearing down on him. Helplessness, the feeling of being unable to take action, and hopelessness, the belief that no action is possible, are states of mind—or parts—that arise frequently when we work with addictive process. They can be pervasive and demoralizing, not to mention contagious. Clients can feel overcome by entrenched burdens and the fear that nothing will change. "Does he know you're with him?" I asked.

"Yes," Dan said quietly. Then he shifted, sat up and looked at me with a sly smile. "So—I had a *lot* of girlfriends."

I said, "The sexy guy helped this sad teenager back then?"

"Yes. He still does."

"Right. He does help. He really does. I wonder though, do you still—right now—feel close to the sad one who felt like a such loser?" I asked. Dan nodded. "Is that okay?" He nodded again. "Then let him know that you understand."

Dan shook his head. "I've felt like this my whole life."

Noticing the lonely teenage boy who felt like a loser, helpless to change his situation, abandoned by an ill, depressed mother and a rejecting, acting-out father finally brought Dan close to the despairing feelings his sexy guy had been working so hard to dispel. Although Dan continued to appreciate his sexy guy after this session, feeling close to the vulnerability and pain of his exiles gave him insight into his childhood suffering and new self-compassion. This eventually helped the sexy guy relax so that Dan could end his extramarital relationships, one by one. But at this moment, the heavy sadness of his teenage boy was in the room with us and I was watching to see if his parts would let him stay connected. I said, "Right, he's always there, just under the surface. Maybe take a breath, pause, and be sure it's okay to stay with him." Dan nodded. "As you see him there how do you feel toward him?"

"I feel bad for him."

"Right, yes, I see that you do. Can you show him, from the inside, that you care about him? And that you get how he feels." Having closed his eyes, Dan was breathing evenly. "And ask this kid if he'd be willing to show you more."

"Well, he's just sitting there. Not sure he can talk to me."

"Then let him know you're with him, just interested in how he's doing."

Dan eyes snapped open. "He's not doing well. Y'know I don't think my mother ever even walked into my fucking bedroom! She was in the house somewhere but it's not like we talked to her." Beyond knowing that his mother had slept on the couch a lot, not getting up in the morning or after school to be with Dan and his brothers, he had not yet said much about her. I nodded encouragingly. "When I was six, she went to the hospital." Dan went on, looking more upset.

"Maybe the loneliness of the teenager has something to do with the feelings of this little guy. Ask the teenager if we can shift over to help the 6-year-old." Dan nodded. "How do you feel toward the 6-year-old?" I asked.

"He's just sitting alone in his bedroom," Dan said.

"What do you notice?"

"He's blanked out watching TV."

"As you see him blanked out on TV, all alone in his room, how do you feel toward him?"

"This is when my mother was gone. I didn't know where she was. My asshole father never told me!"

"This little guy is lonely and scared, right? Let him know, on the inside, that you're with him now. Ask him what it's like to be by himself, not knowing what happened to his mother."

"He thought she wasn't coming home—like ever! I had no clue. My father didn't tell us till later."

Dan was closing and opening his eyes, moving in and out of inner inquiry. I guessed this was because his system was finding it hard to tolerate the depth of the little boy's fear and unprocessed grief. I nodded, "That must have been terrible. And there's a part who feels angry on his behalf. No wonder! He needed someone to take care of him and stand up for him. Let's see if it's okay with the angry part if you go back to the little boy. He may want to show you what it's like for him to be alone, not knowing what's going on."

"He's not talking!" Dan said with an edge of panic.

"That's okay," I said. "He's not used to having anyone to talk to. Go slow and gently, ask him to notice you."

"Okay. Okay. He knows I'm here."

"What does he need you to know about him? See if he can show or tell you, or just let you get a little closer."

"Yeah, he wants me to hang out with him."

"Is that okay with you?"

"Yeah, yeah it is. I'm gonna watch TV with him."

"How close are you to him?"

"Oh, he's right next to me. We're on the bed," Dan said.

"Great. Well you guys just take your time." I waited a few beats before adding, "And if you can, Dan, just breathe together, letting him feel you right there next to him."

Dan continued with closed eyes, breathing evenly, his face relaxing. I waited, just watching him, before saying, "It may not be the right time, so this is up to you two, but if it seems right, ask the little guy if there's more he wants to show you about how it was for him before you came in, when he was alone."

Dan nodded, shifting in his chair. "He's so glad I'm here." Tears began to roll down his cheeks. "He needs me! He really, really needs me."

"Right, yes. Tell him he's so brave to let you know what he needs. Before, there was no one to tell, even though he needed someone so much. Of course he did! Any child would. Is it okay to let him know that he can count on you?"

"Yes, he can," Dan said.

"Let him know it can be different now. He might choose to come stay with you or you can stay with him or we can come back to him. Whatever he wants."

Dan nodded, "Uh-huh, yeah, I'm telling him. Yeah that's what he wants. That's good for him. He can count on me."

Despair

People with addictive systems invariably have parts who feel helpless, hopeless and despairing. They've tried to change so often and feel they failed each time. They've also often experienced the pain of watching family members never achieve recovery. The clinician working with addiction may need to keep an eye out for these despairing parts and for their own caretaking parts who want to rescue clients from their pain. If you notice any intolerance of despair in your internal system, attending to this trailhead is wise. Parts who fear despair will subtly need the client to feel better rather than allowing the client's Self to bear witness to their legitimate grief and sorrow. Providing the attunement these suffering parts deserve means accepting the pain they are currently feeling; this is what will help them eventually unburden and feel strong.

Treating a System, Not a Symptom

To summarize the work of Dan's sessions, when he began therapy a few distractors were blended with him, including a sexy guy who was engaged in several extramarital affairs. Though his sexual acting out created acute stress for him, we needed to treat his whole system, not just his distractors. As he learned about his process, he identified many hard-driving managers and saw how they also unbalanced his system. When he was able to differentiate from this polarity, Dan discovered that the sexy guy balanced out his over-functioning parts and protected his lonely high school basketball star. And he found an even younger part, a child acutely alone and untended, whose feelings of misery, loneliness and panic had threatened Dan's ability to function. These teams of protectors in Dan's system worked continually to try to shield him from his buried, emotional pain. This formed the core triangle of Dan's addictive process.

In our clinical relationship, I focused on helping my managers (and exiles) relax and stay open to Dan's distractors, knowing that his parts were more than willing to get into a lively external polarity with me to avoid the scary feelings of his exile. If my managers had criticized me for being vulnerable (which I was), I would have been too preoccupied to help Dan. If they had shamed him for womanizing, I would have become part of his problem and his protectors would have had no choice but to defend against me. In either case, if my parts blended with me it would have destabilized both of us. For me to be useful, I needed enough compassion and Self-energy to hold us both.

I Am Not Here to Take This Away From You

As we see in Dan's case, there is often a risk that the client's inner rift between managers and distractors will become externalized, that is, between part-ners, between parents and child or between a therapist and client. When a client is compulsive and self-destructive, his lack of judgment pulls for action by the competent, managerial parts of people in his support system, which elicits a central question: Whose problem is this anyway?

In an acute crisis, when acting out behavior is life threatening, others clearly do need to intervene. Yet taking the bulk of the decision-making out of the client's hands on a regular basis can ultimately prove to be coun-terproductive (though it seems to happen in many addiction treatment centers). The risk is that too much external control may short circuit the ability of clients to focus internally and discover parts who do genuinely want to stop using.

I was explicit at the outset with Milo and Dan that it was not my role to control or judge their use of pot, alcohol or extramarital relationships, though neither would I minimize their impact. To understand the inten-tions behind their protective parts we identified the risks and consequences of their behavior as well as the cycle of their addictive process. Clients realize that while their distractors do cause significant suffering, they're commit-ted to the protective task of medicating emotional pain. I believe that the process of change can't be dictated by a timetable; rather, my role is to turn the process of building internal relationships over to the client, offering the hope that they can address their pain in a safer way. The bottom line is that all attempts to control distractor parts by managers in the client, a partner, a well-intentioned therapist or a treatment center—will ultimately mirror the polarity in the addictive process and fortify the client's impasse: Parts can only activate other parts!

OUTSIDE SUPPORT

When it comes to treating an addictive process, one hour of psychotherapy a week may not feel sufficient. Self-help groups and structured group therapy are often a welcome refuge for clients, offering validation and understanding as well as relief from isolation. Other resources include the arts (writing, painting, knitting, dancing, playing music), body-centered activities (yoga, sports, exercise) and meditation. These activities foster self-acceptance, provide healthy distraction, allow safe risk-taking and give the client the opportunity to be creative. Since many people with addictions have been missing-in-action from their lives for periods of time that are critical to normal development, these activities are also an opportunity to negotiate missed developmental stages, acquire age-appropriate skills and build a sense of competence and confidence as a bridge back into the world. Last, consultation on medication with a psychiatrist who is familiar with addiction may be useful at some point during the client's treatment.

CONCLUSION

Rather than defining addiction as the behavior of one acting-out part, I define it as a systemic, cyclical process that is characterized by a power struggle between two teams of protective parts, each valiantly struggling to maintain a balanced inner system. One team is critical and judging; the other impulsive and compulsive. Their chronic, escalating struggle is intended to block the emotional pain of traumatic experiences or unprocessed shame but actually adds acute distress. As a result, when we work with addiction, we need to spend as much time building solid connections with these two teams of hardworking protectors as we do with exiles.

The first steps in IFS treatment of addiction involve creating a safe environment and clarifying that the therapist is not responsible for controlling the client's behavior. Instead we help him (I use the male pronoun because my examples are male, but all of this applies equally to women) track the addictive cycle and build strong, accepting relationships throughout the internal system. Although we typically begin with critical managers who fear the destructive power of distractors, we want to note, as early in the therapy as possible, that exiles exist and drive protector behavior. When the client gets into relationship with his using protectors rather than trying to control their behavior, the energy gradually drains out of the addictive polarity and we gain access to exiles. Throughout this process, I keep in mind that internal systems with extreme parts are weighed down by helplessness, hopelessness and despair. To keep these parts from being a subtle drag on the healing process, I acknowledge their experiences and offer them compassion from the start.

When a client is using too heavily to make progress in therapy, it's time to shift the focus. I offer an honest assessment of the risks I see in his current situation and discuss options like rehab, structured outpatient programs or other parameters necessary for psychotherapy to become useful again. Even when the client is making use of therapy I don't assume there will be a dramatic reduction in acting out or using (though it may happen!), and I do assume relapses will occur along the way. When that happens, my goal is to help the client's critics calm down so we can locate the vulnerability without shaming. Overall, I expect therapy to proceed with small shifts in functioning: softer critics, less acting out and increasingly better decision-making in combination with less emotional charge in the internal system. Distractors will usually improve all along (albeit fitfully), but they may be the last protectors to leave their stations.

Perhaps most important, the therapist will be challenged to stay centered and outside the client's addictive polarity. Parts (and people) who judge the addictive process fortify the client's central impasse and escalate the problem. When we're able to work with our parts to create a nonjudgmental, nonpathologizing relationship, we help the client focus on his inner work rather than on protecting himself from external threats to his autonomy. My focus is to help the client understand his parts and their positive intentions, without denying the damaging consequences of compulsive risk taking.

Finally, I keep in mind that everyone has a singular path to healing, and transformation will happen in the client's own time frame. I feel strongly that each person has an innate capacity for wholeness, yet I know that some will have a very long struggle. I've witnessed deep healing and full recovery, and deep suffering that yields only partially to treatment. Nevertheless, the IFS model helps clients discover their polarities, understand the positive intentions of negative behavior and experience self-compassion, which is the best way I know to safely guide them on their journey toward self-trust, healing and inner balance.

REFERENCES

Schwartz, R. C. (1995). *Internal family systems therapy*. New York: Guilford.
Sykes, C. C. (2001). Why I love my firefighters. *Self to Self IFSA Journal*, 5(6), 1–3.

Chapter 3

IFS and Eating Disorders
Healing the Parts Who Hide in Plain Sight
Jeanne Catanzaro

INTRODUCTION

From the perspective of internal family systems (IFS) therapy, eating disorders (EDs) result from the combined actions of protective parts who strive to shield the client from overwhelming, negative feelings by focusing on food and the body. While extreme EDs are among the most deadly of psychiatric diagnoses, even moderate eating disorder behaviors commonly cause serious physical and emotional impairment. As a result, traditional treatment tends to focus on eliminating or stabilizing the behavior, while family, friends and providers tend to respond with strong emotions like fear, helplessness and revulsion. When power struggles ensue, which they generally do, eating disorder symptoms increase and the client is left feeling even more helpless and ashamed. IFS offers a different—and in my opinion more effective—approach that involves defusing power struggles and addressing the underlying motivation of eating disorder parts.

CHAPTER OVERVIEW

In this chapter, I illustrate how to win the cooperation of ED protectors and help the client reveal and heal underlying vulnerabilities. I give particular attention to characteristic polarizations within the client as well as between the client, therapist, family and concerned medical professionals. While looking at some of the typical complications involving complex external systems I also illustrate how I work with my reactive parts. Finally, I discuss common obstacles to recovery, including the necessity of grieving the inevitable damage of a full-fledged eating disorder.

THE ETIOLOGY OF EATING DISORDERS

Research has identified many factors that may contribute to the development of eating disorders and that probably interact, including genetic vulnerabilities, personality variables, attachment difficulties, psychiatric issues and cultural context (Striegel-Moore & Bulik, 2007; Keel & Forney, 2013). However, what seems clear is that the internalization of a thin ideal is a primary risk factor. Long notorious among white American adolescent females, ED behaviors have been spreading to men (typified by a lean or muscular body type (Bunnel, 2010), to post-adolescent women (Maine, 2010) and across the globe (Pike, Hoek, & Dunne, 2014).

Although most people struggle at some point with cultural standards of beauty, they do not develop clinically significant eating disorders, which are often (though not always) preceded by attachment difficulties and interpersonal injuries, including physical or sexual abuse, neglect, bullying and pre- or perinatal trauma (Brewerton, 2007; Ackard & Brewerton, 2010). Even when the body itself has not been victimized directly, trauma results in feelings and sensations from which the trauma survivor needs to disconnect in order to keep functioning. The bodies of traumatized people (and often those with insecure attachment) are "constantly bombarded by visceral warning signs, and, in an attempt to control these processes, they often become expert at ignoring their gut feelings and in numbing awareness of what is played out inside" (van der Kolk, 2014, p. 97). As van der Kolk says, they learn to hide from themselves, but they also hide from others. Eating disorders help people—mostly women—hide in plain sight.

There are many reasons a person may wish to hide, not least fear. The dialogue clients have with their eating disorder parts is a preoccupying, often comforting buffer that allows them to maintain a safe distance from themselves and others. Thus, an anorexic client can appear engaged while mentally checking off the list of foods she ate/didn't eat that day. But hiding from relational intimacy does not bring peace; over time the individual typically becomes lonelier and more steeped in shame as her inner critic delivers a running commentary about food, weight, body image and other perceived failings. For example, when the proscription of a part who restricts food intake is violated with a forbidden bite (or full-on binge), a critical protector may step up to quash the rebellion and get the client back on track by repeatedly yelling *You fat pig!* while yet another part—whom one my clients often calls *the Captain, the Taskmaster,* or *the Boss*—creates an even more rigid and austere action plan. This all-consuming cycle allows the client to avoid being aware of much else.

AN IFS LENS ON EATING DISORDERS

Schwartz (1995) designates two types of protectors in internal systems: the manager who acts to prevent unwanted feelings from reaching awareness and the firefighter who mobilizes to suppress those feelings once they become conscious. ED behaviors can fall into either category. For example, a part who purges in response to an argument is reacting to painful feelings and would be designated a firefighter. However, if the relief that follows purging motivates a daily habit of purging that effectively suppresses feelings all the time, the purging part is acting as a manager. Similarly, bingeing, restricting, exercising or obsessing about food and weight can be either proactive or reactive in relation to feelings.

Identifying whether an ED part has tried to protect the client proactively or reactively helps to honor and appreciate the part's contribution to the client's well-being. More important, however, is our awareness that ED protectors always polarize into two camps: parts who push for restriction and control of the body and parts who reject this control and push for less restraint. Their tug-of-war keeps the client from being aware of the intense negative feelings and memories of exiled parts. While an individual's specific ED diagnosis depends on which parts dominate at any given time, the overall symptom picture, even if it isn't obvious from the client's physical appearance or self-report, always involves this dialectic between restraint and rebellion against restraint.

Beyond the pitched battles of polarized parts, the foremost challenge of an eating disorder is the cluster of parts who deny or minimize the problem. Even when negative consequences like medical difficulties and co-occurring psychiatric conditions accumulate and worsen, or when the ED actually no longer feels helpful, most clients come to treatment only because family, friends or school administrators urge or mandate them to get help. Of course, some clients initiate treatment on their own. But even then, their committed ED parts who have no wish to alter the behavior will soon show up.

MEREDITH: BEGINNING AN ED TREATMENT

When Meredith was a freshman in college, her therapist told her that her eating disorder was her way of separating from her mother. Looking at me 8 years later, Meredith shrugged and said, "That made sense to me. I was close to my mom and I missed her when I went to college." This narrative about her eating disorder, however, did not affect her behavior. While she was able to return to college after taking a semester off to get help, she continued to restrict and purge. In her second year of a master's program in social work she came to see me, feeling desperate yet declaring, "I doubt treatment can help. It's become such a habit; it's just what I do."

I knew from her current nutritionist that she had gained a significant amount of weight in her second residential treatment, which had inflamed her fear of giving up ED behaviors and prevented her from sticking with any outpatient therapy. To validate her concerned parts, I said, "I get why parts of you would have a hard time believing this work could be helpful. But it also sounds like you were put on a meal plan that was higher than your body needed."

Meredith leaned forward, exclaiming, "I knew it was too much but no one would listen! I felt like I was bingeing all the time. It was so gross. As soon as I got out I lost the weight." Then she leaned back and sighed. "But then I got back into the same old habits. I really don't know how this can ever change."

"I know treatment so far has consisted of efforts to get you to stop the eating disorder behaviors," I said. "But I want you to know that I'm clear about two things: First, your ED parts have been working hard to help you in ways that we need to understand. Second, they'll agree to change only when they no longer feel they need to take care of you this way. I—we—can't make them change."

She looked at me for a long moment before replying, "Well, no one's ever said that to me before!"

As Meredith told me about her life over the next few sessions, I sensed that her protectors, who had been assessing me, were beginning to believe that I wasn't going to try to control them and were relaxing. I learned that her father was a successful businessman who traveled frequently, and that her mother had quit work years earlier to devote herself to caring for Meredith's older brother Bobby, who was developmentally delayed and lived at home. Hers was a family with little overt conflict and much reinforcement for doing well in school and expressing positive emotions. When Meredith did speak about her ED during this early narrative, she described herself as lazy and said the ED was just a way of maintaining a "reasonable" weight.

Patience

After a few sessions a part of Meredith who wanted things to change spoke up. "I'm so tired of all this bingeing and purging!"

"Are you open to hearing from the part who gets you to do it?" I asked.

"It's ridiculous!" she declared, ignoring my question. "I end up ordering all this food online, getting rid of it, then surfing the web for more. Then I break down and binge and purge. It's exhausting."

"Would it be okay to get to know the one who orders food and gets rid of it?" I repeated.

"I suppose," she said.

"Is there an objection?"

"Yeah, but it's okay. It's just ridiculous."

I waited for a moment to see if this *it's ridiculous* part had more to say. Then I went on, "Where do you notice the parts who order the food and throw it out—physically?"

She pointed to her throat and then her heart, saying, "Tightness here, tension there."

"Is it okay to be curious about them?"

"I do want to know why they're doing it!"

"To get rid of them?" She nodded. "Of course. But would the one who wants to get rid of them be willing to give us some space to talk to them instead?" I asked.

"Okay," she said.

"Which one wants to go first?"

"They're always in a struggle back and forth—one gets me to buy food, the other throws it out—and then I go back and order more. The two of them keep me busy."

Typically, protectors are convinced that relaxing will either allow an opposing protector or an exile to take over. Since these two protectors said they worked together, I surmised they were concerned about an exile. Using the most effective hypothetical for detecting polarized parts, I asked, "What would happen if they didn't keep you busy ordering food and throwing it out?"

"Thinking about that gives me anxiety!"

"Can we stay with the anxiety?"

"I don't like it. I hate feeling anxious."

"Tell me more."

"It's so uncomfortable. I don't know what to do with myself."

"Is anxiety the feeling that comes up when you start bingeing?"

"Yeah, but I already knew that."

"What if we could help the one who feels anxious? Would you like that?"

"It's too big."

"I'm sure we can help it not to overwhelm you."

"How?"

"First, try telling it that you want to help but you can't be available if it overwhelms you and see if it's willing to stop."

Meredith looked surprised as she reported, "It agreed. And I notice the ones who hate the anxiety feel better because it's not so intense."

"How do you feel toward the anxious part now?"

"I want to understand it because I don't want to keep doing this."

"And what does it want you to know?"

"Well, it feels different to be asked. I'm always trying to get rid of it."

I nodded and waited a beat before asking, "And what else?"

"My anxiety always makes everyone uncomfortable. When I get anxious my father ignores me or gets mad and my mother tries to fix it by giving me food."

"You've never mentioned that."

"Yeah! Ironic because in the next breath she'll talk about my weight and whether my clothes are too tight."

"What has that been like for you?"

"Well . . . confusing. And it got me in the habit of eating something whenever I start feeling anxious or upset."

"How do you feel toward the anxious part now?"

"What a mess. I feel sad."

"Does the anxious part protect anyone?"

"No."

"Can you see it?"

"I never see this part. I just feel it."

"How's it doing right now?"

"It wants to know where I've been."

"What do you say?"

"I'm sorry! I really didn't mean to leave it alone like everyone else did."

"And what does this part need from you now?"

"Just to be with me without being told what to feel."

"Is that okay?"

"Yes," Meredith said, displaying more Self-energy toward a part than I had seen to date.

As Meredith was finding, her anxiety came from a young exile who had learned that her needs would have to come last in the family and who had been shamed for complaining about that. The part of her who binged, in turn, soothed the anxious one with food. And the purging and restricting parts had been trying to keep Meredith's weight down despite the bingeing. As these parts unblended and Meredith was able to hear from them, her view of the function of her ED changed. She no longer thought of herself as lazy or believed that her behavior was just a tool of weight management. And as the anxious part felt more connected to her, Meredith felt calmer.

Another Exile Emerges

"Even though I'm no longer bingeing and purging, I'm still obsessed with food. And something happened last night. My mother called and I got so angry when she talked about my brother. She said, *At least you can have a life.* I was barely able to stay on the phone."

"Okay to hear from the angry part?"

"Not really. Isn't it ridiculous? Bobby will never get better and here I am making myself sick."

"So there's a part who disapproves of you feeling angry?"

Meredith sighed. "My parents are right. I should get a life. How can I be so weak?"

"Who needs your attention first," I asked, "the guilty part or the angry part?"

Our work continued in this vein over several sessions, gradually getting permission from protectors to approach the part who had been exiled internally for having feelings that Meredith believed were unacceptable to her parents. This was particularly challenging for Meredith because her parents wanted to be involved with her treatment, called her often and were willing to drive a long distance to have family sessions. While they had parts who were pushing her to get better, it was also clear to me that they cared and were concerned. The more they pressed, the more torn Meredith was between anger and guilt, parts who had a hard time unblending. This exacerbated her ED symptoms, which, in turn, stirred her parents' fears and anxieties. ED therapists are often challenged by the gravitational pull of various relationally complex systems that orbit the client. Here is a family session I conducted with Meredith and her parents that illustrates my need to stay Self-led and be "the I in the storm" (Schwartz, 1995).

Family Dynamics: Legacy Burdens and the Push Against ED Parts

Maintaining an open, compassionate stance can be challenging for friends, family and treatment providers when they are dealing with extreme ED parts. Watching someone starve and deny it or repeatedly binge and purge elicits fear and helplessness. I've often seen supportive family, friends and providers abruptly turn angry and rejecting. Meredith's parents, who had just driven several hours, sat down with us but before I could even open the session, Dan, her father, exploded. "We've mortgaged our retirement so we could get you to stop puking, and it's literally going down the drain!"

Meredith and her mother froze. After a painful silence, I said to him gently, "Would your angry part be willing to let you speak for it?"

"It's so frustrating!" he exclaimed. "It's been years! We can't keep going like this. We refinanced our mortgage to pay for the last treatment that was supposed to help."

"I get how upsetting it is to hear that Meredith still needs support. It sounds like you have parts who are discouraged and also parts who are worried about being able to continue helping her financially." He nodded. "Would this frustrated part say more?"

He replied, "I don't know what to do! I'm listening to you and what you're saying makes sense. She likes you and this isn't a setback per se. But

I guess a part of me is thinking *how is this time going to be any different?* I'm not going to work forever. I plan to retire in 5 years. At some point she's just got to stop."

Both Meredith and her mother were looking at the floor, neither moved.

"How about we all take a moment to breathe and notice what's going on inside?" I said. "We can see if there are parts who need to be spoken for."

But Dan was too wound up to pause. He looked at his wife and daughter, who did not look at him. "I guess I'm just scared nothing is going to work. We've lost so much time to this eating disorder. I feel scared about what she's missing out on in life, and I worry about what will happen to her when I can't take care of her." Now Meredith looked up. "I'm sorry, honey," he went on. "I love you. I worry about you. And I want you to be well."

"Thanks," Meredith said.

"I just . . . panic," he said.

Meredith shifted in her chair, glanced at her mother, and then said to Dan, "What I'm learning is that it's okay for all of us to have feelings. I know you didn't mean it to be this way, but you're both so capable and used to handling everything and being upbeat . . ." She glanced at me, took a deep breath and continued, "What I want to do is speak for a part who felt it just wasn't okay to have feelings in our family."

"That's absurd," Peg said sharply. "Of course we have feelings."

"Like I was a bad person," Meredith pressed on. "You've sacrificed so much, Mom, and you never complain. I wanted to be like you but I can't. Maybe I'm not as strong. I have to be okay with that."

Her mother sat stiffly, not looking at any of us. Concerned that a protector was shaming her in an effort to shut down her exiles, I said to her, "When Meredith speaks about her experience, would it be okay to check on what happens inside you?"

"Inside me?" she said looking up, first at Meredith and then Dan. "I'll tell you what's happening. I'm furious! I'm sick of all this whining. I give and give and live like a ghost! I never complain. I take care of you and you and Bobby and that's all there is to my life. How do you think I feel?"

Meredith leaned over and hugged her mother. "I'm so glad you said that, Mom!" she exclaimed. "I really want to know how you feel."

At this Peg melted into tears. But Dan, who was wide-eyed and pale, looked to me.

I said, "Would it be okay to check inside and see what's happening for you right now?"

"I'm . . . scared," he admitted.

After this session we agreed to go on meeting as regularly as possible, and I also referred Dan and Peg for individual IFS therapy in their home state. Over the course of several family sessions, Peg was able to express anger and grief, as well as guilt that she had these feelings and fear that matters could get worse if the pressures on Dan became too much for him. Her protectors, I realized, were far more tuned in to Dan's fragility than he was.

In turn, Dan recognized a pattern in his response to any information about Meredith's needs: a part of him would amplify bad news to protect him against disappointment. This part told Dan that if Meredith still needed treatment, then therapy for EDs was useless and Meredith would never recover. This line of reasoning evoked the terror and helplessness he had felt as a child when his mother was terminally ill, and, of course, later when Bobby was diagnosed as an infant.

Dan had learned to rely on his self-sufficient, ambitious managers, who usually did a good job of keeping him away from vulnerable feelings. So when Meredith's illness was in front of him, they went into overdrive, pushing him to stay longer at work, travel more and try harder to get others to fix her. As he got close to his exiles in therapy, he began to notice a background of continual worry about the welfare of both children along with a belief that their fate, like his mother's, was his fault. As he helped his parts to unburden, he was better able to speak for his concerns about financial limitations without panicking and shaming Meredith. In turn, learning about his exiles and understanding how they drove his critical, angry protectors allowed her to receive this reality check without self-attack.

Meredith's bingeing and purging protectors had worked hard to ward off feelings that were unwelcome in a family culture that was organized around denying negative affect. Family therapy turned out to be key to helping her differentiate from her parents, who started to take stock of the fears and injuries that led them to exile their own vulnerability. This allowed Meredith's protectors to relax so she could finally help her exiled part who had always believed that feelings like jealousy, anger, sadness and loneliness were unacceptable. As she and her parents worked to heal their exiles, family dynamics started to shift toward being more open and Self-led, and Meredith's ED parts started to trust that they didn't need to protect her in this way anymore.

FIONA: SUBSTITUTING ONE EXTREME DISTRACTION FOR ANOTHER

Clients with ED protectors often substitute one distraction for another during the course of treatment. Fiona, now a 29-year-old lawyer, had become anorexic in college after starting a diet due to weight gain while living in the dorm. When being thin generated positive attention from her roommates, a part chose to maintain the behavior. In junior year she spent three months in residential treatment, using IFS to work with parts who were representing her parents' unyielding expectations for high achievement, and she was able to go on with her life. After graduating from college, she broke from her family's long tradition of going into finance, got a law degree and began work at a law firm. She did well for several years, maintaining a healthy weight without hyperfocusing on food or her body. But because all her energy was going into work, she had few friends and was very vulnerable when her boyfriend suddenly ended their relationship. Isolated and lonely, she fell into a depression and returned to me for help.

Around this time a concerned friend introduced her to a type of spin class that was very popular in the city. Studios offering these classes focused on making their customers feel like members of a special community by pushing them to physical extremes. Fiona immediately loved the intensity, energy and camaraderie of this environment. One class a week quickly turned into five, and soon she asked to change our weekly appointment time because it conflicted with the schedule of a favorite instructor. When I expressed curiosity about the part who was organizing her life around her spin classes, she shut the conversation down.

"There isn't anything negative about this. I feel great, my mood is great. I feel strong. There's nothing bad about it."

"I see how the spin classes have been helping your mood. Want to talk about that?"

She said, "It's not just that I feel good. Everyone I know says I look so happy." She went on to describe how she had always had a problem with her stomach protruding but now, without dieting, she had just the abdomen she had always strived to achieve.

"It sounds like this means so much to you. Tell me more about what having the stomach you've been striving for gives you."

"It makes me feel like I've made it. I keep up with the classes. I belong. And I'm less lonely."

"So exercise helps with the loneliness and sadness you started to feel after breaking up with Dave?"

"I thought the relationship was going somewhere. Then all of a sudden I had nothing. I hate my job, which is also going nowhere. But at the studio I belong. Now that I go every day and see the same people I actually have a community."

"You felt so lonely when your relationship ended," I observed.

"Absolutely," she replied. "My depression lifted once I got around other people with the spinning classes."

I said, "So this part does a number of things for you. It improves your mood, makes you feel good about your appearance, structures your day. And it helps you not feel the pain of Dave leaving. Does that sound right?" Fiona nodded. "Sounds familiar, doesn't it?" I asked rhetorically. "Here is a part driven to focus on one thing intensely so you won't notice sadness."

"Yes, it does," she said. "But this is totally different! This makes me happy. And I'm eating really well. Now that I'm taking such good care of my body I just don't feel like having junk."

I realized that my attempt to link her current behavior (spinning) with her past behavior (restriction) was an error. The part who was driving her to spend most of her spare time (and money) at the cycling studio sensed that I wished it to change and responded by listing all the reasons it was helpful. Owning that a part of mine had blended, I said, "Fiona, I'm sorry. I realize I have a part who is concerned about your focus on spinning. I'll work with it so that it doesn't take over again."

When I focused on my concerned part between sessions, it reminded me how sick Fiona had been in college and how responsible it had felt for preventing relapse. I reminded it that if I could remain Self-led, Fiona would eventually see how this ED part had become blended with her. In our next session, I said to Fiona, "I've noticed that I have some parts who feel responsible for you and I've asked them to step back. While I do see similarities between spinning and anorexia, I trust we'll explore the question if and when you want to."

Now Fiona began to have a social life through her gym. She liked being invited to eat out but feared eating unhealthy food and gaining weight. As she had in the past, she went through a mental check-list of the foods she had or hadn't eaten that day while socializing over a meal, which helped her to eat modestly and tolerate being with people. Unlike bulimia, anorexia (which was edging back into the picture now in a franker fashion) tends to evoke pride and a sense of belonging to an elite group. When some of Fiona's non-ED parts began the inevitable rebellion against being careful about calories, Fiona went further. She bought pastries from the most decadent bakery in town and put them on her counter where they remained until she threw them out several days later. She told me that she felt good about having so much self-control, which this blended part insisted was a sign of progress.

Struggles for Control Between Members of External Systems

Throughout Fiona's treatment, I was in regular touch with her nutritionist. While she had lost 10 pounds since beginning the spinning classes, she was eating and I was not alarmed. Her nutritionist, however, was alarmed and began to question whether Fiona was committed to recovery. She pressed Fiona to keep food logs and finally suggested a more intensive level of treatment for her. When I didn't agree, she expressed concern that I wasn't holding Fiona "accountable." I noticed that I had a part who felt critical of the nutritionist, judging her assessment inaccurate and her tone shaming.

Once I got my critic to relax, I was able to explain in a friendly way why I wasn't alarmed and what we were doing in therapy. This calmed the nutritionist's protectors and helped us to align around our mutual concern for Fiona. But I knew that Fiona's ED protectors had noticed our differences.

"What's this like for you?" I asked.

To my surprise, Fiona grinned, "I like it!"

"Oh?"

"Because now you get what it's like with her," she said happily.

"And what's the best thing about that?"

"I don't feel so lonely," she said. "I like that you've got my back. But I think I should find a new nutritionist—someone who isn't so focused on weight and numbers. It's not like I'm anorexic anymore. I'm healthier than I've ever been. I just want support to keep making balanced choices. Do you know anyone?"

I nodded and noticed parts who were skeptical about her request for a referral. Was her decision Self-led or was a part of her hoping to please me while avoiding having to increase her food intake by finding a nutritionist who was less focused on behavior change?

Effective treatment of eating disorders typically requires the coordinated efforts of a multidisciplinary treatment team because there is a reciprocal, often progressive, relationship between biological and psychological symptoms. Although everyone on the team usually agrees on an end goal, philosophies and methods along the way may conflict. The quantitative measures of weight, food exchanges and behavioral contracts used by physicians and nutritionists contrast sharply with the more ambiguous markers of change used by therapists, such as the capacity to tolerate emotional discomfort and to speak for internal experience. These differences, along with concern for the client and for personal liability, can result in finger pointing and power struggles, making it all the more imperative for the therapist to do her inner work so that she can be Self-led. I decided to sit with the concerns of my parts between sessions and find out more.

As I did so, I remembered that Fiona had been apprehensive from the beginning of our work about the style of this nutritionist, whose approach made her uncomfortable. But she had been reluctant to make a change because her inner critics were warning her that she could make a "wrong" decision. Watching me and the nutritionist struggle with our differences seemed to help these parts relax, leaving Fiona more confident about making a choice. After hearing from my parts and checking once more with Fiona to be sure her decision-making process was Self-led, I gave her the names of other nutritionists.

Meanwhile, the weekly waiting list for the marathon spin classes at her gym made it difficult for Fiona's ED parts to see her behavior as extreme. She did have parts who were complaining of exhaustion and worried about the cost of all these classes, but the spinning part was still very blended with her. I had to remind myself to stay curious rather than siding with her critic. Knowing that the spinning part, along with its shadow ally, the anorexic part, would not shift until they felt witnessed and appreciated, I asked, "Would the spinning part be willing to share more?"

"I was really athletic before I had the eating disorder and my body totally deteriorated," the part responded. "I'm impressed with myself. I'm really, really good at this. Other people can't do what I can. The instructor moved me from the second to the first row this week!"

After taking time to appreciate how this part had been working to help her feel better, I said, "I see how the spinning part has been helping you recapture your athletic body. What does it think would happen to you if it eased up on the number of classes you take each week?"

"I hate mediocrity!" she replied.

For some reason, this was the moment Fiona recognized the familiar voice of a critic who had been central to her eating disorder. During her residential stay, because Fiona had healed the exiles who felt shamed for not meeting her parents' expectations and believed they were inferior, her ED parts had shifted and this critic had relaxed. Its reemergence, she now saw, signaled the existence of other exiles. So she was not surprised to find, as we explored, that both the spinning part and the anorexic part were distracting from more fragile parts who felt devastated by Dave's abrupt departure and believed that Fiona (and they) were not good enough.

Staying Self-Led With Extreme Parts:
ED-Related Countertransference

As this vignette illustrates, one ED behavior can lead to another, very much including overexercise. The spinning pinwheel effect of one ED after another can try the patience of the therapist if her parts feel responsible or phobic about disappointment. When Fiona turned to overexercising, I spoke from parts who feared she was relapsing because I had failed her. To regain the trust of her protectors, I needed my parts to unblend so I could return to being curious about how her ED behaviors served her.

In general, I encourage my parts to unblend by reminding them that I will be able to help the client access her Self if they stop trying to manage her symptoms. However, when I'm working with some clients, my inner conversation about responsibility is ongoing. Holding the reality of an increasingly worrisome physical or emotional condition that's being minimized by ED protectors easily intensifies the anxiety and vigilance of my therapist part, who fears the client will experience irreparable physical damage, miss out on critical developmental stages and opportunities or actually die. My interactions with family members, school administrators and other treatment providers who have similar fears and often press me to fix the client can certainly complicate the picture. In addition, I worry for clients who face financial constraints and can't find or afford adjunctive treatment like nutritionists, group therapy or intensive outpatient programs, which can be so important with EDs.

To be effective, therefore, I need to be aware of and work with my parts. When I don't do my work, my parts are far more likely to get pushed by concerned others and locked into power struggles with the client's ED protectors who are vigilant to anyone's need for them to change or be gone. ED parts continually scan the therapist. They will notice, for example, if the therapist says she wants to get to know the ED protectors but then gets excited when parts who are tired of the ED emerge. In short, it's important to be aware that prioritizing the pro-recovery side of the polarization antagonizes ED protectors and hinders recovery.

As well as scanning the therapist for signs that she has an agenda, the client's protectors will try to figure out whether the therapist has her own eating disorder. To detect and work effectively with ED parts, we must be aware of personal burdens regarding food, weight and appearance along with attitudes in general about self-control and excess. A therapist who minimizes or denies her restrictive parts may not notice—or may actually compete with—a client's restricting protectors. A therapist who attributes a client's weight gain to a lack of self-control is likely to discover she has parts who feel intolerant about her own struggles with weight. In both cases, the ED parts of the client will respond by becoming more entrenched. On the other hand, when the therapist works with her parts who judge ED behaviors, she earns the trust of the client's ED parts.

JEN AND HER MOTHER: WORKING WITH THE CLIENT'S LARGER SYSTEM

Popular media lives by the mixed message of the ED polarity: excess on the one hand, deprivation on the other. In families that come down on the side of excess, turning down food is unthinkable. In families that side with deprivation, restricting and overexercising are seen as healthy. Clients who live in environments that support an eating disordered perspective often get confused by the suggestion that their own thoughts or behaviors are extreme. Seventeen-year-old Jen was a good example of this. Just as I started working with her, I got a call from her mother.

"You have to do something about Jen!" her mother urged. "I know she's telling you that she's restricting but she's not. I see her eating all the time. This is what she does. She says she's sick but look at her! Do you really think she's restricting?"

This opening gambit not only prepared me to work on family dynamics, it gave me important information about Jen's childhood and her current environment. As Jen explained to me soon after her mother's call, "It's difficult to understand the school counselor and my doctor who say I have to be in therapy when my parents think I *should* worry about my weight."

The restricting parts of Jen's parents, who pushed her to weigh herself daily and to keep losing weight, could not recognize her ED behavior as a problem. In turn, Jen's loyalty to her family caused her ED parts to believe they were simply doing the right thing. As always, my job was to help my judgmental parts relax so that I could work with Jen in the context of, and not in opposition to, her relational system.

SAMANTHA: A COMPLIANT PART IS AN OBSTACLE TO HEALING

Individuals with ED protectors who oversee achievement or people-pleasing typically do well in residential treatment where they receive lots of positive feedback for being compliant. Their people-pleasing parts enjoy the opportunity to organize around a clear goal, and they like being viewed as "good." However, these clients also typically relapse after discharge when their ED protectors step in again to care for vulnerable parts who remain isolated and unhappy.

Samantha, a 21-year-old woman referred to me by a residential eating disorder program, was adamant that she would never again binge and purge. Family members and treatment staff praised her for being able to stop restricting, bingeing and purging so quickly. Upon discharge, if any of the components of her treatment plan were altered (if, for example, I couldn't meet with her twice in a given week, or she didn't follow her meal plan to the letter), she became very anxious.

When I asked what she wanted to work on, she always replied, "Staying on the plan!"

"Could we hear from the part who wants to be sure you stay on the plan?" I asked.

"I can't go back to that cycle of bingeing and purging again," she said firmly. "The plan protects me."

"Do you notice an urge to binge and purge?"

"The truth is," she looked at me warily, "I miss purging most of all. I'm embarrassed to say this because I know it's ruining my teeth and part of me thinks it's disgusting but another part likes it."

I nodded with interest, appreciating how hard it was for parts of her to acknowledge this, and asked, "What does this part like best about purging?"

"I get it out!"

"What is 'it'?" I asked.

"I don't know," she said, looking lost for a moment. "But that's what's happening and I get so much relief. My mood just lifts afterward and I float. I don't know how else to describe it. I'm not purging now but I think about it a lot and that makes me feel like I'm disgusting. Do you think I'm disgusting?"

"Not at all," I replied. "Relief is very reinforcing, physically and emotionally."

A therapist who feels disgust can't be genuinely interested in the client's experience. But if you do have a part who feels disgusted, help it to unblend so you can ask questions that convey your curiosity and genuine respect for these protectors. The questions I ask in relation to purging include: *Does the vomiting provide a sense of mastery, relief, shame, sadness or a combination? Does the purging mediate depression or anxiety?* Some clients describe feeling exhilarated after purging, which regulates their depression, while others report feeling sleepy, which regulates their anxiety.

"Anyway, I just can't go through that again," Sam said.

"What would happen if you did?"

"I'd disappoint everyone. You'd be really mad at me. Everyone would. My life would be ruined."

"I hear you have a part who wants to purge and parts who feel that I would be mad at you and that disappointing others would ruin your life?"

"Yes," she said sadly.

"Which part needs your attention?"

"Why should I want to purge? Everything is going so well."

"Can you ask, or are you open to me asking?"

"The part who likes to purge says, *Going well for who?*"

"And what do you say?"

"For *whom*. And that would be me. I want to do this the right way."

"Could this be the part who wants to stick to the plan?"

"Of course."

"Can we hear from it?"

"It says, *If we can just behave for once everything will be okay.*"

"And what would misbehaving look like?"

"Getting mad, being stubborn and stupid. You know!"

"I hear you. What if we could help the part who feels like that?"

"Ha!"

And so it went for a couple of sessions, until we got permission to help her exile, a feisty little girl who had been viewed (and punished) as a "handful" by her family and the nuns in the Catholic schools she attended. Her purging part, it turned out, enacted a fantasy her system had developed when she was very young of "getting out the bad." Although Sam's managers began to allow her Self to spend time with this "bad" little girl, it was weeks before they were able to trust that I would accept her and that she wouldn't ruin Sam's life.

Ironically, exiling this part in favor of being compliant and "good" had set Sam up for some traumatic interactions with men as a teenager. But her critical managers, who had blamed the little girl for this as well, were only able to understand the dangers of being too compliant after her Self had become a steady presence. At which point they were able to admit that tight oversight, including restricting and monitoring everything Sam said in social situations, only encouraged the bingeing and purging parts whom they despised. When they gave Sam enough room to respond to a significant binge and purge episode with compassion and curiosity instead of their usual dose of anger, shaming and restriction, they were gratified to see the binge and purge parts relax as well. As protectors on both sides of her ED polarity calmed down and formed a relationship with Samantha's Self, they were able to admit that the "bad, stubborn" part was, after all, just an energetic little girl.

As this case illustrates, protectors work tirelessly to prevent access to feelings, memories and secrets they fear will result in more pain. While they mean well, they often end up creating the dangers they wish to avoid, no matter which tactic they choose. Our job is to validate their good intentions, help them feel safe enough to acknowledge the limitations of their strategies and try something new.

MAYA: WHEN CLIENT AND THERAPIST CANNOT AGREE ON TREATMENT OPTIONS

To eliminate the risk of future power struggles, I tell my clients at the outset of treatment that I will refer them to a higher level of care if they go below a certain weight or engage in a certain level of bingeing and/or purging. Depending on the client, a higher level of care may include regular monitoring by a physician, visits with a nutritionist who specializes in eating disorders, psychiatric medication or intensive outpatient or inpatient treatment. Once we have established these ground rules, I do not monitor ED protectors. Instead, I work on getting their permission for the client's Self to help exiled, vulnerable parts.

In my experience, clients who make important emotional connections in therapy but lack the internal or external resources to make behavioral changes can waste a lot of time, effort and money being seen on an outpatient basis. I feel it is similarly unethical to continue to treat clients when nutritional deficits (due to malnutrition or dehydration) make it impossible for them to use therapy. If I believe a higher level of care is necessary, I remind the client of our opening conversation, I say that I understand the motives of her ED protectors and I encourage her to talk about the limits I'm setting. Although I'm willing to keep negotiating if the client's protectors are, at this point I'm also willing to stop treatment.

Maya, an 18-year-old bulimic woman with an undisclosed history of sexual abuse, was still living with her parents, who were burdened by their own traumas and preoccupied with their own needs. Prior to working with me, Maya had been hospitalized twice. Since then she had refused psychiatric medications and had been wary of therapy. She had a big polarity between anger and loyalty toward her parents, so although she chose to come to therapy, the parts who felt loyal to her parents blocked her from talking about her experiences with them. As long as her symptoms were low key I was able to be patient. But after she witnessed a violent crime in her neighborhood, purging parts took over and escalated rapidly.

"I know you have parts who don't like the idea of residential treatment," I said. "But I'm also sensing that some other parts are scared and would feel relieved."

Maya nodded, but said, "I resent the fact that my parents keep doing what they do while I'm the one in therapy."

"Is that the main objection you hear to residential treatment?"

"It's fucked up! Like I'm the only one in my family who has a problem."

"What do your parts want us to know about that?"

"Going to residential treatment will give my family another reason to believe that I'm the one with the problem."

"I understand why parts of you feel strongly. It isn't fair that your family doesn't get it, and it makes sense that parts of you are furious about needing more help."

"I'm not going," Maya said.

"Okay. I explained the components of treatment that I need in order to work with you as an outpatient when we began. I respect that you have parts who object to residential treatment. So this is your decision? As we've discussed, we need to settle this today."

"I don't need residential treatment. I can do this myself."

"If you reconsider down the road I'd be happy to continue our work. Meanwhile, here are the names of some other therapists who specialize in eating disorders. Please keep in mind that if you give me permission to talk to another therapist, I'll go over these recommendations along with the work we've done."

Maya took the piece of paper I held out, glared at me and walked out of the office. A month later she returned and agreed to go to residential treatment. As this vignette illustrates, I anticipate what will happen in various possible scenarios when I start treatment with a client who has an ED, and I'm willing to be firm if one of those scenarios comes to pass.

ANABELLE AND KRISTEN: LIVING WITHOUT
ED PROTECTORS

Clients who have managed the aftermath of trauma by establishing close relationships with ED protectors often report a profound sense of loss once exiles have been witnessed and protectors shift. As my client Anabelle said, "The anorexia was a relationship that I couldn't have anywhere else. It gave me peace."

For some clients the eating disorder has been their only way of bearing witness to their trauma, and they need to find other ways to acknowledge what happened—often when others around them will not—without resorting to an ED. Many of my clients find a way to honor their experiences through expressive therapies or activities such as writing, dance, art or music. Others become motivational speakers, mentors or therapists. And, finally, some clients find that the changes they make in recovery disturb the status quo with family and friends, which is distressing, sad and threatens more loss.

As Kristen said, "I haven't felt so unsafe in years! Women who know me from the past keep asking how I lost the weight. And when I see my family they watch me eat. I feel preyed on!"

ERICA: MOURNING THE PHYSICAL COSTS
OF EATING DISORDERS

The ED cycle can be perpetuated by guilt, fear and shame about perceived or actual damage to the body. Since many physical effects of EDs can be treated or reversed (Tyson, 2010), even when a behavior is ongoing, I encourage clients to consult with their dentists and physicians. Refraining from brushing teeth after purging and using protective rinses, for example, can help prevent further enamel erosion. However, there are conditions like osteoporosis that can't be reversed. As is true for other losses related to eating disorders (e.g., missed relational opportunities, infertility and disruptions of school or work), many clients come to feel profound sadness about their harsh self-treatment and its cost, and their critical parts can be relentless in attacking them for creating those losses. In my experience critical parts only stop once exiles have been unburdened and the client has grieved.

Erica, a 40-year-old client, came into treatment because she had to stop running marathons, which had seriously damaged both her knees. Her first words to me were, "Any time I think about what I've done to my body I feel like what's the point? There's no use getting better because my body's fucked up." Now 3 years later, she was grieving the loss. "Running was my go-to," she said. "When I ran I didn't have to think about the rape. The feeling of being trapped, not being able to move, the panic—none of it. I just felt the power and the *fuck you* of it all."

Mourning is, at least in part, a process of Self-led recognition and gratitude for protective parts whose strategies have run out of steam, often in the case of EDs because the body can't take any more. Erica had taken up running to survive a childhood of severe physical and emotional trauma and had then been taken to task internally by a critic who was assessing the physical cost of coping. Feeling the compassion of her Self for all parts concerned helped her critic calm down.

CONCLUSION

While traditional eating disorder treatment involves stabilizing or reducing ED behaviors, and some attention to this may be necessary for the client to be in outpatient treatment, pressing her to reduce food-related behaviors is, from an IFS perspective, a mistake. Instead, as I have illustrated, we acknowledge from the beginning that ED parts won't change until they feel the behavior is no longer needed. When ED protectors understand that therapy isn't going to focus on trying to make them change, they can relax and we can concentrate on making progress at the outset of therapy by getting to know and understand the client's parts. As she discovers that she has polarized protectors who fear each other (a restricting protector fears that bingeing parts will take over and vice versa) and also fear that relaxing will allow the intense negative feelings of exiles to surface, the therapist has the opportunity to validate their concerns and negotiate alternate behaviors to reduce the physical threats of the ED and de-escalate the conflict.

Like all protectors, ED parts mean well. Their behaviors may look strange and seem incomprehensible, their stubbornness and determination in the face of such imminent danger and devastating consequences may be disheartening and infuriating, but their mission and zeal are in proportion to the injuries they hide. If we can navigate the obstacles that dot the course of any ED treatment, not least our desire to control dangerous symptoms and eliminate ED parts, our clients have the inner resources they need to heal.

REFERENCES

Ackard, D. M., & Brewerton, T. D. (2010). Comorbid trauma and eating disorders: Treatment recommendations and considerations for a vulnerable population. In M. Maine, B. McGilley, & D. Bunnell (Eds.), *Treatment of eating disorders: Bridging the research-practice gap* (pp. 251–267). San Diego, CA: Elsevier Academic Press.

Brewerton, T. D. (2007). Eating disorders, trauma and comorbidity: Focus on PTSD. *Eating Disorders, 15*, 285–304.

Bunnel, D. (2010). Men with eating disorders: The art of and science of treatment engagement. In M. Maine, B. McGilley, & D. Bunnell (Eds.), *Treatment of eating disorders: Bridging the research–practice gap* (pp. 301–316). San Diego, CA: Elsevier Academic Press.

Keel, P., & Forney, K. (2013). Psychosocial risk factors for eating disorders. *International Journal of Eating Disorders, 46*(5), 433–439.

Maine, M. (2010). The weight-bearing years: Eating disorders and body image despair in adult women. In M. Maine, B. McGilley, & D. Bunnell (Eds.), *Treatment of eating disorders: Bridging the research–practice gap* (pp. 285–299). San Diego, CA: Elsevier Academic Press.

Pike, K. M., Hoek, H. W., & Dunne, P. E. (2014). Cultural trends and eating disorders. *Current Opinion in Psychiatry, 27*(6), 436–442.

Schwartz, R. C. (1995). *Internal family systems therapy.* New York: Guilford.

Striegel-Moore, R. H., & Bulik, C. M. (2007). Risk factors for eating disorders. *American Psychologist, 62*(3), 181–198.

Tyson, E. P. (2010). Medical assessment of eating disorders. In M. Maine, B. McGilley, & D. Bunnell (Eds.), *Treatment of eating disorders: Bridging the research- practice gap* (pp. 89–110). San Diego, CA: Elsevier Academic Press.

van der Kolk, B. A. (2014). *The body keeps the score: Mind, brain, and body in the transformation of trauma.* New York: Penguin.

Chapter 4

From Reactive to Self-Led Parenting

IFS Therapy for Parents

Paul Neustadt

INTRODUCTION

I am the father of a son who has struggled with mental health issues and substance abuse, so I bring personal experience as a parent to my work as a therapist. I often tell the following story to the parents I work with. My son had recently completed a 30-day addiction treatment program and was living in Oakland, California. Because he had stopped drinking, his underlying psychological issues were wreaking havoc. His mother and I were eager to support his recovery by being in close touch, but he hated talking on the phone so we decided to visit. As we got on the plane in Boston, I was acutely aware of my anxiety and fears for him. I carried a list of concerns in my pocket that I felt a need to discuss with him as soon as possible.

On the first day my son took us on a hike. As we walked I started asking my questions. Not surprisingly he shut down. In turn, I began to despair. Did this mean we couldn't even talk in person? But then I was blessed with a moment of clarity: My anxious parent part was overwhelming my son with its intensity, making him feel even worse. What he needed from us, I saw, was to feel loved and accepted. It was most important to relax and enjoy being together.

In internal family systems (IFS) language, helping my anxious parent part unblend allowed me to access the clarity and wisdom of Self-energy. As my part relaxed, I focused on loving my son. When I shared this insight with my wife, she immediately agreed and we dropped our agenda. In turn, our son relaxed and enjoyed being with us. On the last night of our visit, he came into our bedroom and started talking about the things that were on his mind. We ended up talking in depth and covering most of our original concerns—but on his terms and at his initiative.

I share this story to let parents know that I understand what it's like to be taken over by an anxious, reactive part. My goal is to convey what can happen when we help our parts unblend and we access Self-energy. A personal story like this often has a greater impact on parents than anything else I say. In my experience, parents can befriend and transform intensely reactive parenting parts and learn to see that they provide a trailhead leading to their own injured, burdened young parts who can be healed.

CHAPTER OVERVIEW

In this chapter, I describe the difference between reactive and Self-led parenting. Most clients who come for help with their children do not intend to do inner work, but since their own childhood experience is fundamental to their parenting style, parenting work inevitably leads back in time (Siegel & Hartzell, 2014). Using case examples, I illustrate how to help parents differentiate from their reactive parts and change stuck behavioral patterns in favor of being more curious and creative. Further, I describe how therapists are easily inducted into the inevitable polarizations that occur in family systems and how we can navigate these polarities skillfully by working with our own parts.

REACTIVE VERSUS SELF-LED PARENTING

Self-led parenting is perhaps best understood in contrast to reactive parenting, a state in which parts who are blended with us perceive a current situation as if it is a negative experience from our own past. In contrast, a Self-led parent is able to be more present and see the current situation clearly. In a reactive state, we see through the eyes of protective parts who are focused on preventing the repetition of some painful experience from the past. In doing so, they attempt to exert control over the child with strategies that usually create a polarity with the child's protectors and cause the very thing they are afraid of.

GETTING STARTED: LYDIA

Lydia was a single parent who came to me for help managing her anger toward her 12-year-old adopted son. She described screaming horrible things at him and then, in a fit of guilt, telling him that she needed to find him another mother. Fearing more bad interactions, she dreaded being alone with him and was terrified of losing him. None of her friends knew about this behavior, and she was certain they would be appalled if they found out. Having grown up with a lot of screaming and threats, she hated that she was recreating her childhood with her own son, and felt she had become a monster.

Being Human

When Lydia called me to ask for help, she sounded hesitant and uncomfortable. So I asked, "Do you have the privacy to talk for a moment or shall we make another time to talk?"

"Oh, this is fine," she said. "I just . . . What I have to tell you isn't pretty. It's about how I act with my son. Sometimes I don't recognize myself."

"Sounds painful," I said.

"It's awful," she replied. "I need help."

"It takes courage to recognize that you need help. I'm a parent, too, and I know about being reactive."

"Thank you for saying that," Lydia said. "I don't know you and this is hard."

In my experience most parents who seek help with parenting feel guilty and ashamed, and judge themselves harshly. Even if they have buried some parts who feel vulnerable, they still expect to be judged by others. My goal on the phone with Lydia was to communicate, both directly and indirectly, that I was fallible like her. I didn't talk a lot about my experience—just enough to communicate that I could relate and was not judging her.

Mapping

After I have gathered some background and established a therapeutic rapport, I suggest clients focus on the repetitive interaction they most want to change. Using an easel (or whiteboard), I ask them to describe what is going on internally as the interaction unfolds. As I write, I reflect back what I am hearing in parts language and ask if I'm getting it right. I include their perceptions of their child's parts because it helps us to understand what their parts are reacting to together.

Lydia wanted to focus on how quickly she would start yelling at her son when he wouldn't do as she asked. The most common parental firefighter is the one who rages. It can be hard to see the positive intent of this part because it does so much damage. In addition to hurting the child it usually alienates the other parent (if there is one) and any other children. A raging part also

Table 4.1

Lydia's Parts
1. Feels disrespected by Sean and yells at him.
2. Feels uncared for and unloved by Sean.
3. Feels terrible about yelling at Sean and wants to stop.
4. Tells her that she is a monster.
5. Feels ashamed and believes she is a monster.
6. Dreads spending time with Sean.
7. Fears losing Sean.
8. Tries to fix things with Sean but often makes matters worse.

causes the parent's other parts to feel ashamed and remorseful, which stimulates the raging part to justify its behavior. Nevertheless, recognizing and acknowledging the positive intent of raging parts is essential for recruiting their cooperation. As I listened to Lydia describe her relationship with Sean, I made a list on the easel of all of the parts she mentioned (see Table 4.1).

Focusing and Explaining

"When you look at this list of parts," I said to her, "what stands out?"

"Wow," she said, "I know I feel disrespected but I wasn't thinking about feeling unloved. That's kind of a surprise."

"So which one needs your attention first?"

"The one who feels unloved," she said.

"Where do you notice it in your body?"

"My chest," she said.

"How do you feel toward it?"

"Scared, I think."

"Does the scared part need anything from you?"

"It just needed me to know."

"And how do you feel now toward the part who feels unloved?"

"I really wasn't aware of it. I wonder what it's about."

"How does it respond?"

"I'm seeing some stuff from my childhood. My mother could be pretty critical, and my father barely spoke except when he was exploding."

"What does it want you to know?"

"My older brother got into screaming matches with my mother every morning. Once she got so angry she hit him with a frying pan, and he ran away from home. They didn't even look for him. They just didn't mention him. After three days his best friend's parents called and sent him home."

"What does the part want you to know about that?"

"I was the good girl. I was terrified of being like my brother. My mother used to say he belonged in prison." Lydia chuckled, "Now he's a very successful defense attorney—keeping criminals out of prison. He hasn't spoken to my parents since he was fifteen, and he'll never help them if they need money, I know that."

"So watching your brother and mother fight was frightening?"

"Very. And my father was often mean and terrifying."

"What else does this part want you to know?"

"My son scares her."

"Does that make sense to you?"

"Yes."

"Would it be okay for us to check in with the part who rages at your son?"

Lydia nodded and closed her eyes.

"Where do you find it?"

"In my jaw," she said.

"How do you feel toward it?"

"Oh, I understand!"

"What do you understand?"

"It's protecting the good little girl."

"What does it do for her?"

"It tries to get my son to behave."

"And how does your son react to this part yelling?"

"He yells back or just goes totally silent and ignores me."

"And how does the raging part react?"

"It yells louder and says even meaner things. It doesn't know what else to do! Finally, I have to walk away and go to my room. I slam the door and then I start crying."

"So Lydia, now that you see how the raging part is trying to protect you, would you like it if we could work with it to let you take care of the little girl inside, and also help it find different ways to respond to your son?"

"Absolutely! Is that really possible?"

"Yes, you've made a really good beginning, and I'm confident that I can help you do this."

In subsequent sessions, we learned that the part who dreaded spending time with Sean made her very tense, which helped ignite the very conflict it feared. "When parts are responding to something that happened in the past, they don't see the present clearly," I said. "But even so they mean well."

"My raging part acts just like my parents," Lydia observed. "Isn't it ironic? This raging part is trying to protect me from feeling all that fear and shame by being scary and shaming."

"What does it say to you when it gets going?"

"Never again!"

I nodded, "That's often what protectors say. Does it get the irony?"

"No. Well . . . maybe a little now. But it's pointing out how bad things are at work."

This was how I discovered that Lydia was feeling ill-treated by the men at her law office as well. But there she felt powerless to fight back.

"When I'm with Sean this part says, *At least you can discipline a child! Don't let him walk all over you.* And another voice says, *Yeah, if you don't make him behave, he'll end up in jail!* And I just feel determined to win. Like, in the moment, the end justifies the means and I'll do anything to stop him."

"Sounds like one part is angry with Sean and another one wants you to assert yourself, and another is telling you that he needs you to control him for his own good. Is that right?" Lydia nodded. "For the angry part, what's the most important thing about winning?" I asked.

"I hear *I will not be treated this way.*"

"How do you feel when you hear that?"

"I get it," she said sadly.

"So the angry part isn't a monster. But it is motivated by a big problem that you couldn't escape back then—maybe it doesn't understand that this big problem happened long ago," I said.

"I think it's beginning to get the picture," she said. "I'm glad to know all this, but it's hard to realize I can't ever escape."

"What happened happened, that's true," I said. "But your parts don't have to live in the past. We can get them out of there."

Lydia looked surprised. "How?"

"When they're ready, I'll show you."

"They're not ready yet," she said. "I wonder why?"

"I expect they have more to show you," I replied. "They'll know when the time is right."

The following week the raging part also reminded Lydia how badly she felt when her son didn't want to spend time with her.

"What do you feel when he prefers time with friends?" I asked.

"Afraid. Abandoned. Sad. Unloved. Angry!"

"More than one part?" I asked.

"Definitely two parts. The first one—I can see her. She's the good little girl. She's afraid of her father who's yelling at her. The other part is the one who rages at Sean. I'm telling it that I want to find another way to get Sean to listen."

"How does it respond?"

"It says, *Okay but most of the time when you get home you're already tired and annoyed.* It doesn't believe I have the energy to do anything effective about Sean's behavior."

"So it's pointing out that some other parts are having a hard time, is that right?"

"Yes."

"What an important concern! Shall we work on that?"

Lydia and I then took a close look at her daily life and discovered some parts who were causing her to be stressed and irritable by the time she picked Sean up from school. Principal among these was an inner critic who continually told her that she was doing things wrong.

"What is the critic worried would happen if it didn't criticize you all the time?" I asked.

"I'd make an even worse mess of things," she said.

"How would you make things even worse?" I asked.

"This part thinks I have terrible judgment and I don't know how to stand up for myself."

"That means there's another part who this one thinks has terrible judgment."

"The good girl," she said. "But of course it's also concerned about the raging part!"

"So how would the critic like you to be with Sean?" I asked.

"It wants me to be able to be firm but flexible. To let Sean have some of what he wants but stand my ground with some other things."

"How does that sound?"

"Great!"

Since her critic was willing, I was able to help her talk to the good girl and the raging part. Predictably from my perspective but counter to the critic's beliefs, these parts promptly agreed to practice talking to Lydia without taking her over.

"So what would you like to work on during the week?" I asked.

"I'm going to make sure I have time to myself every day to do something I enjoy, even if it's only for a few minutes. I'm also going to check inside and go over all this when I'm on the way to pick Sean up."

"Sounds good. Can I make another suggestion?" I said.

"Of course."

"Let your parts know that anticipating problems with you by communicating every day would make a big difference. The more direct they are with you, the more you can help them. And if you notice your blood rising because a part is taking over, try taking deep breaths, being there with the part and telling it, *Okay, I'm here to listen. What are you feeling or seeing that you want me to notice?*"

The Gifts of Protectors

Although Lydia's critic had offered to take responsibility for noticing when she was getting upset and reminding her to take a time out, she did yell at Sean again.

"I'm so disappointed with myself!" she exclaimed.

"I guess you haven't achieved perfection yet!" I joked. "I have a confession. I'm not there myself. But I do know if we can listen with open minds to the part who yelled, we'll learn something important about how it was trying to help. Any objection inside to you being curious about this?"

Sometimes our firefighters react so quickly we feel puzzled, as Lydia did. "I do wonder," she said.

Staring to the side while attending inside, she took a few moments. Then she looked back up, exclaiming softly, "Oh my goodness! It says he forgot my birthday and yelling at him was a distraction from my hurt feelings. I really had no idea."

"Wow," I said, "it's letting you know about the hurt part it's protecting. Would it like you to take care of the hurt part so it won't have to get angry anymore?"

Lydia said the angry part would like that, but it needed to see if she could really do it, so we agreed to work on that.

Seeing Through the Eyes of the Self

In a session soon after, I asked Lydia if she would like to try seeing her son through the eyes of her wise, compassionate Self. When she agreed, I said, "Bring up an image of your son and focus on him, and we will see if there are any parts getting in the way of you seeing him clearly."

She nodded when she had an image.

"How do you feel toward him?" I asked.

"I notice that I have some pain in my heart because he forgot my birthday," she said.

"Take time to feel the pain of being forgotten. Then ask that part if it's willing to move aside so you can see Sean clearly."

"It's not ready," she reported.

"What else does it need from you?" I asked.

"It wants me to find a way to make things better with Sean," she said.

"I think this exercise will help," I said.

"Okay, then it's willing."

"How do you feel toward Sean now?" I asked.

"I'm afraid he will just keep growing away from me," she said sadly.

"Focus on that feeling and notice where it shows up in your body," I said.

She stayed with the feeling till it moved aside, after which we heard from some other parts, including one who didn't know how to parent a 12-year-old, one who felt despair about her life being out of control and one who reminded her of times when she and Sean got along well and had fun.

After hearing from all these parts, Lydia focused on Sean again and noticed a new calm. "I do see him clearly," she said.

"What parts of Sean do you notice?" I asked.

"I see the 12-year-old boy who's trying to be grown up and doesn't want to feel dependent on his mother," she said. "I see his confusion, fear and hurt when I yell at him. Of course he doesn't understand why I get so mad! And now I see a part of him who's been provoking me. I get the feeling he does that to feel some control."

"And what does he need from you?" I asked.

"He needs me to stop being such an idiot," she said. "I need to let him know I'm taking time-outs to control my anger and, of course, if I lose it he's not to blame. I learned all that behavior from my father. But I'm working on different ways of expressing anger and disappointment. He also needs to know that I do want him to listen to me, especially if I'm concerned about his safety. And if we have a conflict, I want to be able to talk about it."

Lydia felt empowered by this experience. When she saw her son through the eyes of her Self, she found clarity about how to behave differently and how to repair the damage her angry part had done. Once she could see him clearly, she could also have more appreciation for the ways in which her reactive parts were trying to help her and, in turn, they were more open to trusting her and letting her be in charge.

Lydia's experience illustrates how current challenges with our children can activate our most vulnerable young parts, the ones our protectors locked down and tried to make us forget years ago. When their emotional pain surfaces, our protectors swing into action and, without meaning to, actually re-create the childhood trauma. Generally, in my experience, we're not aware of why we are reacting so strongly in the present. As my work with Lydia illustrates, parenting-focused IFS therapy is about fostering secure attachment for both parent and child.

TEACHING SKILLS

My work with Lydia also demonstrates how I focus on teaching parents specific skills so that they feel empowered and confident to meet the challenges of parenting on their own. I keep a list of skills (see Table 4.2) that I want parents to learn, and I often focus on one of them as we process their concerns. At the end of a session, I often invite the client to make a plan for practicing during the week. Whenever I talk with parents about skills, I keep in mind that their parts are learning these skills and will sometimes stumble when implementing them.

Table 4.2 *The Skills*

1. Take time to check in with yourself. Anticipate and prepare for potentially difficult situations by noticing when you are emotionally aroused and pausing to talk to the part who is activated. Acknowledge its concerns and intention to be helpful and ask it to cooperate.
2. Connect with the vulnerable part underneath the reactivity with compassion. Ask what it needs and if it has something to offer you regarding how you parent your child.
3. Look at your child's difficult behavior as coming from one part and remind yourself that her other parts are not visible at the moment. Be curious about her vulnerable parts who are being protected by the difficult behavior.
4. Decline an invitation to join a negative interaction. Take a time-out when you find yourself in an interaction that is not productive.
5. When a problem or conflict arises, focus on your positive intention.
6. Speak calmly to the other person about the parts of you who were triggered.
7. Transform your complaints into requests.
8. Admit when you are wrong or hurtful. Ask about your impact and apologize.
9. Have your parts watch from the side so you can see someone through the eyes of the Self.
10. Mediate internal conflicts between your parts so you can include the perspectives of all of your parts in your parenting.

THE CONTINUUM FROM REACTIVE TO SELF-LED

Even as I guide parents to work with their reactive parts and teach them Self-led parenting skills, I stress being realistic. While it helps to have a vision of ideal parenting, no one is perfect. The degree to which reactive parts are blended or we are Self-led will fluctuate depending on any number of factors, ranging from how much sleep we got the night before to how many other worries are flying around in our minds.

Like anything else, the more we practice being skillful, the more skillful we become. Being Self-led doesn't mean we no longer have reactive parts, but we do notice them more quickly and we are more likely to take time to listen. As a result, our reactive parts trust that we will take their concerns seriously. If a part does hijack us, we can forgive ourselves, apologize, make a repair and, in so doing, model this experience and process for our children.

ACCEPTANCE: RICK

Self-led parenting involves acceptance and understanding of all parts. Many parents have parts who fear that accepting their child as he or she is permits and even empowers bad behavior. In contrast, my premise in using

IFS with parents is that acceptance leads to attunement and clarity about the child's needs, which in turn generally improves the child's behavior.

After a visit with his 28-year-old son, Rick told me the following story. He had flown to Chicago to visit Peter, who had a history of alcohol addiction and substance abuse as well as significant depression. Peter had been in individual therapy for the last year and a half and before that, in a residential treatment program. Although he was not drinking, he was now using marijuana, which was clearly affecting him negatively. Although Rick had told Peter when he was due to arrive, he waited for an hour at the airport and by the time Peter finally showed up, Rick felt angry. Nevertheless, he decided to do what we had been practicing in therapy: speaking for his parts instead of letting them take over and yelling.

"I landed an hour ago," he said as Peter took the handle of his suitcase. He immediately realized that despite his intentions he sounded critical.

"I told you I have trouble getting up in the morning. I did my best," Peter replied, looking ahead grimly as they went through the sliding doors.

Rick later told me that he understood at this moment that Peter's life was still out of control. Peter wasn't being rude or disrespectful. In fact, he felt terrible about being late. "I was able to help parts who have always been so reactive to separate," he said. "It was heartbreaking for me and excruciating for Pete. But I understood what you meant about seeing him clearly and accepting where he was."

Once they were in Peter's car, Rick said, "I forgot and booked a flight that would get in early, just focusing on having more time with you. My mistake. I know you didn't intend to leave me hanging."

"I'm sorry," Peter said.

"Thanks for picking me up," Rick replied simply. "It's good to see you."

COMING HOME TO WORK IT OUT: KATY

In the next case, I worked with a 25-year-old and her parents, sometimes meeting as a family, sometimes meeting with just the parents and sometimes meeting only with the daughter. The family work focused on helping them all identify reactive parts and learn some communication skills. In meetings with just the couple, I helped them identify the ways they were being influenced by their own childhoods and the behavior of their parents.

Katy had come back to live at home a year after getting very depressed and considering suicide due to the breakup of a serious relationship. Although coming home had made her feel better, she was angry with her parents for not having recognized the seriousness of her situation in the past and not having done enough to help at the time. In response, her mother, Ann, felt so guilty, frightened and ashamed that she had trouble staying present and seeing Katy accurately. She reacted as if Katy was still depressed, and she tried to give Katy the response she had needed a year ago. Katy's subsequent frustration with her mother propelled them all to family therapy.

Another feature of reactive parenting is that protective parts often feel compelled to take charge in a family crisis, which prevents the parents from being Self-led. Reactive protectors are always locked into old beliefs and misguided strategies, some inherited from parents and quite unconscious. When we notice a part enacting a painful old script, other parts who swore never to behave that way feel horrified. One of my first moves with a new family is to help them understand that we all have parts who take on detrimental strategies that are nevertheless meant to make things better. I invite them to notice the difference between the part's intention and the effect of its behavior on others.

Ann was surprised when Katy said, "Nothing I do is good enough for you!"

"But I thought you wanted me to show more interest in what you were doing. That's what I've been trying to do," Ann replied.

George said to Katy, "Why do you put up such a wall if you want us to be more involved and caring?"

"I'm just trying to protect myself from all this scrutiny and pressure," Katy said.

"Exactly!" I interceded. "That is what we are all trying to do—protect ourselves from getting even more hurt or disappointed. Or we try to please the other person. But sometimes the strategies we've learned along the way have a different impact than we intend. It's clear to me that the three of you want your relationships to be better, and I'm sure we can find a way for you to communicate more clearly if we all work at it together."

Katy and Ann

When I met with the parents, Ann was still upset.

"That was exactly how I felt with my mother. I always feel like a failure! Whenever anything goes wrong at work or with friends, I still always think it's my fault. How can I be doing this to my daughter?"

"I'm appreciating that you have a part who is here to make things better. Can we take a moment to feel the determination of this part?"

"Yes, I do want this to change. I don't want my daughter to feel bad."

"I'm wondering if you have a part who learned to parent with your mother as your role model?"

"Maybe. I hate myself for doing this. How can I stop?"

"By having a relationship with the part who took on that job. If you can appreciate how it's trying to help, it may be willing to trust you and shift. Would you like to work on that?"

Ann sighed. "Yes please! It would be such a relief to get along better with Katy."

George said he was glad to have me focus on Ann's parts first so he would have time to understand how this worked. After naming all the parts she could notice, Ann chose to focus first on the one who could be critical of Katy.

"So focus your attention on however you experience these critical feelings and thoughts. Do you feel tension somewhere in your body? Is it more in your voice or your mind?"

"It's in my tone of voice. I sound just like my mother!"

"How do you feel toward the part who uses your mother's tone of voice?"

"Intimidated. Afraid. Her voice has so much power to make me feel bad."

"So another part is intimidated by this critical mother part. Does that make sense to you?"

"Yes."

"Experience tells me that the critical part who sounds like your mother is really a part of you who took on the job of sounding like your mother for a reason. Want to ask it how it's trying to help?"

Ann closed her eyes then raised her eyebrows in surprise, "Oh!" she said. "This is a girl. About 10 years old, I think."

"Does she see you?"

"She's squinting at me. She wants to know who I am."

"And what do you tell her?"

"Well, I don't really know what to say!" Ann opened her eyes and looked at me. "You mean that's my critic?"

"Ask her," I said.

Ann closed her eyes and after a moment said, "Yes. She's just a kid."

"Ask who she protects."

"I'm seeing my mother looking so angry and disappointed because I spilled orange juice on myself," she said promptly.

"How old are you?"

"Maybe three. What does this mean?"

"Ask the girl," I said.

After a moment, Ann reported, "She says, *Someone had to do it.*" Opening her eyes again and looking at me, Ann asked, "Why would sounding like my mother and being mean for 30 years be something someone had to do?"

"Ask her," I repeated.

Ann listened. "She says the little girl had to do better or she'd get killed. . . . Killed?"

"Sounds extreme," I said.

Ann took a deep breath and looked thoughtful. "That's true," she said finally. "My mother could be terrifying. And I've spent my whole adult life fearing that terrible things were about to happen."

"Do you have a sense of how this has affected your relationship with Katy?"

"I think I'm always anxious and I can see how she might have felt I was being critical and unsupportive. I guess I was unsupportive! I wanted her to be really good at things so she wouldn't get hurt."

"Like the 10-year-old wants this 3-year-old to be really good at things?"

"Yes," Ann said sadly. "Just like that."

In the family and individual sessions that followed, Ann found out more about the 3-year-old who had been chronically shamed by her mother and had believed she was unlovable. She also got to know the 10-year-old who had reacted to this fear by imposing a harsh self-improvement program. Copying the mother, the 10-year-old had been controlling, intrusive and demanding not only internally but also with Katy. Like many critical parts, once Ann was more emotionally present and open to its concerns, the part was willing to change its approach, and Ann's relationship with Katy improved.

WORKING WITH POLARIZED PARENTS

One of the most common phenomena in parenting is the painful conflict that can develop between parents over how to deal with a very challenging child. Both parents think that the child's welfare is at stake and the other parent is undermining their parenting or somehow making things worse. When parents tell me about parenting conflicts, I tell them this phenomenon is almost universal and I've experienced it firsthand. When a polarization has gotten intense and bitter, each parent is taken over by protective parts who are reacting inside to the feelings of a young, vulnerable part.

Working It Out: Betsy and Abe

Betsy and Abe were in conflict over their 24-year-old son, Dave, who was back home struggling with anxiety and depression. They were worried that he would not be able to take steps to become independent but they were bitterly divided over how to help him. Betsy felt unsupported by Abe in setting difficult limits. Abe felt dismissed and judged by Betsy.

"What I hear is that you each hold an important perspective, and the more you advocate for your view, the more your partner feels obliged to advocate for the other side," I said. "I'm wondering if you would you be willing to experiment with the possibility that both your perspectives are needed to come up with the best way of helping Dave?"

"No!" Betsy said. "I know I'm right about this."

"Okay, I hear you. Let's back up. I need to understand more about what is leading each of you to feel so strongly. I have a few questions I'd like to ask you both. Who wants to go first?" Because each had intense feelings, I spent some time identifying and talking directly to their parts rather than having their parts separate from them. I knew their protective parts would not relax until they each felt understood by me. That is, I had to serve as the Self in the system until their parts felt enough trust to unblend and allow them to access their Self-energy.

I asked them both the same questions, beginning with, "What are you trying to accomplish by advocating so forcefully?"

"I'm trying to mobilize Dave to be more responsible," said Betsy. "He seems content to stay in his room and watch TV or play video games. He never goes out of his comfort zone!"

"I want to help him take steps toward being more independent, too," said Abe. "But I think he needs a lot of support to overcome his fears and anxiety. I'm trying to be patient, though sometimes I get frustrated and annoyed when Dave doesn't do the things he says he'll do."

Turning back to Betsy I asked, "And what are you afraid will happen if you don't do this?"

"I'm afraid Dave will never be able to leave home," said Betsy. "Abe just keeps protecting him from facing the consequences of not taking responsibility. As a result, I'm afraid he'll never be able to mobilize himself and overcome his anxiety."

"And what life experience have you had that leads you to this concern?"

"Well, Dave does remind me of my brother who has always been a good-for-nothing and was never able to make anything of his life. My parents didn't know what to do with him, so they just always let him do whatever he wanted. They've ended up supporting him, and he's never had more than an odd job here or there."

"No wonder you're afraid that Dave won't be able to leave home—you have your brother's example right in front of you. And Abe, what are you afraid will happen if you don't keep doing what you're doing?"

"I'm afraid Dave isn't getting the help he needs to succeed. So he'll just keep feeling overwhelmed and convinced that he can't move forward. Dave is very sensitive, and I'm afraid Betsy's pressuring and criticism adds to his low self-esteem. And to answer the next part of your question, I can't help thinking about how alone I felt growing up and how I didn't get any support or guidance from either of my parents. All I got was irritation or criticism. And I am sure there are things I ended up not doing because I didn't have the encouragement and support to do them."

"Okay," I said, moving into the pitch I often give parents, "so I see how each of you is trying to prevent something bad that happened to you from happening to your son. I can also see that for each of you the other parent seems to be doing the exact thing that was done before that felt wrong.

What I want to suggest is that we create a safe place here for you as partners in parenting. If you agree, sometimes I'll guide one of you to work with your parts who get activated in your relationship with Dave, and sometimes I will help you engage in what I call a Self-led conversation with each other, a conversation in which you can listen to each other with an open heart and an open mind, which I believe will bring you to a deeper understanding of each other. How does that sound?"

They agreed.

"Is it okay with you both if I interrupt sometimes to keep you on track or slow you down? This is especially important when someone starts to feel overwhelmed."

They nodded.

"And please let me know if you think I'm off track. I'll rely on you for that."

We chose an issue to focus on and identified the parts of Betsy and Abe who had feelings about it. I then listed each part and its concerns on an easel, as noted in Table 4.3.

Working With Our Parts as They Get Polarized

When we step into the emotional field of our clients, our own parts inevitably react. When we aren't aware of their reactions, they may influence and induct us into problematic behavioral patterns either from our own or our client's past. For example, I was aware that I had a part who felt critical of Abe and believed he wasn't owning the ways in which he was judging Betsy and how this affected her.

My critical part focused on Abe during one session in a way that brought out his protectors. I noticed, got curious about what I was doing and recognized that I had a part who was challenging him. I apologized and let him know that I would take some time to work with my part. In doing so I

Table 4.3 Listing Parts

Betsy's Parts

- Dave is lazy and avoiding responsibility so he needs to experience realistic limits and consequences.
- Abe refuses to do the hard things in life. He leaves that to me, but then he won't support me.
- Abe coddles Dave, which encourages him to be passive.

Abe's Parts

- Dave is suffering and needs support and encouragement.
- Betsy is harsh, which shames him and he gives up.
- Betsy is dismissive and judging with me and uninterested in other perspectives.

learned that my part still felt guilty about being critical of my wife years ago when we had been at odds over our son. While we had overcome that polarization, this part felt I hadn't fully repaired the damage, and it wanted me to help Abe avoid hurting Betsy in the same way. I was grateful and promised to speak for this part's concerns with Abe and Betsy—and also with my wife. In return, it agreed not to take me over.

In the next session, I shared what I had learned from my part and talked about how my wife and I had resolved our disagreement. "My father had a bad temper and yelled a lot, so when my wife yelled at our son, I had a part who identified with him and was upset with my wife. Unfortunately, at that time I wasn't able to talk about my vulnerable part. Instead I was critical of my wife. My wife also had an angry, shaming father so even before she heard my criticism she felt ashamed about yelling like her father. Like you, Betsy, my wife felt I left her to set the hard limits. Only by understanding our vulnerable feelings were we able to overcome our conflict."

This made sense to Abe, and he acknowledged that he did have a part who was critical of Betsy. But now he could also see how Betsy would feel caught in a bind between setting the limits she felt Dave desperately needed and hating herself for being angry and critical with him.

As she heard this, relief spread across Betsy's face. "Thank you for saying that," she said, "that really makes a difference! And there's something else. As Abe knows, my brother was out of control and violent with me throughout my childhood. I have some anger about that."

"You have a part who feels angry that your parents didn't do enough to protect you?" I asked.

When Betsy nodded, I said, "Could you ask that part how it's connected to Dave and Abe?"

Betsy was silent while she listened inside. Finally, she said, "This part is telling me that I feel abandoned by Abe just the way I felt abandoned by my parents. I have to handle things all by myself."

I could tell that Abe was moved. "What was it like to hear this?" I asked him.

Looking at his wife, Abe said, "Betsy, I'm so sorry. I hope you realize that I had no idea you felt this way. I was too caught up in trying to make things better for Dave. But I see that not supporting you was also not good for Dave."

This was a turning point. We continued to have some rough spots when they found themselves on the opposite side of an issue, but since they now felt like a team, they were able to help reactive parts step back so they could speak for parts who disagreed and focus on the shared goal of empowering their son.

Once we had practiced having a Self-led conversation several times in the office, I encouraged them to begin talking this way on their own. Abe was a little reluctant. "We've been good at focusing on our positive intentions at the beginning. And we've been good at picking an issue to focus on and taking turns saying how we feel. But I'm afraid we won't be able to get ourselves back on track when one of us feels jolted by something the other says. Even when I'm just trying to understand what Betsy is saying I often get it wrong. And it still seems to be so easy for us to feel hurt or offended," he said.

Seeing Betsy's impatience, and noticing that I had a part who feared Abe would feel hurt, I closed my eyes, took a deep breath and asked for guidance from my Self. In a moment I opened my eyes and smiled. "This is perfect!" I said. "I wanted to talk with you about the importance of taking time-outs. Of course you're still going to trigger each other and feel hurt. There is no way you can avoid that completely. What you can do is notice when a part has been triggered and take time out to stop the interaction from getting worse."

"But then what?" Abe asked.

"Then you listen to your parts and talk to yourself like a wise, loving parent who is talking to a son or daughter. And then, when you're both ready, you can come back together and share the answers to the questions I gave you (see Tables 4.1, 4.2, and 4.3). Shall we practice now?"

When they both agreed, I said "Okay, focus on the part who is most activated right now. . . . Notice how you are experiencing it. . . . This is the first step. Once you have a good sense of the part, ask yourself, *How do I feel toward this part of me?*" After a few moments I asked, "So how are you each feeling toward your target part?"

"I'm aware that I'm annoyed," said Betsy. "And I understand why I'm annoyed. I can't stand when Abe is so wishy-washy!"

"Betsy, I can really feel how annoyed you are with Abe. Now can you ask this annoyed part of you if it would be willing give you some space so your calm Self can be here to help you find a way to address its concerns?"

Betsy was quiet for a while. Finally, she said, "Okay it's giving me some space. Now what?"

"Ask yourself, *How do I feel toward this part?*"

"I'm annoyed with it."

"Okay. So that reaction is another part. When that happens you ask the other part to give you space. And each time you ask yourself how you feel towards a part, if another part reacts, you ask that one to give you some space, until finally you feel some calm or curiosity or openness toward your part."

"You mean I do for my parts what you've been doing for us here."

"Exactly! And there are two most important questions to ask your parts when you do this: *What are you afraid would happen if you didn't do what you're doing?* And *What do you need from me so you can let me stay calm and speak for you?*"

I continued coaching Betsy and Abe to help their parts unblend and be in relationship with them until they felt confident enough to try it at home.

Taking a time-out and using it in these ways is one skill I emphasize with all parents. It provides time and space to be in relationship with activated parts so they don't take over, and it demonstrates experientially the need to have a relationship with their own protective parts in order to change their relationship with their child and increase their capacity to co-parent. It also changes the pattern of a polarized conflict between parents (or parents and child), and helps parents feel more capable of talking together on their own, even while they may save more difficult conversations for therapy sessions.

In our next session, it was clear to me that Abe and Betsy felt more trusting and safe with each other, which allowed them to focus on inherited burdens. Abe felt that his parents had failed to take his awkwardness and social difficulties in school seriously, leaving him lonely and often unhappy. Like many parents, Abe had a protector who vowed to parent differently and then erred in the opposite direction from his parents, believing it was unreasonable to expect almost anything from Dave. Through the eyes of this protector, Abe had always believed he was being supportive. When the part stepped back, however, Abe saw that avoiding clear expectations along with not letting Dave handle what he was capable of were forms of abandonment.

We call these inherited conundrums *legacy burdens*. Our parents were on the receiving end of some difficult behavior enacted by their parents and so on up the generational line. Legacy burdens generate Abe's very typical response of leaning too far in one direction in order to differentiate from his parents. Unless we're released from inherited burdens it's hard to avoid passing them on to our children. With Betsy lending her support, Abe was able to imagine and feel that he was passing the belief that he wasn't able to rise to the life's challenges back to his father and grandfather. Finally, he envisioned his forebears expressing their confidence in the young Abe, after which he was able to handle a challenging situation.

In turn, Betsy focused on believing that being strong meant being tough, critical and angry. Those who couldn't take it, so this edict went, were weak and would never amount to anything. With Abe holding her hand, she imagined herself calmly standing up to her parents and then handing the feelings and the belief that there was something terribly wrong with her back to them. Realizing they were just passing on what they had experienced, she invited her parents to pass their burdens to their parents with the same invitation. Then Betsy imagined both sets of grandparents surrounding her, Abe and Dave in order to give Dave their blessing. Betsy and Abe letting their legacy burdens go had a strong positive impact on this family. While Dave continued to struggle, his parents were able to keep his difficulties in perspective and be far less reactive, which in turn supported him to do his best.

CONCLUSION

With guidance and practice parents can learn to be less reactive and more Self-led. Parents often come to therapy with a sense of urgency, wanting help to deal with the ongoing crises of parenting. While most parents do not intend to do their own inner work, understanding the motives of their reactive parts often leads them to their exiled parts. And once they achieve a more accepting relationship with their own young parts, they can develop a deeper understanding of their child's experience.

Accessing our Self-energy is crucial for staying connected with both parents when they're caught in a painful polarization. Since one or both parents inevitably trigger our parts, recognizing the moment when this happened and being transparent with the parents about your experience is also key. When we acknowledge our imperfection and humanity we help parents open their hearts to their imperfection. The IFS approach offers parents practical tools and skills as well as the ability to heal the wounds and let go of burdens that interfere with optimal parenting. Our goal is Self-led parenting, still imperfect and human but characterized by a greater degree of confidence, clarity, creativity, attunement, compassion and the ability to stay calm in times of challenge.

REFERENCE

Siegel, Daniel, & Hartzell, Mary. (2014). *Parenting from the inside out.* New York: Jeremy Tarcher/Penguin.

Chapter 5

Self-Led Grieving
Transitions, Loss and Death
Derek Scott

INTRODUCTION

Loss is not a problem to be solved. It's an unavoidable recurring life event to which we adapt by grieving. Although grief never feels simple, I use the word *simple* in this chapter to differentiate grief that runs its natural course without obstacle from grief that is made complicated either by unresolved prior loss or by the traumatic nature of the loss. When grief is simple and straightforward, the job of the internal family systems (IFS) therapist is to be a companion and occasional guide for the bereaved client, keeping company and embodying *Self-energy,* a state of mind characterized by presence, curiosity and compassion. But when we notice the client isolating and feeling overwhelmed or bewildered by loss, our inquiry is likely at some point to encounter parts who hold stories of unsupported loss in the past, which means we are looking at more complicated grief and our job is to hear those stories and help the parts heal.

CHAPTER OVERVIEW

In this chapter I illustrate common complications that arise in therapeutic work with grieving clients, including their nonacceptance, guilt, shame, isolation, problematic (or absent) social supports, depression, the urge to suicide and countertransference. For clarity, I divide the chapter into three sections. The first describes simple grief. The second describes grief made complicated by unresolved early or traumatic loss, which can show up in the delay, absence or chronicity of grief. The third covers countertransference, which I place in a category of its own because the therapist must be able to help his parts unblend (i.e., not take the lead in the session) if he is to be effective regardless of the client's history of loss. I illustrate how the principles of internal family systems therapy apply throughout the chapter, whether a case is simple or complicated for either the client or clinician.

How Grief Shows Up in Therapy

Therapists encounter bereavement during their work in one of three ways. A client seeks therapy because of a loss, a current client becomes newly bereaved or the therapist experiences a loss in his own life. In the first case, when a client with no experience of IFS seeks therapy after a loss and affect-laden parts are blending and venting as they tend to do in the early stage of grief, we hold the Self-energy for the client's system, that is to say, we offer "compassionate curiosity" (Wolfelt, 2006, p. 85) and support the client with "tenacious caring" (Schwartz, 2013, p. 4). In the second case, when a client familiar with IFS is already in therapy, we help her to understand her protectors and listen for vulnerable parts who have stories to tell. Finally, if we are the ones in mourning, our awareness of parts who have experienced loss along with our willingness to seek support will help us stay present and available to our clients.

History Matters

Over the years I've heard clients new to therapy say things like my *family was good, they never beat me or anything,* and I've often heard protective parts summarize childhood as *not too bad* or *pretty good on the whole.* While I appreciate protectors who gloss over adversity, report no significant early losses and are casual as they mention the death of a beloved one, they may block other parts who have helpful information about the client's distress and ways of coping.

Therefore, I combine a classic bereavement tool with IFS by taking a *loss history.* The loss history gives the client an opportunity to acknowledge his losses, notice how he survived and appreciate his resilience. At the same time, his history may give me insight into his current response to loss. In order to be as complete as possible with this history, I ask about his supports at the time, what he was told about loss and what his parts learned from watching the way others responded to loss.

I also point out that loss is inherent to the many transitions of childhood. When parents separate, for example, a child may lose the future she expected along with her current life. When a family pet dies, a child may have lost a virtual sibling or a magical being who held many confidences. When a family moves to a new house, a child may lose the fabric and structure of her world. When we listen with openhearted curiosity we hear about the client's attachments and the significance of her losses, which may not be what we would have assumed.

SIMPLE GRIEF AND FIRST RESPONDERS: LIZA

Liza had been coming to me for about nine months to work on anxiety when she reported that her father had died from emphysema after being admitted to a hospital with a chest infection.

"It's funny but even though I'd been expecting him to go I can't quite believe it. I find myself planning a visit to the hospital." Liza looked thoughtful as the afternoon sun shone through the window, illuminating the side of her face. "It was good, though. A couple of days before he died he told my boy Kevin that his time had come and he wanted Kevin to grow up and be a man of good conscience like his father. Kevin is only 8. He was so sweet, listening very seriously to everything Dad said."

"How is it to be talking about this?" I asked.

"Strange. After those sessions when I was so sad that he was going and then mad at him for smoking, now I just feel . . . calm. I thought I'd be much worse off than this."

"It takes a while for the whole system to realize what's happened," I offered. "You may notice different parts responding as the information reaches them."

For the rest of the session Liza reminisced about her life with her father.

"It sounds like you have a storyteller part who wants to take the lead today," I said at one point.

"I guess I do," she said. "Is that okay?"

"It's okay with me. Is it okay with you?"

"Yes, this feels like what I need."

I nodded and reached for my tea. In my system I could hear, *But what about focusing on her anxiety? That's what she came for.* I reminded it that parts who have stories to tell often blend soon after a loss, and my job is to witness them with Self-energy. I assured my part that we would track her system and get back to anxiety when it was once again her main concern.

As we see with Liza, first responder parts who react to loss with shock, disbelief, denial and numbness are often closely paired with storytelling parts. They titrate the influence of our more vulnerable parts (who will be revealed only gradually) and allow managerial parts to cope with required practicalities like arranging funeral services.

In early bereavement work I often use an IFS technique called *direct access* in which my Self speaks directly to the client's part rather than me guiding her to talk to the part and helping it to unblend. If she is flooded with strong feelings and parts are blending one after another, using direct access allows me to hold the Self-energy in the session while we hear from them. Since grieving can't be rushed, many sessions of direct access may be needed.

Time Passes

Liza stared out my office window at the rain.

"How have you been?" I asked.

She turned to me with a sigh. "Flat. Now that I'm not going to the hospital any more I could get back to the gym or take a course—or even write that damn novel that my writing part has been twittering about for 30 years!"

She smiled and I smiled back, familiar with her inner writer and its persistent dream.

"But I don't have the energy," she went on. "I don't care. Am I depressed? I lie awake at night and feel like a zombie all day. I miss Dad!" Tears began to stream down her cheeks. "I miss him so much! He was there for me. He had my back no matter what. Even when I made poor choices, which lord knows I have." She blew her nose. "Even when I didn't know what I was doing my father always respected and trusted me." She blew her nose again. "Now that he's gone it feels like . . . no one will ever love me that way again."

I met her gaze and nodded, aware of a heaviness in my chest. "Missing him is painful," I said.

She looked out the window, "It's *so* painful."

We sat in silence. When she finally looked at me again I could tell that another part had taken over.

"You know what really pisses me off?" she asked.

I raised my eyebrows.

"My husband doesn't get it. He loved Dad, too. And now he's all *What's done is done; your dad had a good run.* And I'm like *what the fuck?* My father did so much for Alan, among others, and he gets summed up with five words? It makes me want to smack him."

"Sounds like Alan's not there the way you want him to be right now," I said.

"He's not!" Then softening she went on, "I wish he were more like Dad. Dad's message was always *You're fine. I don't want to change you.* No questions asked. For me, I think that's gone now forever."

Liza put her head in her hands and sobbed, and I felt honored to hold space for her grieving parts. In this session Liza spoke first of having no energy, which is common in bereavement, and then wondered if she was depressed. Andrew Solomon (2002) wrote, "The opposite of depression is not happiness, but vitality," (p. 443). Since vitality is usually absent for a time during bereavement, Liza was not alone in wondering if she was feeling depressed. But since answering her question at that moment would have taken her out of grieving, I chose to mirror her feelings and stay open and present with the parts who showed up.

The Grief Cluster

As we see in Liza's sessions, after first responders we usually hear from the *grief cluster*, the sad parts who are protesting, missing, searching, longing, regretting and feeling guilty. These parts help us on the unavoidable journey after we lose what we need and love. Whether or not they are connected to earlier unresolved losses, grief cluster parts are generally held at a distance until protectors are convinced that the system can tolerate their distress without being overwhelmed. I therefore think of grief cluster parts as neo-exiles. Unlike exiles connected to childhood events whose stories are kept out of awareness until the Self is available, neo-exiles are only held in abeyance at first, so that their experiences can be heard, held and assimilated gradually. I will often share this information with clients as it both normalizes and informs the inner dance between affect-laden neo-exiles and protectors.

Normal Oscillations in Grieving

As I illustrate throughout the chapter, grieving individuals tend to oscillate between being blended (that is, fully identified) with the grief cluster as it seeks to integrate the meaning of the loss and the restoration cluster as it focuses ahead and urges action. This mixture of grieving and planning ensures periods of relief during a process that can be intensely painful (Stroebe & Schut, 2010). When the whole internal system has had as much processing time as it needs and all has gone well, the restoration cluster will begin to dominate and a new reality that accommodates the loss will be established.

Meanwhile, the meaning of the loss to different parts flows through the system slowly, like a wave. Parts can have intense feelings for weeks or months after a loss, as if just realizing what has happened. I call these *grief attacks*. If the person is blindsided by a grief attack, managers may set about distancing and firefighters distracting. Therefore, I make a point of predicting the possibility of grief attacks and we spend time reassuring protectors that these events are not a signal that something is wrong; rather they are an opportunity for the client's Self to bear witness to grieving parts.

COMPLICATED GRIEF: THE INTERFACE
OF BEREAVEMENT AND BURDENS

Chronic or delayed-onset grief affects roughly 15 percent of mourners (Kersting, 2004) and is more likely to occur under certain circumstances: if the individual has experienced significant loss early in life that remains unresolved and/or the lost relationship was a dependent one (Lobb et al., 2010); also if the person had an ambivalent relationship with the deceased (Freud, 1917). Relational factors like a lack of social support or the client's attachment style can complicate grief as well. Wayment and Vierthaler (2002) found that individuals with "an anxious-ambivalent attachment style reported greater levels of grief and depression" (p. 129).

I often notice the protective strategies that Wolfelt (1992) described with complicated grief, including downplaying the importance of a loss by *minimizing;* converting feelings into physical symptoms by *somatizing;* avoiding grieving by *replacing* with a new attachment; feeling anger or sadness in relation to other people and events by *displacing;* and trying to shelve the whole experience by *postponing.* Once we have identified a protective strategy in therapy, I ask the protector if the strategy is working and what it believes would happen if it let the client engage with the loss cluster, as I illustrate in the following case of Susan.

Over the years I've developed great admiration and respect for protectors and I firmly believe that grief, when uncomplicated, has its own timetable. In consequence, I do not believe that folkloric wisdom about how long grief ought to last is helpful. That said, when grief is complex, being curious about which protective parts may be contributing to its chronicity or delayed onset is essential.

Postponing Grief: Susan

When Susan was 19 years old she was the driver in a car accident that killed her older sister and her best friend, leaving the friend's baby an orphan. She came to see me 6 years later because she had a part who would not allow her to love her own young son, Tyrone, for fear of losing him. Susan found it easy to connect with her parts, and by the third session she was familiar with the IFS method.

"Like I told you, the problem is I'm worried that I don't love my son. He's all lovin' his momma with those Christmas and Valentine cards they get him to make at school and I'm all *Whatever!* I'm pretty sure that's not normal, is it?" she peered at me.

"It sounds like you have a part who's concerned. How about if we ask inside about what's going on?"

"Okay. Hmmm. Well, this part is showing me Tyrone and drawing a big red circle in the air and putting a line through it."

"Are you clear what it wants you to know?" I asked.

"I haven't the foggiest! Now it's doing a mime show and . . . now it has a little buddy translating. I swear to God I have the weirdest parts. It's saying I can't love Tyrone because he might die and then I'd be in that mess over there."

"That mess over there?"

"It's pointing to a pile of images from the accident. Did I tell you I collapsed in court? The judge thought I was crazy."

"Would it be okay to get to know the parts who are connected to that pile of images over there?"

Her eyes lost focus. "Oh no! No way! This uber-giant just popped up with his arms folded to say we're not going there. He says his job is to keep me sane and that will make me crazy."

Because parts like Susan's uber-protector are often aware of the client's history and level of Self-energy, they have a good instinct for the right timing to approach a significant loss, and my policy is to expect them to exert a lot of control in therapy and respect their wishes. But in this case Susan's uber-protector was polarized with the part who brought her to therapy— her parenting part—whose concerns were also very important. So I wanted to see what kind of negotiation might be possible.

"The uber-protector worries that thinking about the accident could make you crazy, right? And he doesn't want you to be close to Tyrone in case he dies. But the part who brought you to therapy wants you to be Tyrone's mother."

"Well, yes, I have a part who is worried about Tyrone needing a mother. But the uber-protector is not the one who wants me to stay away from Tyrone. That's a part who works with the uber-protector," Susan explained.

"How do they work together?"

"Well," Susan's eyes lost external focus again, "it's like if I open up to Tyrone and then something happens to him, he goes onto that huge pile over there. And if that happens they're showing me that the pile will wobble and fall and I'll be crushed. No more me."

"Does that make sense to you?"

"Uh-huh," she nodded, her eyes still glazed.

I was not surprised to hear that Susan's protectors had decided to cut off attachments as well as feelings. I assumed her uber-protector's job was to handle some strong, very scary feelings (exiled parts), and that her internal system had little room—after a frightening childhood and the deaths of her sister and best friend—for self-compassion. Although I knew that a client like Susan would have protectors whose goal was to postpone grief or avoid it entirely, I kept in mind that I was also working with parts who longed for connection and balance.

"So the uber-protector and this other one are holding you together, is that right?"

"Yes," Susan said.

"How's it going?" I asked.

"They say they can do it," she said.

"I can see how hard they're willing to work," I said. "But if you could be safe without them having to work so hard, would they be interested?"

"They say only they can be in charge," she reported.

Although I had to respect the uber-protector's wishes, I wondered if it would allow us to work with some of Susan's other vulnerable parts. My idea was to build Self-energy and revisit these more heavily burdened parts later. I wondered if the protectors would allow that or if we needed to spend more time working with them.

"Would it be okay with them if we worked with some of the other young ones you've talked about—from back when you were a kid? Like the ones who got bullied."

Susan listened internally for a moment and then said, "They're okay with that. But this one," she touched her left shoulder and jerked her head in the same direction, "wants to know if all this is gonna make me a better mama."

"That's where we're headed," I said.

"It says *Well, all right then! Let's go.*"

But before we started with grade school bullying, Susan's protectors agreed to let us create a loss history, starting by noting her youngest exiles. They also agreed to let us help her parenting part, who was a determined negotiator at the table, to take better care of her son. After several years in which we focused on creating a sense of inner spaciousness and self-compassion, Susan's uber-protector decided she could attend to the accident without going crazy.

As we see, Susan's trauma history made her protectors extremely vigilant about therapy, and I had to negotiate a fine balance between her urgent need to be available as a mother to her son and her protectors' need to keep her from being overwhelmed with pain, guilt and grief. This negotiation involved validating the concerns of both sides, always seeking their permission equally and, quite often, providing the Self-energy for our therapeutic circle because Susan's parts were so blended with her.

When Oscillations Are Absent: Fran

As therapists we can attend to and support the natural oscillations between the grief and restoration clusters. But when there are no oscillations we want to know why. For example, we may notice that a client is mired in the loss cluster or, conversely, is only looking ahead. If the latter, the person is stuck in the agenda of the restoration cluster and rarely seeks bereavement counseling or therapy until serious consequences build up.

After Fran's adult son, Mark, died of AIDS, Fran came to therapy because, in reaction to their loss, her husband was spending all his time building a garage. On those rare occasions when Peter spoke of his son's death, he would say, *One door closes and another opens; we have to get on with our lives.* Peter's relentless focus on restoration made Fran feel she had lost her partner as well as her son. Yet at the same time Fran was telling everyone that Mark had died of leukemia. As a result, she felt cut off from family, friends and her son as well as her husband. Along with her shame, this self-imposed isolation caused Fran's restoration cluster to step in vigorously, causing her to believe that she, too, should be moving on.

"I just don't know what's wrong with me, Derek. It's been over a year and I keep trying to get on with my life but I feel . . . I don't know, lonely I guess? And I can't stop thinking about Mark. I know I should be over this by now. Sometimes I have nightmares in which he's dying, and the life is literally being sucked out of him by a huge machine-like thing. And his eyes are staring at me, pleading. I wake up with the sweats."

Fran was wringing her hands and shifting uncomfortably in her seat. "The other day I was shopping and I saw some candy Mark liked when he was little, and I just lost it. I broke down and had to leave the store. I left my basket in the middle of the aisle. Now I can't go back there. I think maybe something is wrong with me. Do you?" she looked at me anxiously.

"You're grieving, Fran. And you're trying to deal with this all alone so some parts are eager to put it behind you. But some other parts are missing Mark and they want attention."

Fran nodded.

"I think it would be most helpful to get to know the parts who are trying to get your attention through dreams or what happened in the store. Would that be okay?"

"Ummm. I'm hearing that I shouldn't need to do that. I should be strong."

"Do the ones who want you to be strong have a specific concern?"

Fran listened and then said, "Their concern is that if we open up to all that pain I'm going to be humiliated again like when shopping. They're also talking about how ashamed I felt when people found out Mark was gay."

"I get what they're saying and I'm glad they spoke up. But I also have a concern. Would they be willing to hear it?"

Fran nodded.

"In my experience, not paying attention to a part makes it work harder and harder to be heard. Like the one who took you over when you were shopping or the one who interrupts your social time or disturbs your sleep. But I know from experience that after you spend time with a part who's upset, it will let you listen to other parts too. Let's invite your parts to choose who needs your attention first."

Fran listened inside for a moment and said, "The one who feels ashamed."

Disavowed Grief

Kauffman (2002) coined the term *disenfranchised grief* to refer to losses that are disavowed or not socially supported, and observed that such losses can intensify emotional reactions across the board. He suggested that "self-disenfranchisement" (which IFS therapists would understand as shaming protectors) is more likely with certain kinds of loss, including miscarriage, the death of a pet, and separation from a partner who has perpetrating parts. In Fran's case, her grief was being disavowed by parts who feared that she would be rejected by her stoic husband and shamed socially because of her son's sexual orientation and his illness. In the language of IFS, her protectors were trying to save her from being hurt and shamed while her distressed, grieving parts were getting louder in order to get her attention and were, at times, overwhelming her. In response, her restoration cluster was urging her to move on. As we continued with Fran's therapy, she gradually got more and more access to Self-energy and was able to help her fearful, socially conforming parts relax and to reassure her restoration cluster that grieving Mark's death would help her system stabilize so she really could move on.

Protectors Who Minimize: Gordon

Minimizing is an extremely common protective strategy—not just with loss but with problems as imperative as climate change or as banal as running out of orange juice, so naturally we would expect this protective strategy to be present with grief. Gordon had been seeing me for a while when his dog, Bailey, died. His experience of losing Bailey illustrates how a person with a history of early, unsupported loss can be flooded with grief in response to a current loss while at the same time feeling deeply ashamed of his grief.

"I couldn't believe it was happening," he said. "When she stopped eating I thought it was just because she was old. Then it went on and I realized she was saying goodbye. I felt really bad but reminded myself that she was just a dog." Gordon was sitting upright, tapping his leg rhythmically with his left hand. I wondered if he had a part who wanted to move away from thinking about Bailey's death.

"I hear you have a sad part along with a part who says she was *just a dog*. Would that one be willing to soften so you can hear from the sad part?"

"Okay. But really I feel kind of stupid talking about a dog so much."

"Maybe the part who feels stupid would be reassured to know that I don't judge you for loving your dog?"

After a silence, Gordon sat back and his fingers stopped tapping. In a quiet voice he said, "Oh, wow. This sad part is really, really sad. I feel it now."

Gordon's Struggle

A few weeks later, Gordon told me he had decided to go to a potluck. He had promised to bring his famous bean salad and while preparing it had found half a limp cucumber in his refrigerator.

"I weighed my options," he said. "Either cycle ten minutes to the store to buy a whole fresh cucumber as the recipe said or use what I had. I just couldn't be bothered to go—and that's not me. I felt apathetic."

"Do you think this apathy is about parts who are missing Bailey?" I asked.

"No, I don't think so." He sighed. "There's just no point in going over it—she's gone and that's that!"

"Sounds like the part who feels resigned about her death has a lot of energy," I said. "Where did it get the idea that you should forget someone who has died?"

After a pause Gordon said, "It says that's just the way it goes. Everything dies. If we think about it, we feel bad."

"We could help the part who's feeling bad."

"It doesn't think you can."

"Why?"

"Because too much has happened to him."

After negotiating with Gordon's vigilant protector for a while we got permission to help the part who was feeling bad. This turned out to be a 6-year-old boy. Gordon's family had emigrated to Canada when he was 6. As his parents prepared the new home, Gordon, who was English, was sent to stay with his mother's Irish parents whom he had never met. He found his grandparents to be harsh and mean like his mother and their culture alien. After a couple of weeks in their house, Gordon sat down at the kitchen table to write a letter to his best friend, Jane, who had been his emotional anchor and whom he missed terribly. Halfway through the letter his grandfather asked whom he was writing to and then how he planned to send the letter. Did he have Jane's address?

When Gordon said *no*, his grandfather laughed and called him *stupid*. His grandmother, who was standing at the sink, laughed too. Gordon began to cry and then sob. In a flash of rage his grandmother strode over and hit him on the head, declaring that she would *give the cry baby something real to cry about!* if he didn't stop.

This was the moment in Gordon's life when his resigned 6-year-old took over. Ever since, this part had been reminding Gordon that nobody wanted to hear about his feelings so he should just be quiet. After thanking the resigned part for all his work, Gordon got permission to hear from his sad part. And after listening to the sad part describe his desperate longing and loneliness, along with his fear and hatred of his grandparents, Gordon asked him what he needed.

"I want to turn into a robot and kill my grandparents," he said.

When Gordon was silent in response, I asked, "Okay with you?"

Gordon nodded and with his compassionate witnessing, the sad part turned into a huge metal man who pummeled the grandmother with one fist and the grandfather with the other. Then he grew larger and smashed their apartment building and finally destroyed their entire town. Satisfied, he turned into Superman and flew off to deliver the letter to Jane.

"Now," Gordon said, "he has a mission. He wants to fly around the world righting wrongs."

"What do you say?" I asked.

"I think it's a good idea. And the resigned part is very happy for him. He wants to give up his job and says I can help any other parts who feel bad, too."

"Who needs help next?" I asked.

"The parts who miss Bailey," he answered. "They're crying and saying they want Bailey back." He was quiet for a few moments. "You know, Bailey actually thought I was her puppy." Tears began to roll down his cheeks. "Even though Bailey was blind and crippled from arthritis before she died, if she sensed that I was crying she would struggle up onto her feet and come over to lick my face. This young part is telling me that he was the puppy and she was his mother—his real mother. No wonder I've been so sad." He chuckled, "Oh, that last comment was from my figuring-out part."

A week later Gordon reported how being able to listen with compassion to his grieving young parts had affected his relationship with his surviving dog. "Now I lie down with him in the morning and give him a cuddle. I know he'll die one day, so I'm more determined than ever to love him up while I can."

A few weeks later Gordon described walking in the park when a part, as he said, *hijacked* him with sadness. "I noticed this ball of sadness rising from my belly and I asked it, *Do you just need me to know how sad you are or would you like to express yourself directly?* The part said it wanted to cry real tears with me watching and I was fine with that."

Gordon's main protector had learned early in life that open grieving would bring pain and humiliation. So minimizing his attachments became this part's primary strategy for dealing with loss. When he finally allowed Gordon to access his sorrowful young exiles, he was able to process the real meaning of Bailey's death—losing the unconditional love of a mother—and feel his grief.

Suicide and Early Traumatic Loss: Jack

Jack was a transgendered man who had been my client for a few years. He had taken a break from therapy and then returned to see me after ending the relationship with his girlfriend. He and Rebecca had lived together as monogamous lovers until Rebecca began to seek out casual sexual encounters. This turn of events caused Jack great distress. Although he had transitioned many years earlier, he had a very young exile who felt castrated and other parts who felt inadequate in comparison to what he called *bio-men*. His experience shows how early traumatic loss can eventually convince protectors that suicide is the only option.

Jack appeared in my office at the appointed hour, sullen and slumped. "Hi," he said flatly.

"I hear you're having a rough time," I said.

"I guess." He shrugged. "I guess it's over between me and her."

"I'm sorry. I know how much you wanted this to work. How bad has it gotten for you?" I asked.

He sighed, "Normally I can keep my suicide parts at bay by talking about what it would be like to leave the cats and Rebecca and my family. But this time it doesn't seem to matter."

I sat quietly for a moment. Internally I noticed a part who was talking about loving Jack and not wanting him to die. I acknowledged the part and asked him to soften so that I could stay with Jack. "My guess is that your suicide part is connected to some parts who are in a tremendous amount of pain, is that right?"

Jack nodded.

"So your suicide part believes it can only end this pain by ending your life?"
More nods.

"Would it be willing to give you some space and feel you?"

Looking up, he said, "It's more than one part. They say, *We all want to die.* As far as they can see, nothing can help."

"I know they believe that. On the other hand, I wonder if you have some parts who don't want to die but do want to live without pain."

He shrugged. "They don't think so."

"I get that you have a lot of parts who believe there is no answer to your pain except dying. And I want them to know that we can heal the pain instead of you dying."

"They don't believe that," he said.

"They don't have to," I replied, "but how about giving you and me a chance. Would they agree to seeing what we can do?"

After a pause Jack nodded, "They like you so they agree."

"If you don't mind, just double-check for me on whether the parts who want to die are agreeing? Sometimes a manager steps in."

"No, it's them."

"Great. Please thank them from me."

After this, Jack's suicide protectors stepped down. In subsequent sessions it became clear that his relationship with Rebecca was validating for his parts who wanted to feel equal to bio-men. We had formerly worked with his dad parts and their regret about not being able to father a child, as well as many of the young boy parts who were distressed at being schooled in an all-girl environment. The breakup with Rebecca had triggered a part who felt less than bio-men, which became a trailhead to a deeper exile who was in great anguish regarding the feeling that he had lost his penis, which was so intense that protectors in Jack's system believed suicide was the only reasonable option.

My preferred approach with suicide parts is to negotiate for the time to do exile work, as I did with Jack. However, if suicide parts don't have sufficient trust in the client's Self, they may decide that suicide is the only option and hospitalizing the client becomes a life-saving necessity. Of course, if a suicide protector is determined, it can bide its time, say the right things and achieve its goal with or without hospitalization, but I have not had this experience. The most important element of working with suicide protectors is attending to our parts who over- or underreact to risk.

From an IFS perspective, contracting against suicide is ineffective at best and dangerous at worst. It's ineffective because the part who agrees is likely to be a compliant manager and not the suicide part. It's potentially dangerous because exiling the suicide part can increase its desperation and the risk that the client will be injured or killed. An active suicide part may be allied with some other protectors or claim to speak for the entire system, but whatever a suicide protector says, these parts don't want to die—they simply see no other way to handle the extreme distress of exiles (Richard Schwartz, personal communication, December 12, 2013). Their goal is to stop emotional pain. As I did with Jack in this example, I assess for suicide by asking, *How bad does it get?* In my experience, suicide parts soften when I treat them with respect and understanding, helping them to realize that the Self is around to care for the exile and making sure they feel connected to the Self.

COUNTERTRANSFERENCE: HELPING PARTS UNBLEND

Because attachment, loss and grief are universal experiences, our own loss experiences are inevitably awakened by grieving clients. We may have managers who consider the grieving of clients who are flooded with emotion every session to be excessive. Or our firefighters may start fantasizing about cheesecake or a drink as we listen to their stories. Empathic parts may get overwhelmed when imagining us in a similar situation. The key to IFS therapy is to know yourself. The key to IFS grief work is to know your losses and be able to feel your own grief. Acknowledging our inner life makes us far more able to respond to our client's needs appropriately.

Losing a Child: Alice

Some losses are terrifyingly random and sudden. The violent death of a child is particularly heartbreaking and often evokes a feeling of dread in adults who are parents. After Alice's 21-year-old daughter was killed by a hit-and-run drunk driver, she went to three therapists before coming to me. I asked her why she had not stayed with the others.

Her tone flat and despondent, she replied, "I just didn't like them."

"Can I ask what it was you didn't like about them?"

Alice shrugged, "I guess they were okay. I just didn't feel like they could help me."

I wondered what had prevented Alice from feeling connected to these other therapists. She clearly wanted help with her pain and I wanted to help her, but I had a part who was concerned about being dismissed as unhelpful, too. Reassuring my concerned part that we could learn more, I asked, "What was unhelpful?"

Alice raised her head to look at me. "One said that she thought the pain must be unimaginable." Although her tone was still flat, I could see the anger in her eyes. "The other told me it was every mother's worst nightmare and started crying."

I sensed that my response would determine if she could consider me a potential support or not. Inside I heard parts agreeing with the other therapists. One started to imagine losing my 6-year-old daughter and tears were going to come. I acknowledged this part and asked it to step back. Staying curious was essential to establishing rapport with Alice.

I said, "When they said that, what did you feel?"

Angry tears sprang to her eyes, "I know what a nightmare this is. I'm living it! I don't need someone who has no idea what it's like to sit there and cry. It's not my job to take care of the therapist—I'm here for help!"

I indicated the tissue box and said, "Sounds like you feel isolated in this experience and these therapists made it worse."

Alice, blowing her nose and nodding, added, "I hear the same thing from friends and coworkers. And then they feel completely awkward, and I know they wish I'd just go away so they wouldn't have to deal with me."

After several sessions, Alice was still speaking from a blended part, "Nothing helps. I come here week after week and it doesn't help. My daughter is gone!"

"This part sounds hopeless," I said.

Alice shouted angrily, "I'm sick of hearing you say the word *part.* She's gone. Don't you get it? Gone!" Then she slumped as another part took over. "Of course you don't get it. How could anyone? Why would anyone want to? God, I'm so alone!"

I nodded.

Alice cried softly and then wiped her eyes. "Sometimes I think I should just move. Get out of the apartment with all those memories. But I don't have the energy. I feel trapped."

Using direct access, I met her gaze and said, "This is so, so hard." I've noticed when I shift to using direct access with the client's blended parts that a number of my parts want to take over, particularly my helpful parts who are not my Self so I need to be internally vigilant.

Alice nodded numbly.

Staying Self-Led

A curious, Self-led approach includes open-ended questions that invite the client to share her experience. For example, when Alice described the bleakness of being home alone without her daughter, I asked, *What brings you comfort?* And she replied that sleeping with her daughter's clothes on the pillow helped. If, in contrast, my advice-giver had sprung to life (perhaps offering a suggestion, *How about if you lit a candle by your bed for her each night?*), I wouldn't have been available or curious. His temptation, however, is great. Faced with an anguished client who feels she cannot make decisions, my advice-giver longs to mobilize with helpful suggestions. I remind him that taking over is siding with the client's helpless part against the client's Self and her capable parts, which will just reinforce her despair. He reluctantly steps back, saying, *But this is so hard.* Yes, it is. I offer him compassion, which helps him tolerate feeling helpless. As Wolfelt (2006) wrote, "It is out of your helplessness that you ultimately become helpful . . . 'compassionate curiosity' is what you really need" (p. 86).

I'm also alert to my agreeing part, who gets seduced by the beliefs of *self-evident truth* parts in the client—at least if he agrees with them. These truths are many and varied: *I guess I just need to resign myself to feeling this way,* or *I don't think anybody really wants to know what's going on inside me.* When I catch myself nodding or giving that therapeutic grunt of assent, I know my agreeing part has taken the lead. He blocks me from feeling curious and helping my client to feel curious about the parts who generalize their feeling of impotence.

Over months of work I witnessed Alice struggle with meaninglessness: *I live in a world nobody understands. I don't get how they can care about such ridiculous shit!* and alienation: *I need to leave the conversation whenever people talk about their kids—I know they stare at me. I can't help it!* Her world felt very small to her: *When I'm at work I'm going through the motions; when I'm at home I sit and rock until I'm sleepy or wander around like a zombie.* Each week seemed to bring a fresh aspect of her missing of her daughter: *I still can't cook. We used to cook. We'd put on music and dance around the kitchen chopping and laughing. I mean, I do cook. But I'll never, ever cook like that without her.*

I noticed that I had parts who would prepare for our session. Some were heartbroken at her despair. Some wondered what we would do if Maya (my daughter) died. How would we go on? Some felt we weren't helping her. Some wished she would *get over it.* Others were distressed about not being able to *fix it* for her—they were allergic to feeling helpless in the face of suffering.

I know these parts well. As I acknowledged them, they settled into a big stone semicircle behind me. I also attended to my feelings in my personal therapy. When my intellectual protectors wanted to talk loftily about the existential condition, my therapist would help me catch them. I was reminded by my work with Alice that my grieving clients give me the gift of noticing my own trailheads. In sessions with her, I focused and refocused on her, whose suffering I could not fix, whose unrelenting misery my parts had to endure.

Cultural and Spiritual Beliefs: Go With the Flow

Therapist parts can be challenged when clients share experiences that are outside of our cultural or personal framework, including beliefs about afterlife. The imperative in grief work is to acknowledge and welcome a variety of cultural and spiritual beliefs about death. For example, mourners who feel their experience is being pathologized in therapy will avoid sharing information about the continuing relationship they have with the person who has died. A simple question, *Are you still talking to him? Is she showing up for you in some way?* invites this information. In general, I normalize and welcome discussion about any and all aspects of a person's grief.

CONCLUSION

Grieving typically starts with the shock, disbelief and numbness of first responders. As they give way, the storyteller often steps in, followed by the cluster of parts who are actively grieving as well as some parts who blank out and distract to ensure respite from grieving. Finally, our need for balance after profound disruption is so great that we have another set of parts, the restoration cluster, whose job is to restore equilibrium. Once they get to work, we oscillate between their efforts to welcome new connections and the grieving we need in order to realize the depth of our loss.

The job of the IFS therapist is to be a compassionate companion, a witness to the client's experience and sometimes a guide. The role of guide is most relevant when the current circumstance is extreme (as with suicide, homicide and the death of a child) or complicated by unresolved prior loss. Although simple grieving is a matter of keeping company with the client, when grieving is complicated I apply the usual principles of IFS therapy. I spend a lot of time validating, reassuring and inviting protectors to ally with the Self. I am always on the lookout for suicide parts, who are common with complicated grief. I keep a particular eye out for physical distress because warded-off feelings are often communicated somatically. And my goal is to unburden exiles.

Whether the client's process is simple or complicated, I try always to be aware of my parts. Unlike addiction or childhood trauma, which may or may not be part of the therapist's story, we all have a history of loss. I work to stay in connection with my experience as it manifests in my parts. I notice my therapist parts when they feel they should be *doing more*, and I notice parts who get swamped with empathic distress. The gifts of countertransference are many: One is the opportunity to help our parts unblend and differentiate their empathic distress from Self-energy; another is the opportunity to follow our parts' feelings as trailheads for our own healing. Our capacity to both embrace and facilitate Self-led grief "bolsters a lifelong practice of learning to trust Self-leadership" (Schwartz, 2013, p. 22) and affords us the opportunity to welcome new connections fully—aware of the possibility that we may lose them and secure in our knowledge that the Self will attend to our grieving parts.

REFERENCES

Freud, S. (1916–1917 [1915]). Mourning and melancholia. *SE, 14,* 237–258.
Kauffman, J. (2002). The psychology of disenfranchised grief: Liberation, shame, and self-disenfranchisement. In K. Doka (Ed.), *Disenfranchised grief: New directions, challenges and strategies for practice* (pp. 61–77). Champaign, IL: Research Press.
Kersting, K. (2004). A new approach to complicated grief. *APA: Monitor on Psychology, 35*(10), 51. Retrieved from http://apa.org/monitor/nov04/grief.aspx
Lobb, E. A., Kristjanson, L. J., Aoun, S. M., Monterosso, L., Halkett, G. K. B., & Davies, A. (2010). Predictors of complicated grief: A systematic review of empirical studies. *Death Studies, 34*(8), 673–698.
Schwartz, R. C. (2013). The therapist-client relationship and the transformative power of self. In M. Sweezy & E. L. Ziskind (Eds.), *Internal family systems therapy: New dimensions* (pp. 1–23). New York: Routledge.
Solomon, A. (2002). *The noonday demon: An atlas of depression.* New York: Touchstone.

Stroebe, M., & Schut, H. (2010). The dual process model of coping with bereave-
    ment: A decade on. *Omega, 61*(4), 273–289.
Wayment, H. A., & Vierthaler, J. (2002). Attachment style and bereavement reac-
    tions. *Journal of Loss and Trauma: International Perspectives on Stress and Coping, 7*(2),
    129–149. Retrieved from http://dx.doi.org/10.1080/153250202753472291
Wolfelt, A. D. (1992). *Understanding grief: Helping yourself heal.* Bristol, PA: Accelerated
    Development.
Wolfelt, A. D. (2006). *Companioning the bereaved.* Fort Collins, CO: Companion Press.

Chapter 6

Perpetrator Parts

Richard C. Schwartz

Recently a friend expressed outrage at the increasing number of terrorist bombings in the world. He couldn't understand the mentality of someone who kills innocent children. I asked him to remember what he was like in the sixties. He agreed that, like me, he had had murderous impulses toward government figures, impulses that are still aroused at times. While neither of us ever came close to unleashing those parts, we both knew people closer to the brink, people with whom we strongly sympathized. He said that was different—we were right and the government was murdering innocents. I said that sounded familiar.

While perpetrator parts may become stuck in their roles, they did not start off as perpetrators and they don't really like having to do their jobs. They should be differentiated from ordinary angry firefighters and highly critical managers. The last two can be damaging, but they act without the perpetrator's drive for power or disdain for vulnerability. I define perpetrator parts as a class of protector characterized by particular qualities: (1) the drive to dominate and/or humiliate others; (2) relief when they are able to take over and/or enjoyment in the sense of power; (3) an intense hatred of vulnerability and a desire to punish it inside the client's system and in others; and (4) a lack of concern for the consequences of their actions or the feelings of their victims. Of course these distinctions are not always clear-cut. For example, there are many non-perpetrator protectors who manifest some disdain for weakness or some lack of empathy, and there are perpetrator parts who get no pleasure from dominating but view it as a job instead.

We all have parts who will do whatever is needed to keep us alive. I have experienced having a part like this only once. When I was suddenly attacked in a bar during college, I immediately transformed into a fierce and fearless warrior, protecting myself with cold-blooded efficiency. Up until then, I had no idea I had such a part, but since then I have been alternately disturbed, intrigued and comforted by its existence.

Over the past three decades I've treated many sex offenders, conduct-disordered teens and adults who were sexually abused as children. Virtually all were traumatized, neglected, humiliated and/or betrayed when they were younger. That is, they had been victims of the perpetrator parts of caretakers, neighbors, peers or strangers. In turn, I encountered perpetrator parts in most of them who embodied the energy of the injuring person. Individuals who had highly blended perpetrator parts running their lives would today receive the *DSM-5* diagnosis antisocial personality disorder, whether or not they met the criteria for sociopathy or psychopathy. So for descriptive (rather than diagnostic) purposes in this chapter, I will refer to these protectors as *antisocial.* Although some of these individuals were functioning well in society at the time, in therapy with me they described being preoccupied with memories of former—or with planning for future—victimizing. They had the ability to objectify victims and justify all manner of abusive acts.

Another kind of client knew he was capable of violence, which was a source of constant shame and fear. These individuals spent their lives avoiding situations that might precipitate violence and shamed themselves for any violence that had occurred. They were dominated by a polarity between fearful, self-punishing or highly critical managers and a perpetrator part. Consequently, they had been given diagnoses like anxiety disorder, obsessive-compulsive disorder or depression.

Still others were unaware of a perpetrator part locked away deep inside. They often presented with fearful or critical managers who were struggling to keep their exiles (stuck in abuse scenes) at bay, and they remained oblivious to the perpetrator part until we were well into the therapy. These people had diagnoses like post-traumatic stress disorder, depression or anxiety disorder. They were invariably shocked and mortified to find a manifestation of their abuser's energy inside them.

In general, internal family systems (IFS) views diagnostic categories as descriptions of how inner systems organize for protection. Most clients with severe diagnoses, from antisocial personality to eating disorders to depression, have raw exiles whom their protectors struggle to contain. In the process, the protectors polarize, with one set wanting to shut the person down and withdraw from the world while the other set has the urge to act out in some way. The diagnosis depends on which set dominates.

Based on experience, I expect most clients who have been abused and betrayed by people with perpetrator parts to have a part in a similar role. They will also have parts who hate or are terrified of the inner perpetrator and struggle to keep it contained. All of these parts, the perpetrator and its opponents, are trying to handle exiles who remain frozen in circumstances of abuse.

ANTISOCIAL PROTECTORS

During the course of helping clients dialogue with parts like this, I realized that none of the parts were evil. In every case, the perpetrator part felt forced into the role of heartless victimizer by events earlier in life when the person had been attacked and powerless. The abuse left the part with a strong urge to dominate in order to be safe. Vowing *never again*, it developed a selfish, survivalist mentality and sought to control the environment. As a result, the part would do whatever it took to survive, without regard for consequences. I also discovered that antisocial parts express disdain and contempt for weak, *sissy* parts who are frightened, humiliated and in pain, but that's exactly whom they protect, inside as well as out. To do this job, they must also do continual battle with the critics who seek to control them and the sensitive parts who worry about hurting others.

A TEENAGE RAPIST WITH A PERPETRATOR PART
WHO WAS NOT ALWAYS BLENDED: TROY

Troy was 17 years old when I interviewed him in a treatment center for juvenile sex offenders where I consulted for 7 years. Polite, mild mannered and boyish, Troy could not have looked further from the stereotype of a rapist. I asked him what he was saying to himself before the rape for which he had been incarcerated.

"That I deserve to take what I want. That I should just take it," he replied.

I asked him to focus on that so we could get to know that part better. But he didn't want to because he was afraid. After I reassured him that we could handle the part, he looked inside and saw a sinister, muscular man. Troy's fear was clear. He said again that he hated and feared this part. I told Troy to use his mind's eye to put the sinister man in a contained room. As he did so he reported that the man looked very angry about being put in the room.

So I said, "Here's a useful law of inner physics: your fear gives him power over you. When you're not afraid, that power is gone. I've worked with parts like him for over 30 years. I know how to handle them. I'm not afraid. We can put your scared parts in a safe place and I can help you talk to him." My demeanor was calm and confident, which helped his frightened parts feel they could retreat. He took them to a garden and told them to wait. Now Troy was not afraid. He wanted to know why the sinister muscle man had been urging him to do violent things to women. "Go in the room and ask,"

I said. The muscle man replied that people had deprived Troy, so he should be able to take whatever he wanted.

"Why would you want to rape a strange woman?" Troy asked him. After listening, he reported to me, "Scaring people thrills him."

"Ask him why it's thrilling to commit rape," I said.

"He says he likes the power to make others do whatever he wants," Troy said. "He also likes having power over me."

"Ask the man what he's afraid would happen if he didn't make you feel powerful and if he couldn't get things for you," I said.

"He says he isn't afraid of anything—he just likes power."

So I had Troy rephrase the question, "If he was not doing this, what might happen inside you?"

"He says I'd be a sniveling baby," Troy reported.

"Ask him what would happen then."

"He says people would have power over me."

"And what would happen then?" I said.

"He says people would hurt me."

I said, "Ask him if he's trying to protect you from getting hurt?'"

"He isn't answering," Troy said, "but he looks sad."

Troy's inner rapist ultimately revealed that he protected exiled parts of Troy who had a variety of intense, emotion-laden memories. For example, when Troy was 7, his father was hitting his mother in front of him and he felt powerless to help. Whenever those exiles felt weak or sad, the man attacked them inside and tried to make Troy feel strong or sexual to counter and distract from their feelings. The man also battled with parts who wanted Troy to *be a nice boy* (as I could see from his appearance). The man hated those parts and, in turn, they feared and hated him. Both sides wished they could eliminate the other and feared the consequences to Troy if they failed.

Troy's system was similar to those of many sex offenders and other criminals with whom I have used IFS over the years. Some offenders, unlike Troy, rely on and like their perpetrator part. But once a client becomes Self-led enough to listen to a perpetrator part, the story we hear is remarkably consistent: These parts view themselves as protectors. In later sessions, Troy's perpetrator part revealed that when his violent father was hitting him, the perpetrator part *took the bullet*. That is, he stepped forward and took the punishment to shield Troy's other parts. As a result, he not only felt furious—he also felt helpless and was determined never to let it happen again.

When Troy was being attacked, the perpetrator part saw his father's power. Desperate to have his own power, the part copied the father's behavior and energy—especially his desire to dominate and punish vulnerability. In IFS we call this a *legacy burden,* or a belief or behavior that a part absorbs from a parent or other influential person, who has in turn absorbed it from others in a similar way. Legacy burdens are potent drivers of thought and behavior. Although there are many different kinds of legacy burdens, in my experience the legacy burdens of perpetrator parts come directly from experiences with perpetrators and relate to being powerful. Like the Stockholm syndrome, a part takes on qualities of a torturer when it is terrified and powerless. Although Troy's perpetrator part, this muscle man, would only take him over sometimes, a perpetrator part can be thoroughly blended all the time, in which case the individual is likely to meet criteria for a *DSM-5* diagnosis of antisocial personality disorder. When a perpetrator part stays blended all the time in this way and the client has no access to other parts, we consider it a manager rather than a firefighter.

As we discovered, Troy's muscle man was not particularly interested in sex—he wanted to dominate, feel powerful and scare others. When Troy was in high school, the muscle man took over at times to bully nerdy kids, which got Troy in trouble. In response Troy's managers tried harder to control the muscle man. So the muscle man discovered he could team up with a different firefighter, Troy's sexual part, which was much harder for Troy to resist. The rapes were the collaborative effort of this unholy inner alliance.

As we heard over time, Troy's muscle man, who was polarized with his good boy part, had many reasons to take on the role of perpetrator. First, he was motivated to protect Troy in childhood during a time of dreadful family scenes. Second, he was burdened with rage, the *never again* survivalist mind-set, the desire to dominate and hatred of vulnerability. And the third reason, one I find in most perpetrators, even those labeled antisocial, is that a shaming critic is constantly attacking the perpetrator part internally. Troy's critic used his fear of God's wrath (Troy had been raised in a fundamentalist Christian family) to try to contain the perpetrator part. In order to heal offenders, we must focus as much energy on calming the shaming critic as on transforming the perpetrator part.

Although some authors now challenge the dogma that antisocial individuals lack conscience (Wong, 2000; Loving, 2002; Salekin, 2002; D'Silva, Duggan, & McCarthy, 2004; Stalans, 2004), experts have tended to believe they can't be treated. In my experience, this reputation is earned—and the client is very likely to accept it—when a part who does not have any concern for others dominates the internal system. Nevertheless, I have worked long enough with several clients who were diagnosed antisocial to convince their perpetrator parts to step back. When they did we heard from the client's critical parts, whose savagery encouraged a suicide part, which caused the perpetrator part to insist that it needed to maintain a firm grip.

In addition to critics and suicide parts, we find child parts who are stuck in dreadful scenes of powerlessness, terror, humiliation and grief. I have been tremendously moved as these clients retrieved and healed their exiles. The contrast between their hard exteriors and the gentle love their Self offers their inner children often brings tears to my eyes. This has been some of the most rewarding work of my career, and I believe the reputation of intractability can be highly exaggerated for at least some perpetrators.

The same kind of shame dynamic maintains the behavior of most non-antisocial perpetrators. When exiles feel lonely or afraid, the perpetrating part activates urges, the critic responds by attacking, and the exiles once again feel shamed. Now not only does the perpetrator have to distract from the loneliness and fear of exiles, it also has to suppress their shame. So the perpetrator escalates the urges until the person perpetrates, which brings temporary relief but is followed by an even more scathing attack from the critic, which is followed, of course, by the client's exiles feeling shamed once again. This cycle is vicious and self-perpetuating.

Once caught, the perpetrating person generally becomes an object of outrage and contempt, giving the critic more ammunition. Incarceration is torturous because the perpetrating part can no longer distract from critics and the shame they stir up in exiles. Unless protectors find another way to enforce numbness, the person is likely to be overwhelmed with pain, shame and loneliness, which makes the option of suicide powerfully tempting.

Treatment for people who have perpetrated is often modeled on the relapse prevention strategies developed by addiction programs in the 1980s. In these programs, therapists took an aggressive, shaming stance to encourage accountability. They required participants to detail their offenses, confronted them with the harm they had done and, finally, had them list all stimuli to reoffending (people, places, thoughts and emotions) while planning how to avoid them. That is, efforts were all toward shoring up the critic's ability to contain firefighters.

Since shaming evokes shame rather than guilt, it makes perpetrating parts desperate to act once the client is released from treatment. As a result, when it was assessed a decade later, the shamed straight approach was found to be no more effective at reducing recidivism than no treatment (see Marshall, Marshall, Serran, & O'Brian, 2011, for a good summary of this research). Some who specialize in treating offenders have noticed its inefficiency. Marshall and colleagues (Marshall et al., 2011) in Canada offer warmth while focusing on the offender's strengths instead of shaming. They teach self-regulation and social skills while addressing distorted beliefs, sexual preoccupation or social isolation. Their research indicates that this approach is more effective. For offenders from patriarchal or religious backgrounds whose behavior is primarily driven by isolation, loneliness or distorted thinking, the therapist's support and positive regard represent an important paradigm shift.

However, in my view, both of these approaches are inadequate when it comes to addressing the trauma that drives many perpetrators. Where perpetrator parts are involved (i.e., where offending is driven by the impulse to dominate and hurt others), I strongly advise a focus on healing the emotional pain and shame that derive from earlier abuse. To generalize beyond sex offenders to perpetrators in general, my point is that the more we isolate, shame and treat perpetrators inhumanely, the more likely they are to perpetrate. This vicious cycle helps our prisons overflow. At the same time, I do think perpetrating criminals should be incarcerated. They need to be contained both to protect the public and to break the dominance of the kinds of parts I'm describing. I would like to see our jails become an opportunity for inmates to calm shaming critics, depolarize protective parts, heal exiles and finally unburden their perpetrator parts.

When I consulted at two offender treatment centers, I saw Troy and many other offenders achieve this kind of healing. As my reputation grew, young men lined up outside my door at the treatment center. Everyone else said, *Once a sex offender, always a sex offender.* The offenders were being told they would always have to be vigilant (that is, self-shaming) about their impulses, which seemed impossible to them, and they were desperate for an alternative. My attempts to raise money for an outcome study with this population were unsuccessful, so I cannot say definitively that our work kept them from perpetrating again after release. But I can say that they reported being more responsible for their actions, and they left the center with more Self-leadership. In addition, they felt intensely connected to me, to the staff, and to their fellow detainees (much of the work was done in groups). Before doing IFS-informed group work, many of these inmates had pleaded with staff not let them out of the center, fearing they had no self-control. But after identifying inner perpetrators and releasing them from their extreme roles, these young men reported great reductions in urges to perpetrate (and in some cases the urges were gone), and now they knew what to do if they started to feel an urge. Their self-concept was revised: They did not view themselves as sex offenders but as trauma survivors with parts who tried to protect them in terribly destructive ways.

When I present these ideas, some version of the following question is invariably asked, "By telling offenders that a part is responsible, or that they are survivors not perpetrators, aren't you making them less accountable? Now they can just say, *I didn't do it! That was a part I couldn't control. And besides I was a victim so I was just doing what was done to me.*" My answer is that people can, of course, abuse the message. But my experience is the opposite. Offenders come to IFS therapy highly polarized and unable to exert self-control, and they leave with the inner leadership and compassion (for themselves and others) required to make amends and behave differently. In short, they become accountable.

Many onlookers also feel, sometimes unconsciously, that in having compassion for offenders you fail to recognize the impact of their heinous crimes and you betray their victims. Since I work with many survivors of various forms of abuse I know this feeling well. When I help someone to leave a horrific scene in the past, my parts who feel connected to the victim would like to hurt the abuser. In those moments I could never imagine trying to help such horrible people. But later I remind my parts of the work I've done with offenders and how the offenders are survivors too, and that healing rather than attacking them will save future victims. I keep in mind the story of two men who are sitting by a river when drowning children begin floating by. One rushes into the water to pull the kids out one by one. He looks back to see his comrade jogging upstream.

The man in the water screams, "I can't believe you're so heartless that you would abandon these suffering children!"

The other man replies, "I'm gonna go find the guy who's throwing them in the river."

Troy left the center feeling compassion rather than contempt for himself and his victims. He also reported that he felt (and the staff corroborated that he showed) genuine compassion for other inmates. Whereas his good boy part had previously caused him to do things for the tougher young men in the center, he was now comforting the frailer ones when they felt sad. This corresponds to another law of inner physics: We will feel and relate toward other people in the same way that we feel and relate toward our parts who resemble those people.

The perpetrating parts of many offenders will inflict the same kind of torture or punishment on exiles in the inner world that they experienced as children. There are several reasons for this disturbing phenomenon. First, they have the urge to perpetrate, and if they can't take over externally they will act out internally. Second, when they keep exiles in a state of terror they have more power in the inner world because terror weakens resistance. Third, as many governments know, keeping a person in a perpetual state of fear makes her more dependent. Fourth, like a bad cop parent, perpetrating parts believe that vulnerable parts need to toughen up so they won't be so vulnerable to getting hurt again. Fifth, they blame and want to punish exiles for being vulnerable and needy, which, in their view, got the system hurt in the first place. We see this with Troy, whose muscle man punished his exiles for weakness and also bullied other boys who seemed vulnerable. But once he could love and comfort his exiles, he began to empathize with and comfort those who were suffering around him. At the same time, Troy spontaneously wrote letters of apology to his victims. In short, this work changed him. The staff at the residential treatment center said it was as if Troy's edge was gone, making him softer and more accessible.

I have often seen changes like this as people find and release the pain, protection and polarization produced by their experience. I have also often seen similar changes in families who are dealing with extreme polarizations and are revealing their pain and fear to one another. Their collective edge fades and they can show Self-energy to one another. In a state of

Self-leadership, they can see beyond the limited, survivalist perspective of individual self-interest; recognize the consequences of their actions on the others; and create a common, harmonizing vision for the family.

CRACKED FORTRESSES

While I have a lot of experience working with the perpetrator parts of offenders, these were mostly people who had been caught and imprisoned, which had shattered their worlds. The secret, protective fortresses that their perpetrator parts created to shield them from shame and other scary emotions had been cracked open. Without these cracks, therapeutic work would have been futile in some cases and would have taken much longer in others. This is because when perpetrator parts argue that their behavior is absolutely necessary for our well-being, they are very convincing internally. These committed parts create ethical blind spots that encourage us to minimize or deny the damage they do to others.

This is not just true of perpetrator parts who commit sexual or violent offenses. It also applies to the domineering husband, the racist colleague, the oppressive boss and the critical or abusive parent—the kind of perpetrator parts most therapists find in their offices every day. Like offenders, these clients mostly don't come to therapy voluntarily. Instead, wives, companies or protective services take a stand and require them to have treatment. How do their fortresses crack?

CHALLENGING WITH AN EMPTY BOAT

Being forced into therapy is sometimes enough to crack the fortress. Usually mandated clients arrive feeling put-upon, misunderstood and afraid of being shamed. In therapy we want to create enough safety for their protectors to relax and allow the client's Self to connect with the therapist. If the therapist can remain Self-led when the client minimizes the impact of his actions and blames his problems on others, the client's protectors will sense acceptance and support. In turn, they will begin to trust the therapist. And here is our opportunity to challenge a perpetrating part, a shift in stance that is uncomfortable for many therapists. At the outset of therapy, protectors can easily deflect feedback by convincing the client that the therapist doesn't care. But when it's clear that the therapist does care, a challenge is likely to have impact.

The art of challenging a client involves helping his perpetrating part to separate and recognize the harm it has done while keeping your heart open to the client so he doesn't feel judged. Self-led confrontation is not an oxymoron. The therapist has to draw on qualities of courage, clarity and confidence without losing compassion. Some therapists have parts who are attracted to the gentleness of the IFS approach, but if we fear confrontation we will seem wishy-washy, undermining our impact. On the other hand, forceful, edgy manager parts in the therapist will shame the client, which gives ammunition to the client's internal critics, inflames exiles and reinforces the commitment of perpetrator parts to their roles.

When a member of the Navajo tribe commits a crime, rather than viewing that person as bad, the tribe explains the person as confused, lost and needing love to get back on the path. The community comes together to show the person support. That is, they help their people separate from their perpetrator parts kindly. When we challenge a perpetrator part, we do so to stop the perpetrating activity and access compassion for any victims, not to judge or punish. Thomas Merton (1965) translated a relevant Taoist story:

> If a man is crossing a river and an empty boat collides with his skiff, even though he be a bad-tempered man he will not become very angry. But if he sees a man in the boat, he will shout at him to steer clear. If the shout is not heard, he will shout again, and yet again, and begin cursing. And all because there is somebody in the boat. Yet if the boat were empty, he would not be shouting, and not angry. If you can empty your boat crossing the river of the world, no one will oppose you, no one will seek to harm you. . . . Such is the perfect man: His boat is empty.
>
> (p. 114)

In the same spirit, if you empty your boat of judgment, anger, and fear while keeping it full of compassion, confidence, calm, courage and clarity, you can collide with all kinds of offenders without provoking them to defend or retrench. You can pierce the perpetrator part's denial and offer it a new role.

This, however, is not enough. Beyond seeing a perpetrator part's impact and helping it to separate we must help the client's inner system have less need of its services. That is, the client must heal the exiles who drive protective impulses in the internal system. Too many therapies stop after confrontation and never get to the underlying trauma. I have worked with many clients who knew very well how harmful their perpetrator parts could be, and their perpetrator parts could even separate and sit back, yet if the client felt terrified and worthless, the perpetrator part jumped right back in, strong as ever.

GLASS HOUSES

Working with perpetrator parts in clients is not for those who want to remain self-righteous. While doing this work I was forced to acknowledge my entitled, selfish and denying parts. While never inflicting the kind of pain some of my clients reported, my parts had damaged relationships and hurt people close to me. As the 17th-century Christian mystic Francois Fenelon (1877, p. 27) observed,

> As light increases, we see ourselves to be worse than we thought. We are amazed at our former blindness as we see issuing forth from the depths of our heart a whole swarm of shameful feelings, like filthy reptiles from a hidden cave. We never could have believed that we had harbored such things, and we stand aghast as we watch them gradually appear.

Yet we will be much less afraid to shine that light if we know in advance that these parts are not filthy reptiles—they are good parts stuck in bad roles. If we trust that spotlighting these denizens of our deep and releasing their burdens will transform them into valuable inner citizens, we will not need to recoil from emotional pain, attack inner weakness or run from the perpetrator within. Instead we can welcome their unburdened resources. And at that point, we will be prepared to help the perpetrators of the world.

While some perpetrating behaviors are worse than others, their behavior has a common theme of being self-centered and lacking empathy. I have followed the trail of these parts in me to find and heal the exiles they protected and to help my self-critical managers turn their futile shaming into a conviction not to hurt people again. We all live in glass houses. It's always more comfortable to look out and judge the perpetrator parts of others than to look in at our own. Despite all the work I've done on myself, I know I have more parts like this to find.

SCOTT AND JOEY: A FATHER'S PERPETRATING PART WHO WOULD NOT MEET CRITERIA FOR ANTISOCIAL PERSONALITY DISORDER, BUT IS SKATING ON THIN ICE

After three family sessions, I recognized that I was sitting with what seemed like a typical family triangle involving an overprotective mom, a 10-year-old son who was allied with mom and had been bullying kids at school and an overly tough dad. If I could help each parent speak for the protective parts who drove their behavior, I was confident the parents could negotiate a more united front, which would release their son from his position in the triangle and calm him down. So I asked Scott what happened inside when he saw his wife *spoiling* his son. He described an internal battle between a part who wanted to punish both of them and other parts who told him to let it go.

"How often does that first part win?" I asked.

"Sometimes," Scott replied.

"And what happens then?" I asked.

"I find a reason to spank my son."

Jane burst out, "You call that spanking! You're shaking with rage and screaming at him! I can't stand to see Joey hurt like that."

"You're exaggerating," Scott said. "He has to grow up sometime and you're not letting him."

"It sounds like your punishing part can get carried away sometimes," I observed.

"Well," Scott replied, "I just can't stand how much she babies him."

I said, "I get that—and I can help Jane with her parts who might do that—but right now I want to stay with your punishing part. What's it like for you when this part takes over?"

"I don't know. I feel better. Like I'm not standing around being a coward and letting this happen."

We had to end the session shortly after this exchange, so I asked to meet with each of the parents individually the next week. I wanted to help Scott separate from the part who was abusing his son, which I knew would be harder in Jane's presence. And I wanted to hear more from Jane about the extent of Scott's violence without Scott being present because honesty is often difficult—and can be risky—for someone in her position.

In her session, Jane reported that Scott's explosions were frequent and not limited to her son. Scott had never hurt her physically, but he had often been threatening. In addition, he regularly berated and mocked her about her parenting, and he was on the brink of losing his job because he was abusive with subordinates.

She said, "It's like he suddenly turns into a completely different person when he gets angry—like Doctor Jekyll and Mr. Hyde."

In the beginning of my session with Scott, he talked about Jane's relationship with Joey, calling it unhealthy. I assured him that I would help Jane with her parts but right now I wanted to know more about his inner punisher. Again, Scott tried to minimize its impact, saying that his father spanked him and he turned out all right.

"I get that you feel this punishing part is necessary to counter the way Jane indulges Joey," I said. "But I need you to hear that it's doing a lot of damage in your family. It's only one part of you. I can tell you're a great dad and husband in many ways. You can get to know this part. You can help it let go of this rage and transform. I can show you how to do that if you're interested."

This challenging statement, spoken with the compassion, calm and confidence of my Self, contains several elements that are different from other types of confrontation. First, rather than saying that Scott is abusive, I say that he has a part who can be hurtful, but he is otherwise a good guy. I am also speaking to the part itself, suggesting that it's not bad either and that we're not trying to get rid of it—rather, it feels a lot of rage, which we can unload so it can transform. Finally, through my confidence, I offer hope and assert that change is possible, but I also say clearly that pursuing change is his choice.

I have delivered a version of this message to many people with perpetrating parts, and almost no one has refused the invitation to change. Sometimes it takes a while for them to open up fully, but a challenge embedded in so much hope and caring calms their defensive protectors and elicits their Self, the place in them that knows they are out of control and also has empathy for their victims.

Scott said he had to think about it. He was afraid of feeling the pain under the rage, so he took a couple of sessions to go over all of his fears about what might come up if he focused inside. And before he was willing to work with this big gun part, I had to convince him that I could keep it from overwhelming him and that I would not judge him no matter what came out.

He also worried that without this part he'd be a big pushover who would allow his employees and others to take advantage of him. I heard this as a concern about other parts who cared too much what people thought and were too concerned about not hurting anyone. These externally focused, compliant parts caused Scott's perpetrator part to fear that he'd be ineffective at work. People like Scott who rely on perpetrator parts often believe that they will be spineless and vulnerable to exploitation if their domineering part isn't in charge. And they do usually have overly compliant parts. But I can reassure them, as I did Scott, that everyone has a Self with a moral compass and qualities like courage, clarity and confidence, and that his Self could be firm without alienating people. When I said this to Scott, he found it hard to believe but was willing to wait and see.

Focusing on the protector, Scott said he didn't see any image but he did feel a kind of power in his arms and fists. I noticed that his fists were clenched and his arms had begun to shake.

"Let that part move your body in whatever way it wants," I said, and he immediately punched the air hard. "How do you feel toward it?" I asked.

"Afraid," he said.

"Even though you don't see the rage," I said, "put it in a contained room inside you so that you feel less afraid of it. We can communicate with it while it's in there."

After he had done this, I had Scott reassure his frightened parts that we could get to know the rageful one without letting it take over, and that it couldn't hurt Scott if he wasn't afraid of it. Then we put all of his scared parts into a waiting room.

"I still can't see the rage but I can feel it in the room. I'm not afraid of it anymore so I can tell it's separate from me," he said.

"So how do you feel toward it now?" I asked.

"I could get to know it," he said.

The part told Scott how much it hated and wanted to punish weakness. Scott asked where that hatred came from and the part showed him a scene from his childhood. He was about 9 years old, his father was drunk and Scott was sassing him. Suddenly his father, a huge man, was on top of him, hitting him. In addition to being in pain, the boy was gasping for air. His father seemed drunk enough not to notice that Scott had stopped breathing. Young Scott felt desperate and powerless. He thought he was going to die and wished he were as strong as his father so he could protect himself.

I asked if he wanted me to go into the scene with him to retrieve the boy, and Scott said yes. Scott reported that we were in the bedroom and asked me to pull the father off and take him out of the room while Scott helped the boy.

I said, "Fine and tell me when I've done that."

After a moment, Scott said, "You've got him out of there. I'm holding the boy. He's shaking all over. I'm telling him he's safe now. I'm bringing him home."

After we unburdened the boy, I said, "See if the rage is still around."

"It is," he said. "And I can see it now. It looks a lot like my father and it's very tired."

"Does it want to unburden, too?" I asked.

"Yes," Scott said.

As the rageful part gave up the furious, controlling energy of his father, Scott saw others—whom he assumed were his ancestors—unburdening too. As with Scott's experience, I find that many perpetrator parts carry legacy burdens—the burdens that are passed down through generations. If explored, they often stem from a traumatic event (war, displacement, immigration, famine, etc.) that happened long before the client was born. Often it isn't necessary to witness the source of a legacy burden before unburdening it, so the process can go as easily as it did for Scott. But sometimes parts are reluctant to let go of legacy burdens due to fear of being disloyal to (or losing contact with) the family member who passed the burden along. Since Scott was able to unburden, we didn't explore the origins of his legacy. But if he had wanted to, we could have talked to the ancestors who showed up and he might have gotten more information.

In the next session I had Scott describe unburdening his perpetrator part to Jane and explain what he had learned about its source. She was clearly moved and said she felt for young Scott. She also expressed great relief to hear that Scott was working on his anger. I reminded her of our agreement that she would work with her overprotective parts. She said doing so would be much easier now that Scott had let go of his rage. I also encouraged Scott to apologize to his son, Joey.

Scott replied, "I already have—and I told him what happened to me."

Joey, who was working with an IFS therapist individually, had replied that he understood and was getting to know the same part of himself.

"Before I talked to Joey, though, I felt sick about what I told you," Scott said to me. "I was embarrassed and sure you were looking down on me. I was going to quit therapy. But then I remembered that I'm doing this for my son. So I looked for Joey and we talked."

"Backlash is common," I affirmed, "especially after being vulnerable for the first time, and I'm glad you told me about it. I want you to know that when I thought about you during the week, my only thoughts were how moved I was by your work and how connected I felt to you afterward."

My work with Scott illustrates that we don't just find perpetrator parts in our prisons or treatment centers. They show up in many, many of our clients and have a big organizing effect on their psyches, even when they're never allowed to take over. Women also have perpetrator parts, and most of the female clients I work with who have experienced sexual abuse find them. I've also found many successful business executives and politicians who appreciate the competitive edge they derive from a perpetrator part. An unquenchable drive for power coupled with little concern for others helps them climb to the top. Unfortunately, but not surprisingly, the companies or organizations they run come to reflect their lack of empathy and their perpetrating values. Thus, in working with perpetrator parts we get a lot of bang for our buck. When we unburden the pain and fear of one, we spare others the same fate.

REFERENCES

D'Silva, K., Duggan, C., & McCarthy, L. (2004). Does treatment really make antisocials worse? A review of the evidence. *Journal of Personality Disorders, 18*, 163–177.

Fenelon, F. (1877). *Spiritual letters to men*. London, England: Rivingtons.

Loving, J. L. (2002). Treatment planning with the Antisocial Checklist-Revised (RCL_R). *International Journal of Offender Therapy and Comparative Criminology, 46*, 281–293.

Marshall, W. L., Marshall, L. E., Serran, G. A., & O'Brian, M. D. (2011). *Rehabilitating sexual offenders: A strengths-based approach*. Washington DC: APA Press.

Merton, T. (1965). *The way of Chuang Tzu*. New York: New Directions.

Salekin, R. T. (2002). Antisocial and therapeutic pessimism: Clinical lore or clinical reality? *Clinical Psychology Review, 22*, 79–112.

Stalans, L. J. (2004). Adult sex offenders on community supervision: A review of recent assessment strategies and treatments. *Criminal Justice and Behavior, 31*, 564–608.

Wong, S. (2000). Antisocial offenders. In S. Hodgins & R. Muller-Isbemer (Eds.), *Violence, crime, and mentally disordered offenders* (pp. 87–112). Chichester, England: Wiley.

Chapter 7

Dealing With Racism

Should We Exorcise or Embrace Our Inner Bigots?

Richard C. Schwartz

EDITORS' NOTE

This chapter, in contrast to others in the book, has no case material. Instead, it describes Dr. Schwartz's experience of being shamed for having racist thoughts and becoming curious about the parts who were responsible for those thoughts. It is a revised version of an article that was published in 2001 in Voices: The Art and Science of Psychotherapy.

To discuss race is to immediately evoke polarized feelings in us all. When I work with groups on racism and other forms of bigotry I find the language of internal family systems (IFS) particularly useful. With enough Self-energy in a group, where everyone knows we all have parts and a Self, people can disclose their inner and outer experiences with the belief they will be heard and not judged. In my experience, Self-led conversations mobilize people to heal the injuries of racism at a personal and communal level.

But before I could do this work with groups I had to find and work with my own racist parts, an eye-opening, painful process that began in 1995 when I was invited to discuss racism at a large mental health conference on a panel with the title "Beyond Politically Correct." A prominent African-American family therapist who had presented extensively on racism moderated the panel, which drew a large audience, including many anti-racism activists. He began by showing a video of a young black adolescent talking about how much he hated white people and wanted to kill them. After the video, the moderator turned to me and asked coldly how I felt about this young man. I yammered about different parts having different reactions—one was scared, another identified with his rage and another was saying racist things.

The moderator became very interested in my racist part and asked me to speak from it to the middle-aged African-American woman sitting next to me on the panel. I declined twice, but when he pushed I finally complied with a string of *what's wrong with you people* statements in her direction. As I spoke I heard gasps in the audience. When I paused, the moderator calmly moved on without checking on her or letting me say more. Later in the workshop I was able to explain about parts and recover some of my self-esteem, but the intervening feeling of impotent concern about this woman along with intense shame and embarrassment stayed with me.

As humiliating as this experience was, it cracked open my fortress of denial and I was able to use it as a trailhead to find important, if embarrassing, parts whom I will describe later. Very few people are eager to examine how their actions hurt others. Most white people in the United States are under no pressure to look at their racism. They have the option of ignoring the harsh realities for people of color. And few white people are exposed to any training on the topic.

People of color have tried to combat this denial by describing what life is like for them, compellingly and in many forms. That's an important step. The next step of getting white people to look at their racist thoughts and feelings and to change is difficult for two reasons. First, while denial about racist parts is widespread, flagrant racism is now widely condemned so most of us don't believe we're racist. Second, because we're marinated in a racist culture, we're unaware of the effects of cultural legacies regarding race. Third, who wants to turn the spotlight on their ugliest urges and voices? As you watch what seem like filthy reptiles slither to the surface of your consciousness (Fenelon, 1877), you can easily begin to hate yourself and your race. If hating our parts got them to change, being judgmental about racism would be fine. But my experience has been the opposite: Disdain fosters inner conflict and galvanizes protectors. On the other hand, understanding and loving protectors does help them change.

But how, you ask, can you love your inner bigot? Isn't education more effective and within reach? Certainly there is a role for education and experiences that counter prejudice based primarily on ignorance, but efforts to educate racist parts tend to be about as effective as efforts to banish them. My experience is that racist parts don't enjoy their jobs, and if we take care of the vulnerable parts they protect, they will change. My advice is to first try being curious about how a racist part came by its views. After what happened to me on that panel, I became curious and got to know my inner bigots. They began by showing me scenes from my childhood when I was the victim of anti-Semitism and other scenes from junior high school where my peers were using racist epithets and I joined in. Though it's not pretty, I'll try to be very honest about what I've learned from my own system.

THE RACIST COALITION

I'll start with the angry, scapegoating part who is most commonly associated with the term *racism* and is the one who spoke to my colleague on the panel. While that part no longer has the need to dominate or put others down, there was a time when it did. It was protecting parts who felt worthless and powerless in the past by making me feel powerful and better than others. Because it was not able to inflict revenge on the people who hurt me then, it was always looking for opportunities to hurt people in the present. It had the ability to demonize or objectify anyone who seemed threatening so that I wouldn't care about them and would treat them badly. It rarely took over completely, but in tense situations it was often a loud inner voice.

Once I began to feel more valuable and powerful in my life, this part stopped urging me to actively put other people down and became more defensive. Now rather than attacking, it operates as a sentry, constantly scanning for danger and seeing difference as dangerous. It has a filing system that records the qualities of people who were involved in hurtful encounters in the past, and when someone new has any of those qualities, it presents me with the list. It also keeps files of dangerous events in my environment (for example, it tracks how many crimes in my neighborhood are committed by black versus white people) and it's not afraid to generalize wildly. This part isn't truly racist; it's protective. It will find fatal flaws in people of any skin color or ethnicity if they seem at all threatening. But if I'm headed toward an encounter with someone of another race who it believes is threatening, it won't hesitate to use racial stereotypes.

Another part, the one whose existence I had the most trouble acknowledging, uses an entitled voice and hates weakness in my clients, my family members and me. He has little patience with those who aren't making it in our society, or in my office, and wishes they would all quit sniveling or trying to make me take care of them. He wants me to look out for number one, pay attention to my practice and my family and not worry about people he says don't really want help anyway. He is jaded and cynical and rationalizes inaction either with right-wing (*they're stupid and impulsive*), racist (*it's genetic*) or New Age (*it's Karma*) explanations for the plight of those who are less privileged.

This passage in Michael Lind's description of the American oligarchy captures his attitude:

> We prefer to assign good fortune to our individual merit, saying that we owe our perches in the upper percentiles of income and education not to our connections but solely to our own I.Q., virtue, brio, genius, sprezzatura, chutzpah, gumption. Had we been switched at birth by accident, had we grown up in a ghetto or barrio or trailer park, we would have arrived at our offices at ABC News or the Republican National Committee or the ACLU in more or less the same amount of time.
>
> (1995, p. 39)

Admitting the existence of this entitled guy to myself, much less to anyone else, was hard work. Some other parts detested him, particularly the one who feels guilty about people who suffer while I'm comfortable and the one who feels enraged about injustice of any kind. To justify and ignore inequity, my entitled part says *you deserve more because you're better than those who are disadvantaged,* and it focuses on the apparent flaws of people in that group. My entitled guy is afraid that I won't survive or I'll become depressed if I lose any advantages, and it also fears retribution because I've been in a position of privilege.

My entitled guy teams up with another protective part who wants to keep me from failing or embarrassing myself. This inner pessimist tells me nothing can help less advantaged people or solve their problems, so I'll fail if I try. Or sometimes he says I don't have what it takes to help change anything, and I'll only display my ignorance if I get involved. He keeps a video bank of incidents in which I did embarrass myself, particularly the painful times when I inadvertently said something that proved offensive to a person of color. He asks why would I want to go into that minefield when I can stay in the peaceful, familiar meadow of relating to white people of the same class and education. This pessimist was frequently at my side as I wrote this chapter, telling me that it's not worth the trouble, that people will think these ideas are silly or racist, or they won't pay attention. I think of my entitlement and pessimism as inner survivalists who build a brick wall around my heart.

Denial, the fourth part in this inner racist coalition, is afraid to let me see how I profit at the expense of others for fear that my innate compassion will make me do things to lose my advantages or will trigger my inner judge, which will make me feel bad about myself. This denier can literally cause me not to see, hear or understand obvious injustice in my home or in the world.

To review, I have a racist coalition of four parts: the angry, scapegoating part who is now more a vigilant protector; the entitled part; the pessimist; and the denier. This group is formidable, and they can handle frontal assaults from anti-racism activists or from parts inside who condemn them. They make it hard for me to see not only the injustice of white privilege but also the harm that is generated by insensitive things I say or do. Getting them to differentiate from my Self so that I can know and be with them has been painful but ultimately healing because, when they do make room, I can access so many other important parts, especially those who are playful, loving and sensitive.

THE ANTI-RACISM COALITION

I also have an anti-racism coalition. These three parts polarize with whichever combination of my four racist parts dominates at any given time. One of the three is my inner judge. When this part has the megaphone, it criticizes me for being racist, sexist, homophobic or a bad person for some other reason. It echoes and amplifies outer critics by hammering me with whatever judgment it fears someone else might level at me. As brutal as this critic can be, it's trying to get me to behave so I won't be vulnerable to the judgments of others. So it, too, is trying to protect me. However, the judge isn't always against racism. Chameleon-like, he is simply sensitive to messages from the environment. If I lived among bigots and the judge sensed that by taking an anti-racism position I'd offend people, it would join the racist chorus and criticize my anti-racism coalition as soft-hearted and unrealistic. In short, the judge wants me to fit in and will swing rapidly with public opinion.

Another part in my anti-racist coalition genuinely hates injustice. This part tries to get me to stand up for myself when I'm being victimized, and it wants me to stand up for others who are being oppressed as well. It gets frustrated with parts who advocate passivity and denial in the face of obvious suffering, and it seizes any opportunity to goad me into action. If ignored, this part can become self-righteous and outraged. It remembers well the times when I was the victim of bigotry, growing up a Jew in a Christian environment.

Finally, I have a rebel part who always opposes established cultural discourses and will battle just for the fun of it. This part likes being an outsider, a member of a fringe, far-sighted group who can disdain those whom it believes are less enlightened. This part loved family therapy when it was challenging and avant-garde but once family therapy became widely accepted, this part felt bored. It provided me with some of the courage and impetus to develop IFS.

RACISM AS PROTECTION AGAINST VULNERABILITY

All parts in both of these coalitions are protectors. Despite the sometimes self-righteous or intellectual content of their messages to me, their fights are basically over how best to protect the vulnerable parts my protectors have exiled to inner dungeons. The racist coalition doesn't like taking risks or jeopardizing what I have because that would scare exiles who fear for their survival. The critic protects parts who are sure I'll be abandoned if someone is upset with me. The outraged part was unable to defend me when bullies hurt my exiles, and now it hates seeing anyone get bullied. Similarly, the rebel saw things that weren't right in my family and reacts to exiles who felt powerless to change them.

When I first realized how pervasive my racist coalition was and how powerfully it organized my perceptions from behind the scenes, I was shocked and ashamed. My impulse was to be vigilant about its influence and to stifle its voice. And as my critic and outraged-by-injustice parts took over for a time, I did just that. I also found myself listening carefully for any subtly racist statements made by friends, students or family and confronted the offending person in a self-righteous or patronizing way. I'm sure I was quite ineffective. As Martin Luther King Jr. said, "Darkness cannot drive out darkness; only light can do that. Hate cannot drive out hate; only love can do that" (King, 1963, p. 37). Parts cannot change parts; only Self can do that. So hatred, self-righteousness and patronizing didn't work. But how can we love parts or people who are racist?

Understanding their protective roles helps me. As long as my exiles remain vulnerable, my racist coalition parts will keep their jobs. No matter how many anti-racism workshops I attend, they will cling to racist beliefs because education doesn't reduce my sense of vulnerability. Education is a good first step but I've talked to many people who are anti-racism activists who feel disappointed because, as hard as they try, they can't drown out their inner racist voice. They attribute this failure to the depth of our socialization or a flaw of character and fight harder to counter, eliminate or ignore their racist parts. While I agree that ignorance and socialization are part of the formula that produces racism and that education and sensitivity training can help us become aware of these burdens, I am convinced that as long as our protective parts believe they have to protect us, they will hold on to racism.

The denying parts of white people are supported by a white entitlement that feeds our inner racist coalitions. Our parts believe we are safer and more comfortable remaining blind. But purposeful blindness invites confrontation. While I had to be confronted by some self-righteous, patronizing parts in others before I was willing to look at my racism, it's not an experience I recommend. The humiliating encounter I described at the opening of the chapter evoked an urge to withdraw from dealing with racism, both inside me and in the world. My pessimist and my angry-part-turned-vigilant-protector were insistent that engaging the issue would bring me nothing but pain and shame. Before they let me shine any more light into their caves, I had to reassure them over and over that even if their fears were true, I could handle it.

Self-righteous encounters tend to create this kind of internal backlash. For every person like me whose fortress gets cracked open and responds by looking inside, many more will react by strengthening their defenses. It's by far the easiest and safest (in the short run) choice. I believe fear of judgment deters many people who want to be active on this topic in their communities. A safe environment in which to explore and disclose inner thoughts and prejudices without fear of being judged is the only way I know to avoid internal backlash and avoidance. We can't bring light into darkness if we haven't shone light in our own dark places. But as long as we're afraid of our monsters we will avoid shining that light. We will curse the monsters outside and leave those within stewing and alone. James Baldwin said it succinctly, "One can only face in others what one can face in oneself" (as cited in Collier, 1972).

But it's a lot easier to look if you think you'll find good parts in bad roles instead of monsters. I'm not ashamed to disclose all that I have said here because I know the agendas of my more extreme parts don't reflect who I really am. I'm not a racist. I have racist parts, but even they are just protective. When I say I'm not a racist many will believe I'm ignorant. But I object to all monolithic labels that identify a person with the extremes of their protectors. Consequently, I don't believe there are alcoholics, schizophrenics, borderlines, sex offenders or right-wing zealots. I do believe people have extreme parts.

WHY TRY?

But how can we speak out against injustice when it feels like a thimble of water being poured on a raging bonfire? For most white people there's little motivation to work on racism. The incentive I've heard from anti-racism activists is that white people are missing a lot by not knowing other cultures better. It seems most privileged people are willing to absorb that loss when it's weighed against the risk of digging into dark internal corners and feeling ashamed. I do not believe that sustained action will come from inner or outer critics, or from outraged or self-righteous parts.

But I have found two sources of sustainable motivation. First, as long as my protectors are blended and remain on high alert, they cut me off from my sensitive, creative, fun, intimacy-loving parts. My anti-racism work in therapy has been transformative. When I witness what I do to others and find a way to make a repair, I heal myself. Second, I have a Self and therefore I have an inborn source of compassion and courage. The compassion of my Self will find ways to resist injustice and fight for the oppressed. My Self is unafraid of public criticism or loss of privilege. The clarity of my Self allows me to see injustice while the courage of my Self leads me to speak out or act against it without judgment and self-righteousness because I can also see behind the protective parts of oppressors to the pain that drives their actions. As Longfellow wrote, "If we could read the secret history of our enemies, we should find in each man's life sorrow and suffering enough to disarm all hostility" (Longfellow, 2000, p. 797). When my Self is in the lead, I intuit that secret history. Consequently, my Self tries to bring forth the Self of oppressors rather than further polarizing their protectors by shaming and condemning them. Indeed, my experience as a therapist is that the more racist, entitled, narcissistic or grandiose a client seems, the more insecure and powerless his or her exiles are.

The Self contains what Robert Jay Lifton calls the *species mentality*, the sense that one is interconnected with every member of the larger community of humankind. This meta-perspective permits people to think ecologically about the systems in which they are embedded. With a sense of interconnectedness comes the understanding that when one person suffers, we all suffer, just as my body speaks for the pain of my exiled parts even if I have no conscious awareness of their existence. As I've understood the importance of accepting all my parts, I've seen more clearly the importance of not exiling other people or their parts. When I accept others and myself, I live with the inner certainty that I'm not separate.

A DIFFERENT DISCOURSE

What are the implications of these ideas for the discourse on racism in this country? Conversations regarding race would be enriched if everyone noticed their polarity between racist parts and the parts who disapprove of racism, and could identify who dominates at any given time. Just as the Taoist yin/yang symbol has a black dot in the white and vice versa, we all have polarized parts. Acknowledging what we share would make discussions about race less tense. Anti-racism workshops (or individual therapy sessions) that aim to differentiate from, welcome and befriend all parts would help participants explore their inner conversations about race with Self-energy. Once racist parts are identified, participants would have the opportunity to explore the motives of their parts rather than try to eliminate them. My experience tells me participants would learn that racist protectors are good parts who have picked up bad behavior in an attempt to create safety. If so, they would find that their attachment to racism goes beyond and beneath socialization. My racist parts, for example, believed that racism kept me safe, and they wouldn't agree to change until they saw that I was less vulnerable.

Our protectors will cling to white privilege until we are clear and honest about its internal as well as its external costs. I believe healing inner wounds is key (not the only key, but an important one) to decreasing racism. As I've opened my heart to my exiled parts, I've been more able to open my heart to others. Even so, I haven't had to be fully healed to begin to act. Action itself is healing.

REFERENCES

Collier, E. (1972). A study in chaos. *Black World*, June, p. 33.
Fenelon, F. (1877). *The spiritual letters of Archbishop Fenelon: Letters to women.* Retrieved from https://play.google.com/store/books/details?id=EUc4AQAAMAAJ&rdid=book-EUc4AQAAMAAJ&rdot=1
King, M. L. (1963). *Strength to love.* New York: Harper & Row.
Lind, M. (1995, June). To have and have not: Notes on the progress of the American class war. *Harper's Magazine, 290*(1741), 35–44.
Longfellow, H. W. (2000). *The complete works of Henry Wadsworth Longfellow.* New York: Literary Classics of the United States.
Schwartz, R. C. (2001). Dealing with racism: To exorcise or embrace inner bigots. *Voices: The Art and Science of Psychotherapy, 37*(3), 55–64.

Chapter 8

What IFS Offers to the Treatment of Trauma

Frank G. Anderson and Martha Sweezy

INTRODUCTION

The model of mind used in any form of therapy determines its approach to trauma. The internal family systems (IFS) model of mind taps into the norms of our highly interactive subjective experience and works with internal people—or *parts*—who have feelings as well as agendas that focus on the common goal of warding off psychic pain. As a result, the IFS approach for treating trauma differs from the widely used International Society for Traumatic Stress Studies (ISTSS) guidelines (2011), most importantly for our purposes, from the suggestion that treatment be divided into phases to promote the client's internal resources and stability, and to prevent emotional overwhelm.[1] The ISTSS phases begin by developing emotional and psychological competencies through affect regulation and interpersonal skills, go on to review and reappraise trauma memories, and end with a focus on consolidating gains made in therapy. In contrast, IFS starts from the premise that psychic parts comprise a motivated and purposeful inner community that does not need to be managed. We offer this community our interest and curiosity; in return the parts explain why they believe their behavior, which can seem consistently irrational and destructive to the observer, benefits the client. Once we offer them an alternative way of accomplishing the same goals (for this is our offer), the client's parts must turn to the inevitable post-trauma issue of trust.

Interpersonal trauma is the great destroyer of trust in relationships. It severs external relational ties while initiating an enduring inner assault on self-worth and self-governance. In IFS we aim to undo these effects by getting our clients into a Self-led relationship with their parts, trusting their knowledge, listening to their concerns, validating their experience and honoring their problem-solving attempts while offering them a new solution, the opportunity to unload traumas (*I'm alone and unlovable*) from the past and be loved in the present by the Self. In this way, as we illustrate, IFS relies on relationships, internal and external, rather than preordained phases to stabilize trauma clients who, as a population, tend to become more symptomatic and destabilized when feeling pushed or controlled.

CHAPTER OVERVIEW

This chapter illustrates some relational principles that IFS uses to accelerate healing work with trauma. These include prioritizing the relationship between the client's parts and the Self (Schwartz, 2013); welcoming all parts and seeing their good intentions; helping parts to separate (or *unblend*) from the Self; and getting permission from protective parts before accessing exiles. In addition, we illustrate three foundational guidelines for IFS therapists, including how we avoid taking sides in polarities, help our parts to step back while sitting with clients and heal our own injured parts, which can interfere with the therapeutic process. In our experience, when we do not perform these elements of treatment successfully, our access to our client's wounded parts is hindered, we're likely to feel frustrated and treatment is easily derailed—especially in the case of severe trauma.

THE THERAPEUTIC RELATIONSHIP

In IFS the primary therapeutic relationships are internal, between parts and the Self (Schwartz, 2013). When the client can't access the Self, the therapist is the source of Self-energy in the client–therapist system for as long as needed, which can be months or years in dissociative disorders. Here's an example of being patient yet persistent about accessing the Self with a client who had a severe trauma history.

Nick, who was diagnosed with dissociative identity disorder (DID), had a trauma history that included his parents leaving him in the care of his physically and sexually abusive older sisters while they were busy running the family business. To avoid being with his sisters, Nick spent as much time as he could out of the house, which left him vulnerable to being molested by his tennis coach. Although Nick had many exiles from these traumas, we rarely heard from them directly. Instead, most of my contact was with his frontline protectors. One day I (Frank) said to him, "Can I meet the Nick who is not a part?"

"What?" he said, looking shocked.

"Really," I said, "I know there's a Nick in there who is not a part, and I want us to get to know him."

At first several parts stepped forward who said they were Nick, including the Nick who had protected him when his sisters locked him in the closet or touched him, the Nick who had survived being molested by his coach and the Nick who was running his day-to-day life now. Several months later I was still talking with his parts about unblending when he reported, "My parts really like you and some of the little ones are afraid of losing their connection with you if we let in the Nick who isn't a part."

"Ah!" I said. "That makes sense. But please let them know this isn't an either/or option. They can let us meet the Nick who isn't a part and still have a connection with me."

"Okay. We're scared but we'll try," a part replied. After a few moments of attending inside, the part exclaimed, "Wow! We can see how things could be really different if we were connected to that Nick."

"And he's waiting for you," I said.

As with Nick, in the aftermath of severe trauma protective parts often need to feel safe in the therapeutic relationship before being willing to step back and give access to the Self. Until that happens the therapist serves as the *Self of the system*. The unveiling of the Self can be as dramatic as it was for Nick, or it can involve "passing the baton gradually and naturally" (Schwartz, personal communication, 2014) as parts have the opportunity to experience and feel some trust with the client's Self.

WELCOMING ALL PARTS AND GETTING PERMISSION

Most effective trauma treatments help clients "be with" rather than re-experiencing or "being in" their trauma. The ability to be mindfully (rather than dissociatively) separate from intense affect is an important early step in many experiential therapies, IFS included, because reenactment is not therapeutic. In IFS we can engage a target part (that is, the part the client has chosen to focus on) by helping the client stay open and curious. When that doesn't work we can use *direct access,* a process in which we invite the part who won't separate to come closer by talking with it directly, as we illustrate later. In our experience, this can accelerate the process of connecting with injured parts, especially when we're dealing with extreme protectors.

Because the intensity of the client's affect and/or the degree of her dissociation may leave little room for the Self, especially early on, proficiency at direct access is essential in treating trauma. Once extreme protectors feel safer and the client's Self can take over (with *in-sight*[2]), sessions move more quickly. But whether we use direct access or the open curiosity of in-sight, we always seek permission from the client's parts before tracking the target part. *Would it be okay to . . . ? Would anyone mind if . . . ?* Here is an example of a therapy being temporarily derailed because I (Frank) forgot to ask permission before trying to access the painful feelings related to a client's traumatic childhood.

Peter was 41 years old when he came to me because of difficulties in his marriage, which quickly ended in a contentious divorce. We spent the next couple of years working on his behavior with his children because he was controlling and verbally abusive when they had trouble in school. Although I sensed that his childhood had been difficult due to a critical mother and a binge-drinking father who had abandoned the family when he was young, he rarely spoke of that time in any detail or with any feeling.

Despite his childhood and due in no small measure to a strong intellectual part, Peter did well in college, developed a successful business and provided well for his family. His intellectual part had been in the driver's seat throughout his adult life and was allergic to the slightest hint of emotion. If a feeling was mentioned during a session, the intellectual part promptly jumped in to "understand" it. Although the part was willing to step back when asked, it would interrupt again if feelings came up. Needless to say, the pace of our work was slow and some of my parts were frustrated.

Since the part was always willing to step back, I hadn't felt the need to try direct access, which I usually reserve for parts who refuse to separate. But when I realized I had never actually asked the intellectual part for permission to access parts with strong feelings, I felt that I owed it an apology. So I said to Peter, "I'm aware that I've been trying to access some of your experiences without permission from one of your most important protectors—the one who figures things out. Is it okay with you if I talk with that part directly?"

"Don't you talk to him all the time? I think he's me."

"I don't believe he's you, though he is a really important part of you."

"Well, why not?" Peter shrugged.

"Are you there?" I asked. He nodded. "So you're the part of Peter who helps him to make sense of things?" I asked.

"Yes," the part answered.

"How long have you been doing this job?" I asked.

"Since Peter was 6 years old," the part replied. "He was alone a lot, so he needed someone to help him figure things out. If I hadn't helped everything would have fallen apart."

"In what way?" I asked.

"He didn't understand why his mother was so mean to him. She always seemed angry. And . . ."—the part hesitated before disclosing information that was totally new to me—"just before leaving home for good, his father jumped on him and choked him until he passed out."

"Wow!" I said. "That must have been terrifying."

"Yes. Peter was a little boy. It was confusing. He couldn't understand," the part replied.

"So you helped him?" I asked gently.

"When I fail at my job," the part said, looking at the floor, "the suicide part takes over."

Flooded with compassion upon hearing about the protective role of the intellectual part, I apologized for not having taken the time to understand what it was doing. "With your permission," I went on, "I could help Peter heal the 6-year-old so that you and the suicide part won't have to work so hard."

Softening, the part replied, "I like your idea. It would be a huge relief for both of us."

As we see, Peter's intellectual part could not relax until I understood what it was doing. My impatience and frustration should have been a signal to me that I was not leading with my Self. Only after asking his protector for permission to talk about feelings was I able to help the intellectual part relax. We cannot emphasize enough the importance of asking parts for their permission at every step of the therapeutic process we illustrate. In relationships in general, asking for permission is an essential gesture of respect. If Peter's protector had said *no* at this juncture, I would have honored its decision and continued to be curious about its job. In trauma, which by definition includes a boundary violation, asking permission and accepting *no* if necessary gives power and control back to the client's internal system, which is what protective parts have been trying to achieve. As it happened, however, my shift into Self-energy allowed his protector to feel understood and safe enough to give us access to the feelings he was protecting.

THE ART OF NOT TAKING SIDES

In our experience, parts are as alike and different as people. Although the parts of a client's inner system share goals like safety, survival and belonging, they frequently get into conflict while pursuing those goals. We call these pairs of opposing parts *polarities*. If the therapist takes a side when the client's parts are polarized, causing one to feel supported and the other attacked or dismissed, he can alienate an important protector and the client's inner polarity will simply intensify. Here is an illustration of staying Self-led rather than taking sides in response to a polarity.

An eating disorder specialist referred Angela, a 30-year-old woman, to me (Frank) due to her lack of progress after 3 years in treatment. After a month, Angela came into my office and said, "Is it okay with you if I stand up for a second and ask you a question?"

"Sure," I replied.

"And I want you to be completely honest with me," she said.

"Okay," I said.

She stood up, faced me directly and said, "When I look at myself this way, straight on, I look totally normal, right? I don't look too fat or skinny, I don't look sad, like nothing is wrong with me. But when I look at myself sideways, like this, and see my reflection out of the corner of my eye in a store window as I walk down the street, I don't recognize that person. She looks heavy, dumpy and totally depressed. My question is this. You think I'm the normal one, not the dumpy one, right?" Totally serious, she waited for my answer.

In IFS we view a belief, feeling or bodily sensation as evidence of a part and as the entry point to the client's inner experience. Alert to the relational complexities of the inner system, we ask permission to get to know the part before we proceed. Angela was showing me a polarized relationship between two of her parts. However far from introducing me to these parts, or even really asking me a question, she was directing me to choose one part over the other. Since our goal is to listen to both and avoid alienating either, I replied, "I hear I'm being asked to choose between one part who feels totally normal and another one who feels dumpy and depressed. But I'd like to get to know both."

Angela's face softened and she replied, "Good answer. I think we're going to get along just fine."

As we continued over the next few months I stayed open and curious, and Angela began to make discoveries. For example, the part who felt totally normal was actually working around the clock to block Angela from being aware of bad experiences during her childhood. "If we really admit what happened to us as a little girl," the part said, "I would kill myself in a second."

"I want to be sure I understand," I said. "This part feels that you would have to die if the parts who got hurt shared what they were feeling?"

"The hurt parts hold way too much pain," she replied.

"I totally get that," I said. "Whenever your system is ready we can safely help the ones who hold too much pain."

As I helped Angela's exiles to stop overwhelming her, the totally normal part got to know and trust Angela's Self and allowed her to meet parts who were involved in a more hidden and desperate protective polarity: the one with a sweet tooth who had binged on candy bars after being prostituted by her babysitter in a child pornography ring and the other one who had tried not to eat at all because she associated the sight and smell of food with danger and pain. Angela also learned that her suicidal part took over when she was hospitalized because her eating disorder parts were prevented from bingeing and starving.

Because we are confident that polarized protectors are distracting from the actual problem (an underlying injury), which the client's Self can heal, we don't get involved with trying to resolve inner polarities. Instead, we focus on developing relationships between the client's parts and the Self.

SEPARATING AND NOT OVERWHELMING

As we see with Angela, clients feel as alarmed as therapists by the destabilizing effects of traumatic memories and negative feelings. Emotional overwhelm in traumatized individuals generally stems from an exile blending and causing functional collapse, followed by reactive protectors launching symptoms to distract and suppress the exile's emotional pain. To avoid this outcome, the ISTSS guidelines suggest dividing therapy into phases, starting with affect regulation skills and moving on to processing trauma once the client is stable. From the IFS perspective, increasing competencies along with the ability to tolerate affect through skills training is basically teaching managerial parts new and less destructive ways of distracting from the powerful negative feelings of injured parts.

The IFS approach to emotional overwhelm is different. When we work with psychic multiplicity we focus on building relationships. To build the relationship of the Self with parts, we first ask protectors to separate (or unblend). Frequently protectors are unwilling to separate because they fear the intensity of the exile's feelings. To deal with this concern we negotiate directly with the exile to stop overwhelming the client. Separating and not overwhelming often go hand in hand but are not the same phenomenon. Being asked to create a greater percentage of space (separating) is different from being asked to share a smaller percentage of a feeling (not overwhelming). Parts are capable of doing both.

We're not interested in asking protectors to manage each other or to function better, which will happen naturally once exiled parts are healed. And we also don't need protectors trying to control the intense feelings of exiles. Instead we ask for their permission to access the injured part, which lets them set the pace, and we invite them to be direct about what they fear (often emotional overwhelm), which we assure them we can address. Meanwhile, exiled parts may need to be reminded to tone it down but they don't need to be taught how because this ability is innate. Nevertheless, exiles who seek attention by being intense may not want to stop because backing off has historically meant back to the basement, and they believe intensity is their only way to be heard. The proposition that they can gain longed-for connection by separating and decreasing emotional intensity is a truly novel suggestion that seems paradoxical to them.

Here is an example of supervising a therapist who was struggling with the IFS teachings on emotional overwhelm. Prior to learning IFS, Naomi had been taught to avoid having traumatized clients decompensate by overseeing the content and pacing of sessions, and her attachment to Phase 1 stabilization work was hindering her ability to be Self-led and experience-near with her client. "I'm not sure I can do this model," she said to me (Martha). "It doesn't seem to work for me the way it does for other people."

"Can you give me an example?"

"Okay. I have a client who has this young part in rags. She looks like this little street urchin. She just keeps weeping and holding out her arms."

"And how does your client respond?"

"She's doesn't know what to do."

"And you?"

"I coach Tessa to ask her to wait."

"Until?"

"Until Tessa is stable."

"And what happens?"

"It doesn't work. The little girl keeps crying and holding out her arms."

"And then what happens?"

"Tessa gets frustrated and says she wants to go back to regular therapy."

"And then what?"

"We do that."

"And what do you feel?"

"I wonder if I should be investing all this time and energy when I can't get the hang of this model."

"Shall we check with your parts?" I asked. She nodded. "Can we start with the one who wants the little girl to wait?"

"But I thought we were supposed to ask exiles to wait. She is an exile, isn't she?"

"She might be," I said. "And if she is, her protectors will only let her be with Tessa if she stops being so overwhelming."

"So what do I do?"

"Get permission from her protectors and then ask the little girl to dial it down. And once she does, Tessa's Self can help her."

Naomi shook her head, "I don't get that idea. Paying attention to the exile first seems risky."

"Can we hear more from your concerned part?"

"That's me," Naomi said firmly. "I feel it's appropriate to be cautious. Tessa has a big trauma history."

"Okay. But can we consider your caution as a part for a few minutes just to see what happens?" I asked.

"All right. Then I feel my cautious part is wise."

"And how does it respond?"

"It's glad that I agree."

"So you have a cautious part and a part who agrees with its caution. How do you feel toward them?"

"I agree."

"And how do you feel toward them."

"I feel like I agree."

"Can I ask a question?" I said. She nodded. "Is the cautious part agreeing with itself?"

She looked down at the floor. After a moment she looked up again and said, "I think so."

"Would it be willing to make room for you?"

"It wants me to know that I have to be responsible," Naomi said. "Tessa has had too much heartbreak in her life, and it says I shouldn't add to her burdens by tipping over the apple cart. She'll end up in the hospital again."

"Does that make sense to you?" I asked.

"It does."

"Who does the cautious part think you are?"

"A therapist who can get a too involved, go too fast and make dangerous mistakes."

"What is the overinvolved part concerned would happen if it stopped?"

"I'd feel helpless."

"Would these two like you to help the part who feels helpless?"

Naomi sat up straighter and exclaimed, "I get it! I see where this came from. Of course this helpless part is an exile of mine."

"Will the other two trust you to help it?" I asked.

Naomi closed her eyes for a moment before opening them again and saying, "The cautious part sees me now and is willing to let me handle this. And I thanked the overinvolved part for trying so hard."

"And can you take care of the helpless part on your own time?" I asked.

"Now that I've noticed her, I will definitely help her," Naomi said.

As we see, Naomi had a part who felt helpless with certain clients. In response her protectors had become polarized, with one getting too involved and another trying to balance that overinvolvement by controlling her clients and the content of therapy sessions. I was not surprised to hear that her efforts to make the little girl wait had backfired when she was blended with a controlling part. When exiles get the message that they're unwanted, they tend to either come on stronger or duck for cover with their fears confirmed. And when protectors get the message that they're unwanted, they tend to rebel and become polarized with the therapist. Once Naomi could help her parts separate, she understood that Tessa's protectors would continue to be vigilant until the little girl stopped being so overwhelming. Though exiles often need support, reassurance and practice to do so, they have the ability to calm down and wait in return for the promise of attention. When we know how to help exiles to stop overwhelming and protectors to separate, we can forego the more experience-distant approach of prescribed phases.

THERAPIST PARTS UNDER PRESSURE

As we see with Naomi, although every person's experience is unique, the internal systems of therapists are the same as the internal systems of clients: We have protectors, we have exiled parts and when our parts blend, we do not have access to the Self. As Schwartz has pointed out, internal systems function in patterned ways and abide by certain rules (personal communication, 2012). When traumatized clients lead with hypervigilant, aggressive or critical protectors, our protectors will react. Here is an example of a therapist needing to help his protectors calm down and separate when he feels threatened by a client.

Will was a 45-year-old man who had served two active tours of duty in the Gulf War in the early 1990s, returning in 1992. His father and grandfather had served in Vietnam and World War II, respectively. The family was proud of its military service, but it was a source of conflict for Will whose experience in Kuwait and Iraq had been intensely negative. When he came to see me (Frank), he was divorced and struggling to maintain meaningful intimate relationships. He had become a chronic pot smoker, and when he spent extended time with his 5-year-old daughter, whom he described as *quite strong-willed,* he often got angry and reactive. In addition, he was extremely sensitive about his effect on others and berated himself for having a temper.

"I am a worthless piece of shit," he said repeatedly in the first few months of therapy. "I can't handle life. I keep messing up. I hate myself and my dad thinks I'm a no-good loser."

When we focused on this critical part, it said it was trying to get Will to *do the right thing and be more military* so his father would be proud of him, and it was largely unwilling to separate. During one session when Will was in a particularly bad mood, he reported having had a horrible weekend but wasn't willing to say more. I noticed that I had a part who felt defeated, worn out by the relentless self-criticism and stonewalling of Will's protectors. "I'm sure you'll tell me when you're ready," I offered.

Without missing a beat Will shifted forward in his seat and yelled, "I'm sick of your goddamn calm! You're so high and mighty. You're rich. You have friends. You have a family. You go on great vacations. You don't have a fucking clue!"

Shocked into silence, I was frozen. After a moment I became aware of a part who wanted to run and another who wanted to stand up yell *Get out of my office!* I looked at him. He looked at me. Then his body softened, he slumped back, got smaller and said in a quiet voice, "Please say something nice to me."

But in the grip of the conflicting feelings and impulses of my parts I was unable to speak. Finally, I realized that the best I could do right then was nothing. So I said, "I'm sorry Will. I don't think I'm able to be help-ful right now."

Looking defeated, he got up and walked out, closing the door gently behind him. Fortunately, he had the courage to return the next week. Sit-ting down, he looked at me directly. "When you didn't speak, I felt awful. Inside my head it was the usual: *I'm out of control! I'm such a fuck up!* But at the same time I kept thinking about you. You didn't attack me back and you didn't make excuses for me. I came back because deep inside I know I need your help."

As Will's experience illustrates, when my system was reacting to his anger I was unable to speak for my parts. The best I could do was not speak from them. Although this proved helpful for Will, many different responses would have been true to the spirit of IFS. If I had felt safer I could have been curious about his outburst and helped him be curious; I also could have talked about the reactions of my parts; or I could have used direct access to talk to his angry part. As we were to learn after this session, since Iraq and Kuwait, Will's life had been dominated by a polarity between a critic who shamed him relentlessly and his angry reactive part. Getting Will's Self in the middle to hear the concerns of both sides finally led him to a little boy who desperately needed his love.

TRANSFORMATIONAL HEALING

In IFS the process of transforming exiled parts by healing their wounds is based on the client and therapist tracking feelings and sensations in the body moment-to-moment while we develop the relationship between the client's parts and the Self. Along the way we do not encourage anyone to work harder or better. On the contrary, hard work denotes protectors blocking the Self as they work to keep vulnerable parts, who suffer in pain and isolation, out of awareness. Here is an example of an unburdening that followed several months of negotiation with a couple of hardworking protectors.

At 46, Pippa, a former college soccer star and then high-powered entre-preneur, was unemployed, supported by her parents and crippled with anx-iety. She had a history of sexual trauma in college and had been recruited from a very young age by her mother to *be a little grown-up* and care for her four younger siblings, including one set of twins. She described her father, who was her mother's senior by 15 years, as a distant, preoccupied academic who did not participate in child care.

Pippa's most active polarity was between a harsh critic and a thinking part who worked relentlessly to calm the critic by understanding and fixing Pippa's symptomatic behavior (fear of leaving the house, fainting in public, getting jobs and leaving them abruptly). Needless to say, neither thinking nor criticizing herself calmed Pippa's fears, and her symptoms continued unabated. I (Martha) asked the thinker and the critic to separate. Believing Pippa was the little girl who had been put in charge of her younger siblings, they steadfastly refused. They explained that they couldn't trust her compliant parts, who had collaborated as she was exploited by her mother, to keep her safe at work. They were determined to protect her from being taken advantage of again. I accepted this and spent a few months working around it, getting to know her system and being the "hope merchant" (Schwartz, 1995) by inviting her fainting, fearful part (through what we called *emails* for we had no direct contact) to stop overwhelming Pippa. I also befriended the thinker and the critic with direct access. One day quite abruptly these two powerful protectors bowed out and Pippa was in contact with her parentified 4-year-old in her childhood home.

"She says she protects someone else," Pippa reported.

"Who?"

"Innocence got hidden in a Cracker Jacks box and is sleeping," Pippa said.

"What needs to happen?" I asked.

"No one is ready for innocence to wake up," Pippa said.

"Would it be okay to help the 4-year-old?"

"Yes."

"How do you feel toward her?"

"I care."

"What does she want you to know?"

"I see my father dragging her down the stairs by her hair. Bump, bump, bump. He says she was irresponsible. That's when innocence went into the Cracker Jacks box."

"What's it like for her to show this to you?" I asked.

"She's taking my hand," Pippa reported. "She doesn't want to be alone there anymore."

"How do you feel toward her?" I asked

"I love her."

"Let her know," I said.

"Yes, I picked her up," Pippa said. "I'm telling her that we can leave and take the Cracker Jacks box with us whenever she's ready."

There was a long silence. "What's happening?" I finally murmured.

"She wants me to explain to her mother why she can't stay, so I am," Pippa said. After another few moments she went on, "We're leaving with the Cracker Jacks box."

"They're coming to be with you in the present?" I asked.

"Yes."

"Ask if she has burdens," I said.

"Yes," Pippa said. "She's handing me stones that have been in the pit of her stomach to throw in the ocean."

"Let me know when you're done," I said.

"Okay," Pippa said. After a few moments she nodded.

"Is that everything?" I asked.

"Yes."

"And what has she been missing that she'd like to invite into herself now?" I asked.

"Courage and love," Pippa said.

"Anything else?"

"No. She's happy."

"Can we check with her protectors?" I asked. "Were they watching?"

"They feel relieved," she said. "They're tired and quiet. They need rest."

"What about the Cracker Jacks box?"

"We'll open it after we rest." At the end of this session Pippa reported feeling lighter and freer. "She was afraid but she knows now that I'm not," she said.

As this vignette illustrates, injured parts transform as the Self witnesses their history without question or judgment, validates their feelings and needs and follows their lead while challenging (implicitly or explicitly) all negative verdicts about their value.

CONCLUSION

Trauma has many disturbing aftereffects, including harsh self-shaming, dissociation, addiction, self-harm, suicidality (protectors) and intense feeling states like loneliness, emptiness and worthlessness (exiles). These sequelae influence the traumatized individual's body, emotions, thoughts and relationships, all of which can be addressed in IFS therapy. Often beginning by forming relationships with whichever parts show up, we move through the body and emotions and end when traumatized parts are released from immobilizing feeling states and crippling beliefs. We believe that taking this therapeutic trek through the domains of experience that have been altered by trauma reconsolidates traumatic memory, unlocking, revising and reorganizing the synapses that encode the memory in the brain (Ecker, Ticic, & Hulley, 2012).

Along the way, we find certain guidelines in IFS to be especially useful with trauma work: (1) assuming that all parts (even those who are impulsive, compulsive or dangerous) have good intentions; (2) seeking permission from protectors before trying to access exiles; and (3) guiding parts to separate from, not overwhelm and be in relationship with the Self. We're also guided by a couple of consistent observations about internal systems: that taking a side in a polarity will reinforce the polarity and be anti-therapeutic and that we function just the way our clients do. This means that the therapist and client are always in a parallel process. When we feel threatened by parts who are overwhelming the client, our job is not to control the client's parts but to help our parts tone their feelings down and separate from our Self.

Feeling overwhelmed by virtue of reliving—or abreaction—is an ever-present risk for traumatized individuals. To address this risk, the ISTSS guidelines recommend dividing treatment into phases, with a first phase that focuses on developing emotional and psychological competencies so the client can go on to tell her story safely in a second phase of treatment. We know, however, that the client's hardworking managerial team tends to hear the call to be more skilled as an invitation to work harder at constraining both vulnerable parts who are overwhelming emotionally and extreme parts who react to that overwhelm. Vulnerable and extreme parts experience Phase 1 strategies like grounding, distress tolerance skills and staying within the window of tolerance as further efforts to banish or constrain them. Since all this effort reinforces a broken system and encourages backlash, IFS takes the alternate tack of asking overwhelming parts to dial their intensity down so they can experience the benefits of feeling connected with the Self, and inviting protectors to try something new and different by allowing the Self to take the lead.

As we have emphasized throughout this chapter, the therapeutic process must gain the cooperation of protectors. If we take steps without their input, we navigate blindly and risk reprisal. Nothing authentic can happen without their permission. Therefore, we don't argue with protectors over failed strategies; we welcome them and build trust to speed the pace of therapy. We appreciate their heroism, grant the importance of their work at one time in the client's life and note discrepancies between their positive intent and negative consequences. We tell them *You're the boss* (Schwartz, personal communication, 2012), and then, because in IFS we believe that post-trauma burdens can be permanently released by self-acceptance and love, we offer all parts the alternative of a loving relationship with the Self.

NOTES

1. Frank Anderson teaches an advanced training on the topic of IFS, trauma and neuroscience for the Center for Self-Leadership with Richard Schwartz.
2. See glossary.

REFERENCES

Ecker, B., Ticic, R., & Hulley, L. (2012). *Unlocking the emotional brain, eliminating symptoms at their roots using memory reconsolidation.* New York: Routledge.

International Society for the Study of Trauma and Dissociation. (2011). Guidelines for treating dissociative identity disorder in adults, third revision: Summary version. *Journal of Trauma & Dissociation, 12,* 188–212.

Schwartz, R. (1995). *Internal family systems therapy.* New York: Guilford Press.

Schwartz, R. C. (2013). The therapist-client relationship and the transformative power of self. In M. Sweezy & E. L. Ziskind (Eds.), *Internal family systems therapy: New dimensions* (pp. 1–23). New York: Routledge.

Chapter 9

Expanded Unburdenings
Relaxing Managers and Releasing Creativity
Pamela Geib

INTRODUCTION

Lisa's attention was deep inside as she silently worked with the young child who was so terrified of her chaotic home. As she returned to the room and prepared to leave, she said to me matter-of-factly, "I don't have to punish myself anymore. I'm not bad." As we would discover, her silent inner work in this session had ended a decades-long struggle with bingeing and purging. Her exile and its primary protector were now at rest. In my astonishment, I was beginning to learn about spontaneous unburdening.

Unburdening is at the heart of the healing process in the internal family systems (IFS) therapy model. Its purpose is to help an exiled part release painful emotions and memories, as well as the negative and constricting beliefs generated from these memories. When the exile releases its acute pain and clears the negative beliefs, it can "transform into its original vital state" (Schwartz, 2001), while also allowing protective parts to let go of their extreme roles. The IFS protocol clearly delineates the steps of the unburdening process, which are listed in Table 9.1.

Though the protocol is straightforward, the concept of unburdening is radical. It posits both rapid and sweeping change of a kind not considered possible in most therapies. The radical nature of this change can be seen in Schwartz's description of unburdened exiles. "Exiles contain qualities like liveliness, playfulness, spontaneity, creativity and joie de vivre" (2001, p. 125) that emerge when the child is unburdened. Releasing joyful qualities is a far cry from the more ordinary clinical goal of symptom relief. Clinicians who have been taught that therapeutic change is gradual may have parts who

Table 9.1 *Unburdening*

- Therapist facilitates the relationship between the client's Self and protector parts.
- Therapist facilitates the relationship between the client's Self and exiled parts.
- Client's Self witnesses the exile's experience.
- Client's Self retrieves exile, if needed.
- Unburdening ritual.
- Invitation to take in new, positive qualities.
- Invite protectors to unburden and choose less extreme roles or retire.
- Exile is invited to integrate back into the system.

Adapted from Schwartz, R.C. (1995). *Internal Family Systems Therapy*. New York: Guilford.

are skeptical or intimidated by the idea of dramatic change, or who view the idea of swift transformation as magical thinking.

As Jack Engler noted, "Even some IFS therapists have trouble believing unburdening is possible. Among those who accept the notion, there is controversy over whether an unburdening will hold over time" (2013, p. xxii). Many IFS therapists are inspired by the possibility that we can facilitate dramatic transformation, but many are also concerned about unrealistic expectations. In my roles as teacher and supervisor I have heard a variety of concerns, ranging from disbelief *(I don't want to lead my clients down the garden path)* to discouragement *(I'm not mystical enough)* to fear of being incompetent *(I'm afraid I won't do it right)*.

Over the years, I've also heard from supervisees who never use the standard protocol for unburdening. Some believe in the concept but drop or change the protocol and then feel ashamed and judge themselves *bad* for making this choice. Shame often makes therapists reluctant to speak about their actual practices in peer groups or with colleagues, and this can be isolating. As I've become increasingly aware of these struggles, I invite more discussion about unburdening in my role as teacher. I encourage my supervisees to be mindful of any inner shaming so they can attend to their own parts and then help clients clear burdens creatively, in whatever ways are most natural and effective.

CLIENT RESPONSES TO THE IDEA OF UNBURDENING

Therapists are not alone in feeling skeptical about unburdening. The idea can be equally challenging for client parts. I have heard client's critical managers say things like *You're not getting there fast enough!* Or, *You don't know how to do it right!* Or their fearful parts wonder *But who will I be after an unburdening?* And their shamed parts object *I can't do this!*

The mission of this chapter is to demonstrate that any therapist or client with a part who feels anxious or ashamed can benefit from an expanded view of unburdening. I know from experience that when my managers adhered to a rigid view of the protocol, their anxiety created an obstacle to my clients' ability to unburden in whatever way worked best. Recognizing the validity of all manner of unburdenings—be they spontaneous or built on the foundation of incremental change—has helped my system trust Self-energy, my own as well as the client's.

THREE EXPERIENCES OF UNBURDENING

Here are examples of some different approaches to unburdening that developed naturally from the inner dynamics of my clients. I call the first *spontaneous* because it may emerge, without ritual, any time during therapy as an organic, unguided event. I call the second *unburdening as practice* because creating and maintaining a new Self-led identity can require repetition, especially for clients whose deeply embedded dysfunctional patterns do not release in a single stroke. I call the third, which involves a series of unburdenings, *serial unburdening*. Although serial unburdening is not unique, this case illustrates how my own constrained parts learned to have a broader understanding of this process of release and clearing.

SUSAN'S SPONTANEOUS UNBURDENING

In our first round of work, prior to IFS, we had focused on trauma. Susan, who had begun a new relationship, had come to therapy after her partner commented that she seemed "checked out" during lovemaking. "I was sexually abused by my grandfather," she explained, "and I wonder if this is still affecting me?"

After developing a secure attachment to me, Susan had gotten in touch with her experience of being molested as a young child. Once she had more compassion for herself as a little girl, she questioned her belief that she had been bad and gradually felt less fearful and more present during lovemaking. Since this had been her goal upon entering therapy, we agreed that the treatment was finished and we were not to know for some time that her work was not complete. Her subsequent experience using IFS illustrates how the patience of the client's Self allowed an exiled part to transform in an unexpected way.

Susan Returns

Ten years later Susan called me because her partner had left with another woman. She felt devastated and memories of early trauma had resurfaced. I explained the IFS approach and she agreed to try it. We started with the parts who were flooding her system: a grieving old woman, a critic, a furious firefighter and a hopeless part who believed Susan could never recover. As I held Self-energy in our sessions, Susan's Self emerged and developed relationships with these parts until they finally gave her access to the girl who had been sexually abused. "Can you invite her to be present in whatever way makes her comfortable?" I asked.

There was a long pause. With evident confusion Susan said, "It's hard to describe. I'm not seeing images. She's not showing me what happened. In fact, I'm not sure I can sense her at all."

"How are you feeling toward her right now?"

"Lost."

"You're in touch with a part who feels lost. Can it trust you?"

"I'm asking it to relax back," Susan reported.

"Can you feel a difference in your energy now?"

"The curiosity is coming back, and I feel as caring as I've always felt toward her."

"Let that energy flow to her."

After another long pause, Susan said, "This is different! I'm getting vague feelings, as though she's communicating psychically, not using words or showing me memories like she did before. It's weird."

"Is it okay?"

"There's this impatient manager who's saying that she's not doing it right—he wants her to use words."

"What do you say to him?"

"I'm asking him to trust me. If we let her do things her way it will be faster in the end."

"How does the part respond?"

"He's relaxing. He'll wait and check it out. And now I can feel into this. It's as though she doesn't want to be close. But she's sending messages that I just *know*. I'm getting her experiences, and I have to form them into words on my own."

"Let's see what words come to you."

"Okay. Well, she believed in me and then I left her. That's what I'm getting. It feels like she's letting me know that I left therapy and focused too much on the relationship with George. She started to feel hopeful and then she felt awful," Susan started to cry. "I abandoned her."

"What are you feeling toward her right now?"

"Guilty!"

"What needs to happen?"

"I'm apologizing. She didn't deserve to be treated that way. I was taken over by that relationship and forgot her."

"How does she respond?"

"Hard to tell. I sense she's grateful that I noticed."

"So what needs to happen now?"

"We can continue."

"Let's ask her if your words are accurate. Let her know that she can communicate in any way she wants."

Susan replied, "Well, again it feels like intuition and not too clear, but I believe my words are pretty accurate for her."

"How great that she's letting you know! Is there anything else that's true for her?"

After another long pause, Susan said, "I'm not certain but I get the sense that she still needs help with what happened," she paused. "But now she's gone! All I'm getting is the image of a closed closet door. I'm guessing she's behind the door but I can't be sure."

Fortunately, we both knew better than to push the girl to use words. Although witnessing is regarded as an essential part of unburdening, in this case it seemed that the part needed a kind of silent bystanding. "I can regain her trust by following her lead about repairing our relationship," Susan said. "I have to be patient. She needs my heart energy. I'm beaming it into the closet."

We sat in silence for a few minutes, which can feel like a very long time in a therapy session, but nevertheless felt right to me. Susan eyes were closed and she looked calm. Just to make sure the process was on track, I finally asked, "How's it going?"

"Good," she said. "Oh! Now that manager guy is back. He says we should forget about her. She's a brat who's playing games."

"How do you feel toward him?"

"His bark is worse than his bite. He's just worried. I'm reminding him that if we don't rush we can help everyone. He's willing to let me do that." We sat in silence for another minute. "I feel her again," Susan said. "The door is opening—just microscopically." After another silence she added, "I think that's as far as she'll go today, which is fine. I'm telling her I'm here and I feel patient. She's waited a long time for me. I can wait for her."

It was months before the girl allowed Susan to see her, after which she spent many sessions just gazing at Susan in silence. This drawn-out interaction never involved language. We were open but not attached to the idea that she would one day speak and allow Susan to hear about her pain directly. At this point, Susan was so Self-led that she could stay patiently with the girl and let her choose, without a managerial agenda.

Accepting an Alternative Unburdening

As it happened, the girl never did speak. One day Susan went inside to find her and discovered the closet door wide open. "She's gone!" Susan exclaimed with rising panic. "I can't find her! I even went in the closet and looked around."

"Does it make sense that you have a part who's really upset about this?"

"Yes, I need to breathe and ask the part to relax. Ohhh! It's really upset. It's telling me I've lost her again.

"Taking some breaths is a great idea. Let's help the part calm down so we can be curious about what's happened."

As Susan turned her attention inside, her breathing became more regular. After a while she said, "Okay, I have more room. But the part needs me to look for her. I don't want to lose our connection now." After scanning internally, Susan found the girl playing in the grass with her dog. She looked at Susan from time to time and finally came over to show her a stone. "She seems delighted to be playing," Susan reported. We were silent while Susan watched the girl. Finally, Susan added, "I'm just using intuition to find out what happened and I'm getting that she released her burdens. They're gone."

What had happened? At the time I was surprised to hear that the girl's burdens were gone. My hypothesis now is that she was able to unburden once Susan's patient, consistent, nonjudgmental presence prevailed. I believe the tipping point came when Susan's love felt more present and real than the girl's trauma, so she could finally go out and play. We were surprised and thrilled by her liberation, which proved lasting.

How Susan's Experience Expanded My Thinking

First, the exile in this case communicated nonverbally. Both Susan and I accepted this intuitive communication and silence as valid. We came to realize that, instead of witnessing through images or words, this unburdening required focused and heartfelt bystanding. Second, the release of burdens was organic to the child and unknown to the client until she saw the result of the unburdening. Finally, as with her unburdening process, the girl was the one who invited in the positive elements of play and joy that were her birthright. Neither Susan nor I assisted. So without verbal witnessing, without an unburdening ritual and without an invitation to invite in positive qualities, the girl was liberated and filled with joy. All of which illustrates how exiles who feel connected to the Self and experience their own Self-energy can create their own unburdenings. Thus, as I illustrate throughout the chapter, the protocol guidelines for unburdening can be used as suggestions, but we need not feel any imperative to follow a script. Trusting in the Self is the key.

ALICIA'S SPONTANEOUS UNBURDENING

Alicia, who had retired in her 50s, was now in a marriage that felt like a gift. She and her wife, Sheila, shared many interests, including an array of outdoor sports and a satisfying network of friends. Yet when they tried to negotiate differences, Alicia became angry and argumentative. One part of her was bewildered by this anger while another, a critical manager, disapproved. "Your anger is unacceptable," the critic said to Alicia. "You have a good life! You're being selfish and childish."

I asked, "How are you feeling toward this critic?"

"I'd say it's pretty accurate," she replied, indicating that the part was blended with her.

After we helped it unblend, I said, "Can you ask what it's concerned would happen if it stopped criticizing you?"

"It's afraid my anger would get even more out of control."

"So it doesn't want the angry part to have so much influence over you?"

"That's right."

When there was a sudden death in her wife's family two weeks later, Alicia's critic and her angry part got into an argument in my office. "She wants me to go with her to the memorial for her nephew's wife. But it's a long trip," the angry part complained. "I'm planning to run the Boston Marathon and I'd miss some crucial training if I go. I'm feeling resentful."

"What does the resentful part want you to know?"

"It's telling me this trip would be no fun, and I shouldn't be pushed around by a family I don't even like. It'll be really mad if I do this." Then, before we could question this part any further, the critic jumped in. "But I should go."

"Is this another part?"

"It's my *should* part," Alicia said.

"The one who can be so hard on you?"

"Yes."

"Would it be willing to let you help the angry part first?" I asked. She nodded. "Where do you notice the angry one?"

She took a moment and then pointed to her temple, "I have this huge pressure in my head. It's like my head is going to explode. It's my temper."

"How do you feel toward it?"

"I'm okay. I can do this. I can see the angry part now—it's like the steam coming out of an engine. I'm letting it know that I'm curious. And it's saying, *I don't want to take care of everybody! I just don't want to do things I don't want to do!"* I nodded. "It's showing me a 6-year-old feeding her baby brother, and it's saying, *She worked so hard! She was like Cinderella. No one asked about her feelings. She shouldn't have to do anything that isn't fun ever again!"*

"And what do you say?" I asked.

"I'm asking the angry part if it takes care of this little girl," Alicia said. *"That's my job,* it says. *If I'm not angry, she gets used.* So I'm asking if it will trust me to help the girl," Alicia reported. I expected the angry protector to say yes, after which I thought Alicia would witness the little girl's story and help her unburden. Instead the angry part surprised us both by exclaiming, "Don't leave me! I have a lot of parts who need your help!"

Parts Within Parts

After agreeing to help the angry part's subparts, Alicia said to it, "What do these subparts want me to know?"

In answer, a subpart, appearing as a large red presence, replied, "I'm the leader of the anger system. I have altitude on all this. I can see what's happening and I care about everyone in my group. They've all had to work so hard to help the girl from being used again, and they've taken many blows of criticism and contempt. Will you let me counsel you about their situation?"

"Of course!" Alicia said. "Please tell me."

The Tumble Dryer

In reply, the leader of the anger system said to Alicia, *Things are spinning out of control.*

"Let me just tune in to this," she said to me. "I'll see what I can get." After a few moments she reported, "I got the image of a tumble dryer with many little angry parts spinning and tumbling inside. The leader told me, *Turn off the dryer right now!* So I did, and after they all landed they climbed out. Then they just stood still."

"What do you say to them?" I asked.

"How can I help?"

A representative of the group from the dryer stepped forward and replied internally, *Thank you. We're grateful to have firm ground under our feet. We need to rest. We don't want to return to the past! If the dryer is accidentally turned on again, will you help us?*

"How should I help?" Alicia asked the representative.

The leader of the anger system stepped in again and spoke, *If the dryer starts tumbling again, I will stand behind you, put my right hand on your left shoulder and say, Stop! And you turn the dryer off.*

Alicia nodded, "I'll do exactly as you say."

Also, it went on, *after you turn the dryer off, please drink a glass of cold water and stay with the parts who were tumbling until they feel safe on the ground.*

The pressure in Alicia's head, which had receded during this session, subsided entirely over the next week. In subsequent sessions, the subparts from the dryer set up camp in a lovely meadow far from the dryer, which, they reported, helped them to feel stable. They never spoke about the past, and their trials were never witnessed. They did, however, ask Alicia to help them improve their camp, after which they asked her to remove the dryer entirely. Finally, the leader of the anger system let Alicia know that it was extremely pleased.

The Exile

So far the alliance between Alicia's Self and the leader of the anger system gave all of the anger system subparts a newfound sense of stability and relief. Although both Alicia and I were surprised and a bit disoriented by the whole procedure, our managerial parts didn't take over. When Alicia tried to turn her attention back to the burdened 6-year-old, the leader of the anger system stepped in again with advice. *The girl has been watching*, it said, *and she feels safer knowing that you've helped us. At first she was frightened that we wouldn't protect her anymore, but now she feels you're a force for healing. She's also very close to me, and at some point I would like a chance to talk to her.*

"You're welcome to talk to her whenever you want," Alicia said.

Fine, it replied internally, *I'll wait and you may speak to her now.*

Alicia immediately saw the picture of herself at the age of 6 taking care of her baby brother. She waited. She began to see other images of herself as a child, burdened with responsibilities and deprived of parental protection and warmth. After witnessing this, Alicia asked the girl if she would like to release her burdens but she wasn't ready.

"She's looking around as if someone is missing," Alicia said. "Oh! The leader of the anger system just showed up and it's telling me, *She's missing me. I was her only protector and parent.* Now it's sitting down with her," Alicia reported. "It's saying *You never had a choice about being responsible and you had way too much to handle. Now you can let Alicia decide. She's grown up. And I'll always be here helping.* And now she's going to sleep!" Alicia looked up at me with tears in her eyes. "I can feel her in my heart."

In subsequent sessions, the girl told Alicia that she felt safe and comfortable so she was no longer upset about the neglect and overwork she had endured. But she did ask after her little brother, and Alicia explained that he was now 49 years old and out of harm's way. "She tells me that she loves being in my heart, and she wants me to visit sometimes to read her to sleep," Alicia reported.

How Alicia's Experience Expanded My Thinking

This particular unburdening differed from the protocol I had learned in three important ways. First, Alicia's assertive primary protector stepped in with its own Self-energy, providing important information along with compassionate and clear advice. Second, her exile left the past with no formal retrieval. And third, her exile unburdened without ceremony. All of which helped my managers tolerate these unorthodox variations on what I had been taught, and demonstrated to me the importance of respecting the internal system's wisdom and ability to heal spontaneously.

UNBURDENING AS PRACTICE: LEAH AND HER IDENTIFICATION WITH A PAST NARRATIVE

Leah's experience demonstrates the power of habits of mind and heart to keep a system in stasis and the power of practice to move beyond that stasis. The narrative Leah's protectors repeated to her about her childhood was so narrow and constraining that change was almost impossible. As a result, Leah only came to see me under pressure from her family therapist. She did not understand why she needed therapy, and we began with the only story she had to tell: a constricted story, narrated by a part who explained, "I had a very good childhood. My father was a doctor and money was never a problem. We lived on a lake, and I got to swim and sail as much as I wanted. We didn't have the kinds of problems my kids had. But thank goodness they're over all that now."

From talking to Leah's family therapist, however, I was aware that Leah's husband and two adult children had a very different view and were puzzled by her continuing inability to see the deprivations of her childhood. "So in your vision your childhood was pretty ideal?" I said.

"That's not just my vision—that's how it was," she responded.

It was clear that this protector was blended with her. Yet I was certain that with time other parts, and eventually Leah's Self, would emerge. With the intention of making room for other parts to speak up, I asked, "Would you tell me some memories from your childhood?"

"Well, I remember that Mom would drop me off at the country club swimming pool while she had lunch with the other ladies. I got to swim for almost the whole day," she replied. Then a part who dared make a small complaint added, "I did get sunburned a lot. Sometimes I was really red. My mom was so busy at the club that she gave me a lot of freedom."

"Who took care of that little girl when she was out in the sun too long?"

"Oh, the sunburn went away."

As we slowly began to hear from parts with negative memories, her mini-mizing part invariably cut them off, which irritated one of my managers who wanted things to keep moving. But I grounded myself in Self-energy and practiced respecting all sides: the good childhood minimizing part as well as the complainers who were starting to peep out. As Leah's sys-tem learned to trust my calm patience, more parts with painful memories stepped forward. Here is an example of what emerged.

"I see a little girl," Leah reported one day. "She was lying in bed, listen-ing for her mother to come out of the bathroom. She knew her mother was drunk, and she was afraid her mother was going to kill herself."

"Are you making contact with her?"

"Yes, I can feel how scared she is."

"How do you feel toward her?"

"Someone's telling me she's just making this up to get attention," Leah reported.

"I wonder if that part would tell you what it's worried about?" I asked.

"It says it's just the truth," Leah reported, the minimizer entirely blended with her. Several sessions later Leah said, "I'm seeing the girl at home after school. She's waiting for her older sister to come home. She's really anxious. She's watching her mother who has passed out on the couch, drunk." Barely missing a beat, the minimizer declared, "She's a liar! She makes up stories to entertain you because she knows you're bored. Don't pay attention."

I said, "Now I hear two parts. Do you hear them? There's the one who wants to tell you about the little girl, and there's the one who says she's a liar. Which of these two needs your attention first?"

"It's true that I have a lot of parts who just want attention and make things up," Leah said.

"Should I speak directly to the one who says so?" I asked.

"Okay," Leah said.

"Are you there?" I said.

"Yes."

"What do you do for Leah?"

"I make sure she doesn't get in trouble by whining all the time."

"What kind of trouble would she get into?"

"They'd be mad."

"Really? Then you've had an important job. But do you know that Leah is grown up now and the people who get mad can't hurt her anymore?"

After a long silence, the part said, "I don't think you know what you're talking about."

"Would you like to meet Leah and find out if what I'm saying is true?" I asked.

The minimizer was not ready to meet Leah's Self at this point, and its powerful presence kept Leah's work looping. We continued meeting parts who wanted to eat, drink and exercise to excess, along with some contemptuous managers who criticized them severely. Leah could not connect with any of these parts long enough to quiet their inner turmoil. How did this strong minimizing part get so much power in her system? As our work continued, an unhappy part of Leah reported, "My father was controlling and distant. He made fun of me whenever I cried. He thought feelings were for weak, stupid people and he kept us in line with strict rules. The minimizer sounds a lot like him."

"Can we ask the minimizer what's important about sounding like your father?"

"He says his job is to make me see things Dad's way so I won't get hurt."

"He's very protective, isn't he? He doesn't want you to cry, or feel pain, and he particularly doesn't like it when you offer help to young parts who feel lonely and scared in case they might get too close to you."

"I understand," she said, more unblended from the minimizer than ever before. "He thinks it's dangerous."

Living Into the New: Repeated Retrievals

Although the minimizer continued to press his views as energetically as ever, Leah's Self emerged more consistently, and with a growing understanding of his character and a big dose of patience and persistence, she built a relationship with him. Finally, she let him know that she had decided to make some changes and wanted his agreement. She invited him to join her at her father's deathbed (some years back) where she said, "I hope you understand that my intention is to honor the way my father tried to keep the family together under difficult circumstances. Now that Dad and Mom are gone, Dad doesn't have to keep fighting all the chaos and maybe you'd enjoy relaxing a bit as well. Will you trust me to change the rules now that we're all safe?"

"What do you have in mind?" he asked.

"I plan to retrieve parts who are stuck in the past by revising my father's rules," she said.

"Well I'm glad you finally understand what your father did for you," he replied. "And I'll stand by and watch what you're doing. But I reserve the right to stop you if I think it's getting out of hand."

With this permission, Leah set about challenging her father's unspoken rules. The first step was to make a list. Starting with *No one is allowed to cry*, she asked her system, "Please tell me how you feel about this rule." They replied *It's wimpy and weak to cry*, and *You look ugly when you cry*, and *Other people won't respect you*, and, finally, *If you cry you'll lose control completely.* When they fell silent, she appreciated their experiences and then took them on a field trip to her bedroom. "Now we're going to look in the mirror," she said. "And when we do I'm going to send you all loving kindness." Then she stepped in front of the mirror and after a few moments of sending compassion to her parts, she said, "Can you see me? I'm 58 years old. I'm a grown-up and I can take care of all of us. I will make sure you're safe and I will love you. You have a home with me." Then she took them on a tour of her house and described her adult life. "Now," she said finally, "I propose that we sit down together and rewrite this rule so it makes sense for us."

They agreed and within a few minutes *No one is allowed to cry* became *It's safe to cry when something makes you sad.* In the same way the next rule on her list was transformed from *Never ask for help* to *Help will be available if you ask for it.* During this process (there were 12 rules!) Leah took as many days with each rule as her parts needed, and she would only move from one to the next when she was sure that all parts who had been attached to a particular rule were oriented to the present. She continued until every rule had been revised and her whole system was oriented away from her father in the past and toward her Self in the here and now.

Here is an example of Leah's work with an exile at home in one of her independent sessions of retrieval and reorientation. Leah described connecting with the girl who lay awake, terrified that her mother would die in the bathtub. "I was working with a group of protectors who were involved with the rule about no one being allowed to cry. After our time at the mirror and our trip around the house, the protectors were softening the prohibition against crying. One of them said that he wanted to make it safe to cry. As he was saying that, a little girl emerged with tears in her eyes. She said she was scared that her mom would die in the bathtub and that the door to the bathroom was locked. She was very scared, but she was aware of who I was. I told her *Your mom is living in heaven now. She asked me to take care of you from now on, and I will.* The little girl needed to go see the bathtub to make sure her mom was no longer there. She asked me several more times if her mom was really okay, and then she relaxed and wanted to know where her new bed was. I picked her up and took her to my meditation room. It's a place where other parts go sometimes to take comfort. She just curled up on the couch and went to sleep. The part who had wanted to make it safe to cry felt relieved and pleased that she could now cry and be comforted."

Like this one, some unburdenings happened at Leah's home; a few happened in my office. In both cases we were open to whatever emerged. Leah continued to check with her unburdened exiles. Anticipating that her protectors would bring back old habits when they felt she was under pressure, Leah continued to remind them that the new rules were safe.

How Leah's Experience Expanded My Thinking

Leah's way of unburdening illustrates that practicing new habits of mind and heart is sometimes necessary to counteract the stasis created by the constraining narrative of a powerful protective part. Leah herself created a ritual of retrieval and reorientation. She collaborated with her parts to co-create new versions of the old rules imposed by her father. With daily practice, her parts were able to let go of long-held harsh beliefs, develop positive meanings in their place and create a safe environment in which exiles could emerge and spontaneously unburden. These unburdenings often happened outside the office. As with other unburdenings described in this chapter, Leah's Self found what was right for her system.

EXPANDING MY PERSPECTIVE: BETH'S
SERIAL UNBURDENINGS

I treated Beth before I'd had the advantage of working with the clients described earlier who also served as my teachers. At the time, I expected complete healing once all the steps of an unburdening protocol were accomplished. So in Beth's case, after we unburdened one cluster of parts (an exile and its protectors), we considered the work complete. When reality proved different, some of my parts felt very upset, which prevented me from appreciating the positive changes that had already occurred for Beth. Her story demonstrates how I learned to let go of managerial expectations and become more Self-led.

Beth had a history of sexual, physical and emotional abuse by her father, and spoke of her mother as weak and unable to offer any protection. Despite this dangerous childhood, Beth had a stoic protector who kept her traumatic history at bay and helped her go to college, develop a career and marry. She only sought therapy when problems developed in the last two. She described the way in which her elderly husband had become depressed while she was being marginalized and sexually harassed at work. Despite her stoic protector's advice to *buck up*, she realized she was feeling overwhelmed and was getting depressed as well.

In therapy, Beth discovered that her depressed part was trying to keep her connected to her husband. *If she has an active life away from him, she'll be completely alone in the world. So I help her join him to watch television in silence. That's all she can do*, the part explained. Eventually Beth was able to access the little girl who had felt so desperately unloved and alone throughout her childhood and unburden her. After this successful unburdening, she began to feel strong and competent again. She ended her marriage on

friendly terms, began a new relationship and orchestrated an internal trans-
fer within her company. With the little girl unburdened and many protectors released from extreme roles, we agreed to bring our work to a close.

An Unexpected Return

I was surprised therefore when Beth called eight months later urgently
wanting an appointment. Although she was happily remarried, her new
husband's father was a bully. He intimidated his family and Beth found
him intensely distressing. She also noted that some of her more powerful protectors were back, especially an angry part who caused her to feel
enraged with waiters, store clerks and on the road with other drivers.
Because the same protectors were present, I hypothesized that the same
exile needed more help. So I sadly concluded that her exile was still
burdened by the trauma with her abusive father, and my inner critics
berated me for having been so pleased for having assumed that her work
was done.

As I listened to Beth, however, a new picture began to emerge. Instead of
having memories of her father, she was now seeing images of her mother—
previously described as weak and ineffectual—who now appeared cold,
indifferent and randomly sadistic, meting out physical and emotional abuse
without compunction. "I feel this weakness in my core," Beth said. "It's a
young child. It's like all her blood has been drained out, and she feels completely helpless, unable to move."

In retrospect, it is clear that Beth was experiencing a different exile,
triggered by different stressors, but at the time my system was in a state
of confusion, still oriented to the previous successful completion of our
work. Now my managers who had been so proudly basking in the golden
glow of success gave way to a shaming part who accused me of being
naive and incompetent. To be useful to Beth, I needed to help them
unblend. Although my protectors didn't want me to talk to colleagues
about the case, I challenged their urge to hide, spoke to my peer supervision group and helped my critics relax so that I could work with my
shamed exile.

In the inner calm that followed, I could see and honor how much Beth
had accomplished and I was now free to be of help. As we worked, I was
happy to hear that Beth's system was responding differently than mine. She
was not discounting her previous transformation, and she reported that
the former exile was still unburdened. Our first round of therapy had laid a
solid foundation of trust between Beth's Self and her parts, which provided
the support her system needed for healing the new exile who had emerged
from new stressors.

How Beth's Experience Expanded My Perspective

The unburdenings in this case were not different from other protocol unburdenings. However, their serial nature revealed some rigid expectations in my managerial system. I was reminded that although a treatment may seem complete after an unburdening, the inner experience of trauma survivors is often layered. If unseen exiles exist, they will find the opportunity to emerge later. When Beth returned, urgently asking for more help, my pride and pleasure at the dramatic positive changes at the end of our last therapy set me up for managerial dismay and inner shaming. Once I had done my own inner work, I could be present with Beth for another round of witnessing and unburdening.

CONCLUSION

A typical unburdening in IFS involves a ritual of transformation. The cases in this chapter illustrate how unburdenings can happen at any time and in various ways during treatment. The clients I've described gave me the opportunity to accompany them as their Self-energy generated its own unique options for unburdenings. Several of these were unguided and spontaneous, another was a product of practice and yet another took place sequentially as the stages of a trauma treatment unfolded according to the wisdom and timing of the client's internal system. In all cases, when I was open to their creativity, had self-compassion and took care of my exiles, I learned new ways of unburdening and was myself transformed.

REFERENCES

Engler, J. (2013). An introduction to IFS. In M. Sweezy & E. L. Ziskind (Eds.) *Internal family systems therapy: New dimensions* (pp. xvii–xxvii). New York: Routledge.

Schwartz, R. C. (1995). *Internal family systems therapy.* New York: Guilford.

Schwartz, R. C. (2001). *Introduction to the internal family systems model.* Oak Park, IL: Trailheads Publications.

Chapter 10

Legacy Burdens

Ann L. Sinko

With case material from Kay Gardener

INTRODUCTION

Some families talk about their history while others neglect or hide it. In either case our forebears' lessons regarding safety and survival are conveyed verbally and nonverbally, consciously and unconsciously down the generations. These transmissions may be positive, creating connection and resilience in a family, or they may be limiting and constraining. I routinely expand on the usual internal family systems (IFS) work of unburdening clients by focusing on *legacy burdens*, the intergenerational transmission of constraining, negative feelings and beliefs. In my experience, IFS is equally effective at healing the burdens we develop through personal experience and burdens we inherit.[1]

THE ROOTS OF THE CONCEPT OF
UNBURDENING: SHAMANISM

No description of the IFS approach to legacy burdens would be complete without reference to Shamanism, the spiritual discipline from which the IFS concept of unburdening hails. All spiritual traditions make some mention of the unresolved and unforgiven that elders bestow upon their children. Shamans use the metaphor of energetic cords to describe this phenomenon (Drake, 2003). In my experience it's not uncommon for clients to describe their legacy burden as a cord that connects them with their ancestors. Some ancestral cords are strong, loving and clear while others (legacy burdens) are negative. Some of these ancestral cords are attached to outside energies like oppressive religious institutions, immigration trauma, slavery, genocide or any form of oppression based on difference (racism, patriarchy, homophobia, etc.). I think of the latter as cultural legacy burdens.

CHAPTER OVERVIEW

In this chapter, I illustrate some of the many ways in which legacy burdens are transmitted between generations, including keeping secrets, shaming, enforcing the family code of behavior with threats or rewards and exploiting a child's fears of abandonment and bonds of loyalty. At the same time, I illustrate how we can help clients identify, explore and release legacy burdens. If we include legacy unburdening in our treatment paradigm, know what to look for and ask the right questions, legacy burdens are easily identified and easily unburdened. Along the way, I hope to inspire readers to try this simple and effective technique. For an illustration of how to unburden a legacy burden, see Table 10.4.

BURDENS

IFS posits that people possess what they need to lead balanced, harmonious lives but, when we are constrained by burdens, these resources get blocked. Burdens are typically created under a couple of circumstances: First, catastrophic events that threaten survival are often burdening, particularly if no comfort is at hand inside or out to soften the experience; second and more commonly, when a person feels judged and devalued the stage is also set for burdening. Shaming judgments can be about anything, but typically they focus on a person's physical or psychological characteristics, feelings, beliefs, behaviors, ethnicity, race or culture. In short, a devaluing or life-threatening event that generates overwhelming feelings and negative beliefs can devolve into a burden.

LEGACY BURDENS

In my opinion everyone is subject to legacy burdens, but the dynamics and resources of any given family help either to mitigate or increase the likelihood that burdens will be transmitted between generations. Many legacy burdens develop directly through parent–child interactions. I call these *overt legacy burdens*. Other legacy burdens are absorbed indirectly through a family's emotional process. I call these *covert legacy burdens*. Overt legacy burdening develops in parent–child relationships because children naturally copy and comply with the wishes of their parents. When the protective part of a parent rejects or encourages other parts internally and then rejects or encourages similar parts in the child, an overt legacy burden is created.

Covert legacy burdening is created by contagion because we are all capable of having feelings and absorbing beliefs when we have no knowledge of their origins and because children are highly susceptible to the feelings and beliefs of their parents. I think of covert legacy burdens as free floating, energetic in nature, often experienced physiologically as anxiety, fear and shame—feelings that have become disconnected from a story. When we have no story to give a feeling relational meaning, we're at greater risk of viewing ourselves as physically, morally or psychologically defective. When a client reports that her whole family (*my mother, father, sister and brother all have anxiety*) struggles with a particularly challenging feeling, it may be genetics or a covert legacy burden or, most likely, some combination.

HOW TO IDENTIFY LEGACY BURDENS

Over the years I've noticed that certain statements point toward a legacy burden (see Tables 10.1 and 10.2), and once we hear one of these statements we can ask about legacy burdens. The good news is that we can trust the client's parts to know how much of a feeling or belief belongs to someone other than the client. The questions I ask to ferret out a legacy burden focus on when the problem developed, how much sense it makes to the client, whether there is a discrepancy between the severity of a symptom and the client's personal experiences and whether the client experiences an internal or external source for the energy that drives her feelings.

Table 10.1 *Client Statements That Indicate a Possible Legacy Burden*

- *My mother* (father, grandmother, etc.) *had this too.*
- *It's always been with me.*
- *I will be bad, if I don't . . .* (caretake, accommodate, be nice, follow the rules, etc.)
- *It's unsafe to shine.*
- *I always knew it wouldn't be okay for me to get too big for my britches.*

Table 10.2 *Questions to Ask to Identify a Legacy Burden*

- Does the severity of your symptom fit with your life experiences?
- Do your symptoms make sense to you?
- Do you feel like this energy belongs to you and you alone?
- When did you start to believe this? (If the answer is *always*, keep an ear out for a legacy burden.)

HOW LEGACY BURDENS GET REINFORCED

Events and behavior do not cause shame. Rather, that which is acceptable to one person, family, generation or culture may be entirely unacceptable to another. Nevertheless, sex and sexuality, substance abuse and mental illness are all topics that frequently summon shame and encourage secrecy. Parts who are marked as shameful are exiled internally, while anything that is stigmatized culturally (either in the culture at large or in the family) is exiled externally. As the literature on addiction spells out (Black, 1981; Wegscheider-Cruse, 1981; Elkin, 1984; O'Farrell, 1993; Brown & Lewis, 1999; Anonymous, 2006), a family that is replete with substance abuse is caught in an intergenerational chicken and egg cycle, with shame encouraging secret keeping and secrets generating shame.

Alcoholism is a clear illustration of the role of secrecy and shame in legacy burdens. At 54, Holly sought treatment with me for anxiety and plaguing urges to drink. She had been in active recovery from alcoholism for 5 years and was discouraged that she wasn't feeling better despite continued abstinence, ongoing involvement in a 12-step program and *things going pretty well in my life right now.* She described her anxiety, which had always been with her, as free floating and constant. She had difficulty identifying her feelings and described her whole family as *vibrating* with intense anxiety. As a result, the only safe topic of conversation at family events was the weather.

Holly described her deceased father as a *functional, mean drunk* (he and several of his siblings had died of sclerosis of the liver), her mother as *ineffectual and cold* and her two siblings as substance abusers with long psychiatric histories. She knew very little family history and had no contact with any extended family. In childhood she had been told that her maternal grandmother had died before she was born, but in her 40s she learned that her grandmother had actually died recently in a state psychiatric hospital.

Holly's story is full of symptoms and behaviors that hint loudly at legacy burdens. Her family illustrates Imber-Black's (1993) rules of shame (see Table 10.3). A family's unconscious adherence to these rules can maintain a burden of shame through generations. In IFS, we think of these rules as the edicts of *managers,* or protective parts who cling to the status quo and work hard to banish the unruly feelings of exiles.

I began by talking with Holly about shame and the process of family secret keeping. She was enormously relieved at the idea that much of her anxiety could stem from her family's way of coping with unresolved trauma up the generational line. "In my 12-step program," she said, "we say *you're only as sick as your secrets.* But even though I like what you say, I'm also noticing that I have a part who feels disloyal and concerned that my family will be mad at me if I really get sober. If I want to recover, I guess I'm going to have to break some family rules."

Table 10.3 Rules of Shame

Adapted from Evan Imber-Black's 8 Rules of Shame from *Secrets in Families and Family Therapy* (1993, p. 37).

1. Control: be in control of all behaviors and interactions.
2. Perfection: always be "right," do the "right" thing.
3. Blame: if something does not happen as you plan, blame (self or others).
4. Denial: deny feelings, especially negative or vulnerable ones like anxiety, fear, grief, need, loneliness.
5. Unreliability: do not expect reliability or constancy in relationships. Watch for the unpredictable.
6. Incompleteness: don't bring transactions to resolution or completion because you might have to face the feelings and honest revelations you're protecting against.
7. No talk: don't talk openly and directly about shameful, abusive or compulsive behaviors.
8. Disqualifications: when disrespectful, shameful, abusive, or compulsive behavior occurs, disqualify it, deny it, or disguise it.

This statement signaled to me that we were now ready to begin working with Holly's inherited anxiety directly. Legacy burdens, which parents transmit to their children consciously and unconsciously, are reinforced by binding but invisible loyalties (Boszormenyi-Nagy & Spark, 1973; Hellinger, 2011) of the kind that Holly cited. Fearing banishment if family rules are broken, children learn to comply with secret keeping. When unspoken rules are held in place by loyalty and fear, they generally can't be understood or challenged until they're made explicit, so they can remain obscure and unchallenged for generations.

WITNESSING AND LEGACY BURDENS

Because protective parts cannot distinguish between burdens and legacy burdens, they respond to both in the same way. However, therapists can and should distinguish between them for a number of reasons, primarily because legacy burdens are (most often) easier to unburden than personal burdens. Although *witnessing* exiles is key to healing in IFS, once a legacy burden has been identified as belonging to someone else, protectors are usually eager to let it go. So we ask whether any exile or ancestor wants to be witnessed, and if not we move on to unburdening. If, however, the answer is yes, then we add witnessing in to the mix.

ATTEND TO LEGACY BURDENS BEFORE
PERSONAL BURDENS: AMANDA

My work with Amanda illustrates how I work with legacy burdens before turning to the client's personal burdens. Amanda was a licensed marriage and family therapist who sought me out for consultation when she was feeling unsuccessful in her work with couples. After identifying a part who got frustrated when progress seemed slow or absent with a couple, she noticed that she had a polarization between a caretaking part and a problem solving part. Whenever they sensed her frustration, these parts would vie for floor time and dominate her consciousness.

"The problem solver," she reported, "believes his way is the best strategy and he's really good at it. He says if problems don't get solved things will get worse so he needs to continue."

"What does he mean by *things will get worse?*" I asked.

"He means the caretaker would start in."

"And then what would happen?" I asked.

"I would be ineffectual and helpless. Oh I see! The problem solver is my father and the caretaker is my mother. My father really wanted me to be self-reliant and practical. If I expressed concern about someone else, this contemptuous look would come over his face and he would give me the silent treatment. That's because I was acting like my mother. She always focuses on the needs of other people. She does it in this very sweet way, but really she is super controlling because she can't tolerate conflict. And my father can't tolerate being controlled. So, ha ha, they were—are—in conflict all the time."

"So your problem solving part doesn't want the caretaker getting involved?"

"Yes."

"Ask them who they protect."

After a moment of listening, Amanda said, "Worthlessness."

"Let's try something. Here is a piece of paper. I want you to draw a circle that represents all the worthlessness you feel. Now without thinking—just allow your hand to decide—draw the pie piece that represents the inherited portion of your worthlessness."[2]

Amanda quickly drew a line straight down the middle of the circle and nodded, "Fifty, fifty."

"So your burden of worthlessness is 50 percent inherited and 50 percent from your life experience," I said.

"Yeah," Amanda said. "Why do I need it?"

"You don't need it," I said. "And you can send back what isn't yours. But first let's ask your parts if they would have any concerns about unloading it."

If any part is fearful about some aspect of the unburdening process, we address it prior to initiating the healing steps. Does any part believe the client needs the inherited burden? If no, continue. If yes, ask *What would happen if the burden were gone?* Although protectors are usually eager to let a legacy burden go, they do have three common fears. The first concerns disloyalty, the second identity and the third disconnection, which are all easily addressed.

After consulting the problem solving and caretaking parts to be sure they understood that half of Amanda's burden of worthlessness had been created before their time, they were eager to let it go. "And after that," I said, "we can tend to your parts who carry the other half of this worthlessness. Shall we start? Let's invite the highest positive potential of your mother and father to join our process, along with the highest positive potential of any ancestors, known or unknown, who share this burden."

"What does that mean?" Amanda asked.

"If they were able to be at their best, being the people they would have been had they been less burdened and more able to have self-compassion and feel confident—that's their highest positive potential," I said. When we ask for the highest positive potential of ancestors, we are essentially asserting that the person had a Self upon whom we can now call (Michi Rose, personal communication, 2002).

Since we need Self-energy for unburdening, we must address the fears and concerns of reluctant parts. Some clients report difficulty or disbelief about inviting ancestors to participate, or thinking they might have positive potential, in which case I say it's fine just to imagine the ancestor's Self or highest positive potential. On the other hand, some clients simply have parts who aren't interested in any interaction with ancestors, in which case the legacy can be unburdened in the traditional way to one of the elements. Although I prefer working with the ancestral line, many IFS therapists proceed through legacy unburdenings with little or no direct work with ancestors. I encourage you to try both approaches.

"I'll ask them to participate in their highest possible state," Amanda said.

"Let me know when they're here."

"Okay, I see my mother, my father, my grandparents, and some other people I don't know."

"How do you feel toward them?"

"I feel kind of mad at my parents. But I also have some compassion for them now that I know they have this same worthless feeling. They've been so unhappy. It's powerful to see how far back this goes."

"Would you like to invite your daughters to unburden, too?"

"Absolutely! I'm sure they haven't escaped the curse." By including the client's children (as Barb Cargill taught me to do[3]), we can clear the burden from the whole generational line. Parents are usually eager to unburden their children, who don't need any direct involvement. In my experience, when the parent lets the burden go and also consciously releases the child from responsibility, both parties benefit. "Let me know when your daughters are here. Now invite them, if they feel ready, to take the inherited burden of worthlessness out of their bodies and give it to back to you. When that's complete, take the burden out of your body and give it back to your parents."

"But I don't want them to have any more hardship! They've suffered enough," Amanda said suddenly. Then she added, "I'm afraid of losing my only connection to my father."

"You know because this is their burden you won't be adding anything to it by giving it back to them. You're just returning the burden to its source. Then we'll invite your parents to do the same thing."

Although I could have gone on to reassure her concerned parts that authentic heart connections blossom once burdens are released, I find reassurance from the horse's mouth to be most effective, so when the fear of disloyalty comes up I invite the ancestor in question to address the client's concern directly. If the ancestor's Self, or highest positive potential, is present the answer will be in the best interest of the client.

"So ask your parents if it's okay for you to pass this burden of worthlessness back to them," I said.

Amanda started to weep. "They're nodding," she reported, "and I feel so close to my father."

"Ready then? Take the burden out of your body and give it to your parents. Now invite them to do the same and let the burden pass all the way back. Tell me when it reaches the end of the line."

"Wait a minute! I have a part who thinks if I give this burden up I won't know who I am."

When a burden is about to be released, protective parts often interrupt. In which case we shift our attention to the concerned part until it feels reassured and willing to let us proceed. "I'd like to reassure your worried part that you'll feel more confident and more yourself without the burden. But since seeing is believing, ask if it would be willing to try an experiment in which you release one drop of the burden at a time so it can check at each interval to see if you feel more like yourself or less like yourself."[4]

"Okay." Amanda was silent for a few moments and then said, "After releasing about six drops the part could see me more clearly and it relaxed."

"Great. Is it okay to continue?" Amanda nodded. "Then let's start with your children giving the legacy burden back to you. You pass it to your parents and then it keeps going until the end of the generational line."

Amanda was quiet for a couple of minutes before saying, "I saw my girls take this gooey gunk out of their bodies and give it to me. I took it happily, it was mine and I didn't want them to have it. So then I did the same thing and the gunk went up the line. It went back many generations. No one even needed words! Everyone just smiled and nodded as they passed it back."

"How do you want the ancestor at the top of the line to unload the gunk?" I asked, letting Amanda be the director.

"I want to bury it."

"Before your ancestor does that, let's honor, in whatever way makes sense to you, the hardships that created this burden." After a long silence Amanda described seeing scenes of people in indentured servitude, impoverished and starving. While my suggestion led to Amanda witnessing some of her ancestors, things could also have gone in a different direction. I had no particular expectations. "Ask your ancestors if they have more to show you," I said.

"No that's all."

"Okay. When you're ready, invite your ancestors to bury the burden and let me know when they're finished."

"Done," she said after a few more moments. "We all gathered together and buried it under a massive oak tree and marked the spot with a headstone to honor the struggles of generations."

"And now you can invite the qualities that got pushed out by worthlessness to come back in."

"Love and self-confidence!" Amanda said.

"Invite love and self-confidence to come into the ancestor at the top of the line and ask that person to pass them down all the way to you. Then you can pass them on to your daughters. Let me know when that's complete."

Amanda was very still and deeply attentive to what was going on inside. "Done," she said after a few minutes.

"How's everyone?"

"More relaxed."

"Great. Thank them all for showing up."

"Yeah, they're thanking me too!"

Before ending the session, we checked back with her problem solving and caretaking parts to be sure they had witnessed the legacy unburdening. They both reported some relief and were ready to change even though Amanda had more to unburden personally. The problem solver wanted to be creative while the caretaker wanted to take a vacation and focus on self-care. After agreeing to these suggestions, Amanda asked around inside about the 50 percent of worthlessness that was personal and a part who felt unloved by her parents appeared. This young exile believed she was doomed because she couldn't live up to each parent's expectations. Since we were out of time, Amanda made a commitment to return to her.

Although Amanda had not yet unburdened her exile, she reported after this session that she felt more present in her work, better able to tolerate anxiety in her clients and more curious and compassionate when working with difficult couples. She also noticed that she was no longer inclined to problem solve for anyone, clients or family.

As we see, Amanda unknowingly revealed a legacy burden when she noticed that her caretaker and problem solving parts sounded like her parents. We used the circle drawing to see how much of her burden was a legacy and then checked for concerns about unloading it. After addressing her parts' concerns, we invited her ancestors and children to participate and we checked on their Self-energy. When we had a critical mass of Self in all participants, Amanda was ready to let go of the legacy burden and clear the generational line. When we returned to her protectors at the end, they said unburdening the 50 percent that was legacy gave them enough relief to take on new roles. Finally, we made a commitment to return to Amanda's exile who was burdened with her own sense of worthlessness.

NO NEED TO WITNESS: MEG'S EXPERIENCE
WITH INHERITED SHAME

When stories are lost due to shaming and secret keeping, what remains is the habitual stifling behavior of protective parts. Silenced experience is encrypted and passed down through generations until "the unspeakable becomes unthinkable, because it can no longer be represented; it becomes a 'ghost' that haunts a person who shows unexplainable symptoms, hinting at a secret a parent unknowingly projected" (Schutzenberger, 1998, p. 144). The more the event in the previous generation was perceived as shameful, the more likely it is to be shrouded in secrecy, and the more likely the story of the burdening will be unknown, unrecoverable, vague or (like the game "telephone") significantly distorted. In contrast, families with healthy boundaries are less likely to transmit legacy burdens because they have open communication and a habit of sharing family history in stories that include both failure and success.

Meg, a 40-year-old married woman, came to see me (Kay Gardener) because she had never enjoyed sex with her husband. Instead, a part kept telling her that if she enjoyed sex she would be a shameful slut. When she did have sex, instead of being present and feeling intimate with her husband, she thought about chores, laundry, the kids and other mundane details of her life. Since she had been exposed to feminism, had taken a class on female sexuality and had open-minded friends, she couldn't understand why sexual encounters had always felt shameful to her.

I learned that her family was Irish Catholic and sex had never been discussed at home; there was no hint that her parents were sexual with each other or that she and her seven siblings would develop sexual lives after puberty. We proceeded to explore parts who had negative feelings and beliefs about sex. Meg found and unburdened exiles who felt ashamed about her premarital sex and masturbation. But her experiences did not strike me as having felt shameful enough to explain her phobic response to sex.

"Any chance this fearful energy belongs to someone else?" I asked.

Without hesitating, Meg replied, "I inherited it from my mother, my grandmother, my great grandmother, and many generations of women before them. I just grew up swimming in this water."

This type of response is not uncommon from clients when we begin to explore the possibility of a legacy burden. We are looking for symptoms that persist after repeated unburdenings, and beliefs that appear to be immutable. Given her answer, I knew we were on the right track. When unburdening a legacy takes more than one session, we can set an intention to return to the process and ask the client what might be helpful between sessions. If the client is inclined, releasing legacies can also involve family-of-origin work (Schutzenberger, 1998), visiting meaningful historical places and collecting external confirmation of ancestral experience.

"Would you be willing to bring this up with your mother?" I asked.

Meg closed her eyes and wrapped her arms around her shoulders. "I actually started to shake when you said that," she said. "I don't know if I have the courage."

After several weeks of working with the parts who were afraid, Meg did find the courage to speak to her mother, who was more open than she had expected. Her mother agreed that Meg's dislike of sex was not her burden alone. "She actually laughed when I asked her if she thought sex was a problem for the women in our family, which kind of surprised me," Meg reported. "It was a sad laugh. She said she had never known a time when she didn't feel sex was dirty, bad and shameful, and she was always afraid of having sex with my father, though she did care about him. She was sure that her mother felt the same way."

"How did you feel when you heard that?"

"I was relieved. I have no reason to feel this way. Yet it's so strong! Now it makes sense."

"Is it okay to find the part in your body who feels this inherited fear?"

"It's here," she said, putting her hand over her pelvic area.

"And where in your body does it connect to your mother?" I asked.

"Same place," she said.

"Shall we go all the way up through the women of your family?" I asked. She nodded. "Imagine your grandmother standing behind your mother and notice where this fear hooks back to her," I said.

"Same place," she said again.

"Okay. Let's line up the women from your family as far back as the generations need to go," I said.

"I see several generations," she said. "They all have the same burden in the same place on their bodies and we're all connected by a thick cord. The burden feels really heavy and dark in my pelvis."

"Ask if they need to show you anything?" I said. When dealing with a legacy burden we can simply ask the client's system if witnessing is needed. The answer ranges from *no need* to *yes please*, which can mean either brief or expansive witnessing. In Meg's case no witnessing was required, and Meg shook her head. So I continued, "Okay, now I want you to imagine a healing force in back of all of these women—it can be anything your system wants to use."

"Light?"

"Certainly. Light is good."

"A bright golden light," Meg said. "It's in back of the whole line, as if the sky is bright gold."

"Now gather all your inherited shame about sexuality and pass it to your mother."

"It's like a shadow stone—it's heavy but has no substance."

"Did you give it to her?" Meg nodded. "Okay now have your mother gather all her shame, add it to yours and pass it back to her mother," I said. "She can tell her mother to do the same. Let it go all the way back so the last mother can hand it off to a healing place."

"They want to know what kind of healing place?"

"They can decide."

"They want it to be transformed in a clear, cold lake on a mountaintop."

"Good. The clear, cold lake on the mountaintop will transform their shame into joy and pleasure to be passed back all the way down to you and your daughter, so everyone can experience sexuality and the body in a new way," I said.

"They're dancing and laughing!" Meg reported.

"Please thank your parts and your ancestors for allowing us to honor and help them," I said.

"They're smiling and bowing to you," Meg said.

"Now, what does the part of you who was burdened need?" I asked.

"She wants to try it out," Meg said, a little sheepishly.

"Of course!" I smiled.

A few weeks later Meg reported back on the impact of our work. "It's fun, I feel . . . well, more alive on many fronts. And so much closer to my husband! But I also feel sad. I think about all those years of fear. It was like living in a box underground and not being able to move. My husband and I watched *Philomena* and the *Magdalene Laundries* and even right now I could weep. All those girls punished, tormented and humiliated. I think of everything we missed."

Meg's work illustrates how illuminating and validating it can be for clients to talk with family members about their legacy burdens, though we may need to work with fearful parts first. We can also look at the social and political climate of our ancestors' homeland in various ways, including by subtracting 50 years per generation from the current date and googling what was happening during each ancestor's lifespan.

Table 10.4 *In Sum: Steps for Unburdening a Legacy Burden by Ann Sinko*

Beginning:

1. Identify the legacy burden (or the percentage of the burden that is legacy).
2. Ask the client's parts if they would like to unload the legacy burden.
   a. Ask the parts if they have any reason to hold onto this burden.
3. Address any fears or concerns about unloading the legacy burden.

Preparation for unburdening:

1. Ask the client to invite the Self or the highest positive potential of the parent(s) in along with any and all ancestors, known or unknown, who also carry this burden.
   a. Siblings and other family relations can also be invited to participate and unburden if they are ready.
2. Check with the client for activated parts and help them to unblend, if needed.
   a. How does the client feel toward the parent(s) and ancestors?
3. Ask if any part needs witnessing? Are there any stories, feelings, et cetera that need to be fully seen and understood?
   a. Witnessing is possible at any time during this process.

Unburdening:

1. Ask the client to take the legacy burden out of her or his body and pass it back to the parent from whom it was inherited.
   b. Parts are often hesitant about this request because they do not want to hurt/burden the parent. Let them know that this burden belongs to the parent and will be returning to its source. Then reassure them that the next step is to invite the parent/ancestor to pass the burden back as far as it needs to go.
   c. Or, ask the ancestors to address client's concern about passing the burden back.
4. Invite each ancestor to take the burden out of the body and pass it back.
5. Ask the client to have the ancestor continue this process and let you know when the burden reaches the end of the generational line.
6. Ask the client how the ancestor at the end of the line should release the burden.
   a. Have the ancestor release the burden.

The invitation:

1. Ask the client what qualities he or she would like to invite in now that the legacy burden has been released.
   b. Have the ancestor at the end of the line take in the qualities and pass them forward down the generational line to the client.
7. Check to see how everyone is doing.
8. Ask if anything else needs to happen.

Integration:

9. Invite all parts to notice and be updated about the legacy unburdening.
10. Thank all ancestors and parts.

Note: If the client has children who carry the legacy burden as well, invite the child's Self to participate at the beginning along with the ancestors. If the children are ready, they can unburden what they inherited and the process of passing the burden back begins with them. After the unburdening, when the qualities are being passed back down the generational line, the client passes the new qualities down to the children as well.

CONCLUSION

Legacy burdens involve family values, rules and loyalties. They are transmitted in patterned interactions within the family and larger culture and often involve prejudice about various kinds of differences: being different in any way from the family norm or the dominant culture or being made to feel inferior due to gender, body weight, sexual orientation, race or culture. The implicit contracts we make with our parents govern everything from how we eat to how we respond to death (McGoldrick, 1982). When a contract is age appropriate and the family system has good leadership, it provides helpful role expectations and structure. But all members are at risk when the family lacks the balancing effect of compassionate leadership. Under these circumstances, children simply accept burdens in order to survive.

In my opinion, few if any of us escape burdening. We take on personal burdens from many sources, anywhere from apparently ordinary misattunements in childhood that affect our sense of self-worth deeply to overwhelming life circumstances. Legacy burdens are much the same but are inherited. They come from our families, our cultures and our catastrophes. Our parents pass burdens that originated with their forebears down to us in the form of feelings, beliefs, energy, symptoms and behaviors. When psychic or physical demands outweigh resources, modes of adaptation grow more extreme, and generations can become more and more polarized, inside and out. Loyalty to various modes of protection will lock burdens in place, organizing everything, including our choice of profession, mate, level of survival guilt (can we be happier or more successful than our parents?), separation guilt (can we be independent of our family?), self-care, health and way of dying. In IFS we do not pathologize these efforts. We see all dysfunctional behavior as an attempt to adapt and cope. And though we honor the attempt, we do not feel constrained to live with the outcome. Instead, IFS offers strategies for releasing all burdens, even burdens that hail from an unknown past.

NOTES

1. Systemic family therapy, which has long focused on the multi-generational nature of human problems, and Shamanism, which has long focused on the transmission of energy, have both had a major influence on the concept of legacy burdens in IFS.
2. I learned this technique from Michi Rose, a biologist who later became a therapist and trained in Shamanism as well as energy healing. Michi also incorporated unburdening, a crucial step for healing in IFS, into the IFS model.
3. Barb Cargill is a senior IFS trainer and yoga and dance teacher. She has made major contributions in training IFS therapists to work with legacy and cultural burdens.
4. I thank Michi Rose for this *One Drop* technique and Michael Elkin for his *Advanced Unblending Techniques* for working with unburdening.

REFERENCES

Anonymous. (2006). *Adult children of alcoholics fellowship text.* Torrance, CA: Adult Children of Alcoholics World Health Organization.

Black, C. (1981). *It will never happen to me.* New York: Random House.

Boszormenyi-Nagy, I., & Spark, G. M. (1973). *Invisible loyalties: Reciprocity in intergenerational family therapy.* New York: Harper & Row.

Brown, S., & Lewis, V. M. (1999). *The alcoholic family in recovery: A developmental model.* New York: Guilford Press

Drake, A. (2003). *Healing of the soul: Shamanism and psyche.* Ithaca, NY: Busca.

Elkin, M. (1984). *Families under the influence: Changing alcoholic patterns.* New York: Norton.

Hellinger, B. (2011). *Laws of healing; Getting well, staying well.* Bischofswiesen, Germany: Hellinger Publications.

Imber-Black, E. (1993). *Secrets in family therapy.* New York: Norton.

McGoldrick, M. (1982). *Ethnicity and family therapy.* Needham Heights, MA: Allyn & Bacon.

O'Farrell, T. (1993). *Treating alcohol problems: Marital and family interventions.* New York: The Guilford Press

Schutzenberger, A. A. (1998). *The ancestor syndrome: Transgenerational psychotherapy and the hidden links in the family tree.* New York: Routledge.

Wegscheider-Cruse, S. (1981). *Another chance: Hope and health for the alcoholic family.* Palo Alto, CA: Science and Behavior Books.

Glossary

Although parts are considered autonomous and their behaviors motivated, there is no empirical view in IFS on the nature or origins of psychic multiplicity, nor is there a consensus among practitioners about the nature of parts.

Blended When a part is undifferentiated from another part or from the Self.

Burdened When parts have taken on painful beliefs and feelings about themselves from external sources and have no relief until they are unburdened.

Direct access The alternative approach to in-sight. When a protector will not unblend, the therapist speaks directly to the clients' parts. In direct access the therapist can speak *explicitly* to a part (e.g., *May I talk to that part directly? Ok. Why do you want Charlie to drink?*). Or, when the client rejects the idea of parts, or says, *That's not a part, that's me,* the therapist can speak to it *implicitly,* without direct acknowledgment that it is a part. Direct access is the usual method with children although some children are able to use in-sight.

In-sight The primary approach used with adults to understand parts, in-sight requires that the client be aware of parts (often aided by visual, kinesthetic or aural experience) and have enough Self-energy to communicate with them directly. When in-sight is blocked by protectors, direct access can be used.

Parts Internal entities, or subpersonalities, who function independently and have a full range of feelings, thoughts, beliefs and sensations. These entities, who have their own Self-energy when they feel understood and appreciated, vary in appearance, age, gender, talent and interest. They exist and take on various roles within the internal system. When not exiled or in conflict with each other over how to manage exiled parts, they contribute in a variety of ways to our efficient functioning and general well-being.

Three types of parts

IFS classifies parts in three broad categories according to how they function in relation to each other. An injured part, or *exile,* is primary in its influence on the behavior of other parts. Orbiting around exiles are two categories of protective parts. The proactive protector, called a *manager,* has the role of maintaining the individual's functioning despite what the exiles feel. The reactive protector, called a *firefighter,* has the role of suppressing the emotional pain of exiled parts, which breaks through despite the best efforts of the manager.

1. *Exiles*   Revealed in feelings, beliefs, sensations and actions, these parts have been shamed, dismissed, abused or neglected, usually in childhood, and are subsequently banished by protectors for their own safety and to keep them from overwhelming the internal system with emotional pain. A great deal of internal energy is expended to keep exiles out of awareness.

Protectors

2. *Managers*   Proactive helpers who focus on learning, functioning, being prepared and stable, and are therefore vigilant in trying to prevent exiles from flooding the internal system with emotion. As a consequence, they often use a variety of harsh tactics—not least, relentless criticizing and shaming—to keep us task-oriented and impervious to feelings.

3. *Firefighters*   Reactive protectors who share the goal of exiling vulnerable parts and extinguishing emotional pain. Firefighters get activated when the memories and emotions of exiles break through despite the repressive efforts of managers. They tend to be fierce and use extreme measures that managers abhor, like alcohol and drug abuse, binge eating, excessive shopping, promiscuity, cutting, suicide and homicide.

Polarization   An adversarial relationship between two protectors who are in conflict over how to manage an exile. Over time, their opposing views tend to become increasingly extreme and costly. However, when the intentions and contributions of each part are acknowledged by the client's Self, polarized protectors generally become willing to allow the Self to take over the job of caring for, protecting and repatriating the exile. Protectors are then freed from an onerous job and can find their preferred role in the internal family or retire.

Retrieval After being witnessed in whatever way it needs, an exiled part leaves the past where it has been living and comes into the present.

Self The innate presence in each of us that brings balance and harmony along with certain nonjudgmental, transformative qualities (curiosity, caring, creativity, courage, calmness, connectedness, clarity, compassion, presence, patience, persistence, perspective, playfulness) to our internal family. Parts may blend only partially, in which case there will be some measure of Self-energy present. Even when they blend completely (overwhelm and therefore obscure), the Self nevertheless continues to exist and is accessible as soon as parts unblend.

Self-energy The perspectives and feelings that the Self brings to the relationship with parts and other people.

Self-led When an individual has the capacity to hear, understand and be present with parts, acknowledging and appreciating the importance of their roles in the internal family system and with other people.

Unblended The state of being in which no part (e.g., feeling, thought, sensation, belief) is overwhelming the Self. When unblended parts remain present and accessible but are not vying to dominate, we have access to Self-qualities. This state of being unblended is often experienced as internal spaciousness.

Unburdening When the painful emotions and harsh self-judgments of an exiled part are ceremonially released, often using imagery that involves one of the elements. After unburdening, the part can invite qualities of its own choosing to fill the space formerly occupied by the burden. The qualities of Self (calm, confidence, clarity, connectedness, creativity, compassion) are common choices.

Witnessing The process in which a part shows and/or tells the client's Self about its experiences until it feels understood, accepted and self-accepting.

Index

Page numbers in *italics* refer to figures and tables.